CLAIMING LINCOLN

CLAIMING LINCOLN

Progressivism, Equality, and the Battle for Lincoln's Legacy in Presidential Rhetoric

Jason R. Jividen

NORTHERN ILLINOIS UNIVERSITY PRESS
DeKalb

© 2011 by Northern Illinois University Press

Published by the Northern Illinois University Press, DeKalb, Illinois 60115

Manufactured in the United States using postconsumer-recycled, acid-free paper.

All Rights Reserved

Design by Shaun Allshouse

Library of Congress Cataloging-in-Publication Data

Jividen, Jason R.

  Claiming Lincoln: progressivism, equality, and the battle for Lincoln's legacy in Presidential rhetoric / Jason R. Jividen.

    p. cm.

  Includes bibliographical references and index.

  ISBN 978-0-87580-435-4 (clothbound : alk. paper)

  1. Presidents—United States—History. 2. Presidents—United States—Language—History. 3. Rhetoric—Political aspects—United States—History. 4. Political oratory—United States—History. 5. Lincoln, Abraham, 1809–1865—Influence. 6. Progressivism (United States politics) I. Title.

  E176.J58 2011

  352.23'90973—dc22

                            2010037739

To Wesley and Rebecca

Contents

Acknowledgments ix

Introduction 3

1 — Lincoln and the Idea of Equality 9

2 — Theodore Roosevelt's Lincoln 33

3 — Woodrow Wilson's Lincoln 64

4 — Franklin Roosevelt's Lincoln 97

5 — Lyndon Johnson's Lincoln 134

6 — Barack Obama's Lincoln 154

Conclusion 174

Notes 181

Bibliography 213

Index 229

Acknowledgments

This book would not have been possible without the efforts of my teachers. For his direction and support, I owe much gratitude to Professor Larry Arnhart. Thanks are also due to Professors Gary Glenn, Christine Dunn Henderson, and Gregory Schmidt for their guidance and inspiration during the writing of this book and beyond. I would like to acknowledge the efforts of the late Professor Morton Frisch, who remains an inspiration as a teacher, a scholar, a citizen, and a human being.

This project began while I was in the political science doctoral program at Northern Illinois University. During that time, I was fortunate to have the assistance of H. B. Earhart Fellowships, and I thank the Earhart Foundation for their generous support. For their support during the revisions of the manuscript, I am also especially grateful to Gary Quinlivan, Bradley C.S. Watson, and my colleagues at the Center for Political and Economic Thought at Saint Vincent College. Many thanks are due also to Sara Hoerdeman and Susan Bean at Northern Illinois University Press for their invaluable advice and enthusiasm. I am grateful to the anonymous reviewers for their helpful suggestions, and I would also like to thank my former colleagues at the University of Saint Francis for their support during the editing of the manuscript. For their conversation and support over the years, I thank my friends from my graduate program at Northern Illinois University. For their advice, comments, and friendship while writing this book, I must particularly thank Steve McCarthy, Andy Schott, Chris Whidden, and Lauren Hall. Of course, any errors or deficiencies in this work remain my own.

Above all, I must express my deepest gratitude to my wife, Marcie. This book would not have been written without her unwavering support. Her love and patience continue to amaze me.

CLAIMING LINCOLN

Introduction

ABRAHAM LINCOLN REMAINS ONE of the most frequently mentioned figures in American political rhetoric, and we have witnessed Barack Obama's appeals to the Lincoln image during his recent campaign and in his early speeches as president. Beginning on the eve of the two-hundredth anniversary of Lincoln's birth, Obama's appeals have created interest among scholars, politicians, and journalists who rush to affirm or debunk the president's invocation of Lincoln's legacy, yet this phenomenon is nothing new in American politics. American politicians' attempts to appropriate the Lincoln image have often turned on an appeal to the American promise of equality, said to be proclaimed in the Declaration of Independence, vindicated in the Civil War and the Reconstruction Amendments, and developed through the Progressive Era, the New Deal, the Great Society, the civil rights movement, and beyond. Throughout, politicians have claimed to continue Lincoln's unfinished work in the name of the American promise. Yet many who have invoked Lincoln's name have profoundly misunderstood or misrepresented Lincoln's political thought, particularly his understanding of equality.

In his widely influential *Lincoln Reconsidered,* prominent Lincoln scholar David Donald discussed the American political tradition's attempt to "get right" with Lincoln. Donald's fundamental insight is that, as of the 1950s, the jury was still out on the question of Lincoln's political thought and its influence upon the American political tradition. Until the beginning of the twentieth century, the claim to Lincoln's political inheritance had predominantly been in the possession of the Republican Party. However, during the Progressive Era, the claim to the Lincoln inheritance became a partisan issue in the 1912 presidential election. William Howard Taft, Theodore Roosevelt, and Woodrow Wilson all publicly claimed to follow in the Lincolnian tradition. Likewise, in 1932, as part of their heated debate over what could and should be done to address the challenges of the Great Depression, Herbert Hoover and Franklin Roosevelt engaged in a similar disagreement about just who could plausibly claim to follow in Lincoln's footsteps. The claim to the Lincoln inheritance had become a major component of presidential rhetoric.[1] Given Obama's appeals to Lincoln in recent years, it appears this is still the case.

The dispute over Lincoln in political rhetoric would find a parallel in academia, wherein scholars often disagree, sometimes vehemently, about the nature and scope of Lincoln's influence on American political development. One finds that sharp, sometimes bitter disagreements persist between serious and thoughtful people as to the character of Lincoln's political thought. Central to these debates is the meaning and influence of Lincoln's opinion, famously declared in his Gettysburg Address, that we are a nation "dedicated to the proposition that all men are created equal."[2] Many observers, both critical and supportive of Lincoln, suggest Lincoln was central in establishing a modern, leveling egalitarianism in American politics. This modern pursuit of equality is said to focus not upon securing the formal equality of individuals before the law or equality of opportunity but, rather, upon equalizing substantive outcomes among both individuals and groups. Generally this pursuit calls for the presence of a strong, centralized national government to pursue such ends. Its proponents often seek to alter or abolish fundamental constitutional structures and procedures (for example, various aspects of federalism, representation, separation of powers, among other institutions) thought to be antidemocratic or reactionary obstacles to the goal of greater equality in American society.[3] However, in reality, Lincoln's pursuit of equality was very different from the egalitarianism often espoused by modern-day academics and politicians, in both principle and practice. Arguing against the institution of slavery and defending the idea of free labor, Lincoln sought to secure individuals' equal liberty to exercise diverse and necessarily unequal talents in pursuit of their interests, under the rule of law, while expecting an inequality of results or outcomes among individuals in that pursuit. Lincoln understood that this pursuit of equality is moderated by the limited government constitutionalism that follows from the premise that all men are equally endowed with natural and inalienable rights. Moreover, Lincoln understood that this pursuit must be tempered by a prudential appreciation for the circumstances of political practice.

However, beginning in the Progressive Era, political rhetoricians nevertheless looked to Lincoln's rhetoric of equality to articulate and justify modern egalitarian claims and proposals. In particular, U.S. presidents and presidential candidates appealed rhetorically to the Lincoln image only to mischaracterize and distort his understanding of equality in the process. Lincoln's understanding of equality became divorced from its grounding in the constitutionalism and natural rights thinking of the American Founding and came to be reinterpreted in light of the Hegelian notion of progressive, rational history. This rhetorical use and abuse of Lincoln, I argue, has profound consequences not only for how we understand Lincoln but also for how we understand equality as a goal to be secured in American society.

In Chapter 1, I examine a representative snapshot of studies in relevant literature on Lincoln and American politics, all of which posit a relationship between Lincoln's pursuit of equality and the equality espoused by the progressives and their political heirs. Focusing on Lincoln's political speeches and writings, I explain his understanding of equality and begin to distinguish this idea from the egalitarianism that will emerge in twentieth-century American politics. In subsequent chapters, I trace out the manner in which later presidents appealed to the Lincoln image in their pursuit of equality, only to reject Lincoln's principles. In examining this rhetorical use and abuse of Abraham Lincoln, I largely focus upon three general periods in American political development—the Progressive Era, the New Deal, and the Great Society. In each case, the idea of equality as a political, social, and economic goal was publicly debated and redefined in presidential rhetoric and American political discourse. Clearly, it is not my intention to write an exhaustive account of the rhetorical appeal to Lincoln among American presidents. I limit myself to the speeches and writings of Teddy Roosevelt, Woodrow Wilson, Franklin Roosevelt, Lyndon Johnson, and to a lesser extent Barack Obama. I hope to show that these presidents help us to understand larger themes in American political thought and development, themes that necessarily involve the idea of equality as a national commitment. Above all, their use and abuse of Lincoln is wrapped up in a more general rhetorical trend, in which our fundamental political principles and institutions are redefined in light of a faith in progressive history rather than articulated in light of an enduring and imperfect human nature.

In Chapter 2, I discuss Theodore Roosevelt's frequent and well-documented appeals to the Lincoln example. I focus primarily upon Roosevelt's controversial claim that the Bull Moose Progressives were alone the rightful heirs of Abraham Lincoln. Roosevelt claimed that, like Lincoln, he believed the purpose of American democracy was to secure all individuals an equal chance in the race of life.[4] In the name of equality, Roosevelt sought to promote and legitimate progressive reforms of the American regime by arguing their supposed kinship with the Lincoln legacy. However, the mere fact that Roosevelt appealed to the Lincoln image does not mean he rightly understood—or rightly represented—Lincoln's political thought and deeds. On the contrary, I argue that Roosevelt's understanding of what equality is, and the means by which that equality ought to be achieved, departed from the Lincolnian tradition. Ultimately, Roosevelt's attempt to claim the Lincoln inheritance hinged upon a selective and incomplete presentation of Lincoln's political thought.

I begin with Teddy Roosevelt because his claims to Lincoln's legacy represent what I believe to be a common theme in twentieth-century rhetorical appeals to Lincoln. Building on the work of progressive journalist Herbert Croly, Roosevelt offered a version of Lincoln that deemphasized the natural rights principles and the limited government constitutionalism that informed Lincoln's understanding of equality. Roosevelt seized upon themes in Lincoln more useful to the rhetoric of American progressivism, wherein the natural rights principles of the Declaration of Independence were rejected in favor of a historicist understanding of our political tradition. In this, Roosevelt helped to lay a foundation by which the Lincoln example might be historicized and ripped from the first principles that defined Lincoln's political thought. Roosevelt's Lincoln serves as a touchstone for the modern egalitarian use of the Lincoln image.

In Chapter 3 I examine Woodrow Wilson's rhetorical use and abuse of the Lincoln image. While Wilson appealed to the Lincoln legacy less frequently than Roosevelt did, I argue that his attempt to appropriate Lincoln into the rhetoric of American progressivism was no less significant. As one of the premier architects of American progressivism, Wilson rejected the natural rights basis of Lincoln's political thought in favor of Hegel's philosophy of history and the concept of the modern state. Wilson tried to incorporate Lincoln into this vision, but like Teddy Roosevelt he offered a mistaken, misleading interpretation of Lincoln. As part of his project to alter fundamentally American political institutions in the service of progressive notions of equality, Wilson offered a Lincoln that no longer served as an example of constant dedication to principles of natural rights and constitutionalism. Rather, Wilson's Lincoln became the very personification of the doctrine of progress and the historical overcoming of these principles. This overcoming, Wilson believed, demanded a new role for the American presidency to serve as the embodiment of the will of the people, a rhetorical leader of men necessary for national progress. Although Wilson claimed Lincoln as one of the chief models for this popularized, rhetorical leadership, I argue that Wilson's own rhetorical efforts to incorporate Lincoln into the vision of the modern plebiscitary presidency are highly problematic.

In Chapter 4, I discuss Franklin Roosevelt's appeal to the Lincoln image. I argue that FDR offered a spin on Lincoln similar to that of the progressives. His use of Lincoln is thus subject to similar criticisms. But Roosevelt did introduce a new element into the rhetorical appeal to Lincoln—an increased focus upon the idea of "rights," especially economic rights in the pursuit of equality. FDR suggested that *the* task of statesmanship consists not in securing natural and inalienable rights held to be true everywhere and always but, rather, in the continual "redefinition" of our most fundamental rights in light of a growing and changing social order. In his New Deal rhetoric, FDR praised Lincoln as this kind of statesman, as "a character destined to transfuse with *new meaning* the concepts of our constitutional fathers and to assure a Government having for its broad purpose the promotion of the life, liberty, and happiness of all the people."[5] FDR offered another step in the incorporation of the Lincoln image into the modern rhetoric of equality. Following the template laid by the progressives, FDR associated his Lincoln with the ends and means of the New Deal and thus with an expanded notion of equality that rejected the core principles of Lincoln's political thought and practice.

Chapter 5 turns to consider Lyndon Johnson's frequent appeals to Lincoln's legacy in the rhetoric of the Great Society and the civil rights legislation of the middle 1960s. Johnson often appealed to Lincoln but would eventually depart fundamentally from Lincoln's individual-regarding equality of opportunity. Speaking at Howard University in June 1965, Johnson declared that, whatever the civil rights legislation of the middle 1960s might have contributed to individual freedom in America, ultimately freedom is not enough. It is not enough, Johnson claimed, merely to "open the gates of opportunity." Rather, we must see that all our citizens "have the ability to walk through those gates. . . . We seek not just legal equity but human ability, not just equality as a right and a theory but equality as a fact and equality as a result."[6] Despite his claims to continue Lincoln's unfinished work, Johnson abandoned Lincoln's understanding of equality, and he did so upon theoretical and political foundations laid by the progressives and the New Deal.

In Chapter 6, I briefly examine Barack Obama's recent and widely discussed rhetorical appeals to the Lincoln image. Obama's frequent attempts to incorporate Lincoln into his political rhetoric have sparked new interest in Lincoln among many. However, despite the popularity of Obama's appeals, they are nothing new. Rather, Obama's rhetorical appeals to Lincoln are a rather standard, repackaged version of the progressives' Lincoln, vaguely dedicated to the idea of equality as a political goal but ultimately divorced from the natural rights and limited government principles that serve as the basis for Lincoln's political thought. Despite his eloquent appeals to the Lincoln example, Obama's use of Lincoln is complicated by the fact that his understanding of the first principles of American democracy owes more to the progressives and the New Deal than to Abraham Lincoln. To understand Obama's Lincoln, one must understand the progressive appeal to Lincoln. Indeed, I argue that it is really the progressives and FDR that did the heavy lifting to render a modern egalitarian Lincoln, a version of Lincoln readily available for Obama to incorporate into his presidential rhetoric. As such, I concentrate more heavily upon the use of Lincoln prior to Obama, during the Progressive Era, the New Deal, and the Great Society. It is during these periods that the use and abuse of Abraham Lincoln really takes shape.

ONE
Lincoln and the Idea of Equality

ABRAHAM LINCOLN EMBRACED AN IDEA of equality that sought to secure individuals' equal liberty to exercise diverse and necessarily unequal talents and abilities in the pursuit of happiness, under the rule of law, while expecting an inequality of results or outcomes among individuals in that pursuit. Lincoln recognized that this pursuit must be moderated by competing political and constitutional goods, including the fundamental principle of government by consent of the governed, and subject to the practical limitations of political life. This notion of equality—rooted in the Laws of Nature and Nature's God, and tempered by the realities of political practice—distinguishes Lincoln's equality from many variants of modern egalitarianism, which often seek to secure equality of substantive outcomes or results, sometimes at the expense of competing political and constitutional goods.

Nevertheless, many academics attempt to connect Lincoln's understanding of equality as a binding national commitment to the pursuit of modern egalitarianism that springs from the American progressives and their modern liberal heirs. On the one hand, many on the American left praise Lincoln as a precursor to modern egalitarianism, as a visionary who ushered in new and improved ideas of equality and national responsibility. On the other hand, many on the right condemn Lincoln as a revolutionary who destroyed the federalism and limited government of the Founders' Constitution in the name of the necessarily abstract, centralizing, and dangerous principle of equality. While they might disagree about the merits of modern egalitarianism, these observers fundamentally agree about Lincoln's supposed contribution to it. This connection between Lincoln and modern egalitarianism would seem to be bolstered by the fact that progressive and modern liberal politicians—most visibly U.S. presidents—have routinely sought to appropriate the Lincoln image in their writings and speeches. In this study I will attempt to demonstrate, however, that even though progressive and modern liberal presidents have tried to adopt Lincoln, they have in the process misunderstood, misrepresented, and even ignored Lincoln's notion of equality. My purpose in this chapter is to examine this supposed connection between Lincoln and modern egalitarianism and to explain Lincoln's actual understanding of equality. In subsequent chapters I will examine how progressive and modern liberal presidents have misinterpreted, misrepresented, and distorted Lincoln's equality in their rhetorical attempts to claim Lincoln's legacy.

Lincoln's Equality as a Precursor to Modern Egalitarianism

The idea that there is some relationship between Lincoln's understanding of equality and the modern egalitarianism of contemporary American politics is commonplace. For some, Lincoln is to be praised as a revolutionary who introduced a new regime into American life by establishing the supremacy of the national government over the state governments and by elevating equality as the paramount political goal to be secured by that national government. A representative example of this view appears in Columbia law professor George P. Fletcher's *Our Secret Constitution: How Abraham Lincoln Redefined American Democracy*. According to Fletcher, Lincoln departed from and improved upon the constitutional order bequeathed to us by the Founders. "At the heart of this postbellum legal order," Fletcher claims, "lay the Reconstruction Amendments—the Thirteenth, Fourteenth, and Fifteenth Amendments. . . . The principles of this new legal regime are so radically different from our original Constitution . . . that they deserve to be regarded as a second American constitution."[1]

According to Fletcher, Lincoln is to be praised for supplanting the Founders' Constitution, which was based upon "the principles of peoplehood as a voluntary association, individual freedom, and republican elitism." Lincoln's second constitution, on the other hand, would be guided by "organic nationhood, equality of all persons, and popular democracy." For Fletcher, the Founders' Constitution "stood for a maximum expression of individual freedom," which included "the right of white persons to assert themselves freely to seize and control the lives of certain other people known as Negroes." The second constitution, Fletcher claims, "is dedicated to the proposition that all men are created equal." As president and rhetorician, Lincoln is said to have laid the groundwork for this new regime with the Gettysburg Address. According to Fletcher, Lincoln's efforts to refound the nation on the proposition that all men are created equal culminated in the Reconstruction Amendments. However, Fletcher claims, the courts rejected this new constitutional order during the age of substantive due process. It was not until the twentieth century, Fletcher argues, that the new regime finally reasserted itself, "first in constitutional amendment, then in academic discourse, and finally, in the rhetoric and decisions of the Supreme Court," particularly in equal protection law.[2] For Fletcher, Lincoln is to be venerated for having introduced the germ of a modern egalitarianism that would continue to develop in the twentieth century.

In his *Abraham Lincoln and the Second American Revolution*, noted Civil War historian and Lincoln scholar James McPherson also argues that Lincoln and the Civil War improved upon the Founders' regime by ushering in a new and deeper understanding of equality. According to McPherson, "with the new birth of freedom proclaimed in the Gettysburg Address and backed by a powerful army" Lincoln helped to move American democracy toward deeper and expanded notions of "equity, justice, social welfare [and] equality of opportunity."[3] As Steven Hayward has observed, a similar view is expressed in filmmaker Ken Burns's wildly popular PBS documentary series on the Civil War. Historian Barbara Fields contributes to the film's commentary, suggesting that Lincoln and the Civil War established a new standard of equality that "will not mean anything until we have finished the work. . . . If some citizens live in houses and others live on the street, the Civil War is still going on. It is still to be fought, and regrettably, it can still be lost."[4] Burns endorses Fields's comments, and argues that America is "constantly trying to enlarge the definition and deepen the meaning of 'all men are created equal'" and that "we have not fulfilled the promises that we made at the end of the war."[5] Such views are commonplace among academics, politicians, and journalists. According to this line of thought, the idea of equality is continually redefined, and good government is defined by the extent to which it seeks out new and expanded means of fulfilling the promise of equality and continuing Lincoln's unfinished work. According to this view, Lincoln is to be praised and remembered for introducing an ever-deepening, ever-expanding notion of equality into American life.

But this supposed transience, this seeming open-endedness associated with equality, also animates some of Lincoln's most serious critics, many of whom are associated with various strains of American conservatism. Libertarian economist Thomas DiLorenzo, for example, condemns Lincoln for destroying the limited government and federalism of the Founders' Constitution in waging the Civil War. "Before the war," DiLorenzo suggests, "government in America was the highly decentralized, limited government established by the founding fathers. The war created the highly centralized state that Americans labor under today." DiLorenzo argues that some "left-of-center" commentators such as Fletcher, McPherson, and Garry Wills have largely abandoned the effort to "portray Lincoln as someone who was devoted to preserving the Constitution." Rather, as modern egalitarians, they praise Lincoln for destroying the Founders' Constitution. Central to this destruction, DiLorenzo reasons, is Lincoln's assertion that we are a nation dedicated to the proposition that all men are created equal. While DiLorenzo condemns this supposed destruction and Lincoln's contribution to it, we should note that he agrees fundamentally with his left-leaning opponents that Lincoln's exaltation of equality as the "the principal feature of the federal government really was revolutionary."[6]

DiLorenzo claims that historian Garry Wills in his popular *Lincoln at Gettysburg: The Words that Remade America* is "obviously thrilled" with "Lincoln's emphasis on 'equality' in the Gettysburg Address," which "redefined the primary purpose of American government as the pursuit of egalitarianism." This pursuit, DiLorenzo argues, "always requires a large, activist, centralized state." DiLorenzo asserts that the equality Wills attributes to Lincoln refers "not merely to equality of treatment for the ex-slaves, but also to the whole twentieth-century socialist enterprise of using the powers of centralized government to attempt to force all types of 'equality' on the population." Although he disagrees as to the desirability of this egalitarianism and its centralizing effects, DiLorenzo agrees with Wills's assertion that Lincoln performed an open-air sleight of hand and a great swindle on the American people by elevating equality to a supreme national commitment in the Gettysburg Address.[7] Wills's arguments on the lasting impact of the Gettysburg Address are particularly illustrative of the view that there is some connection between modern egalitarianism and Lincoln's presidential rhetoric. Wills suggests that, because of Lincoln, we live in a "different America" than the one that once saw "states' rights" as a defensible position. Because of "the values created by the Gettysburg Address," Wills claims, "original intent conservatives" cannot act as if there never was a Fourteenth Amendment, even though they may wish to do so. Wills seems to assume that Lincoln's understanding of equality, the Fourteenth Amendment as originally intended, and the Fourteenth Amendment as interpreted by the modern Supreme Court are necessarily identical. Wills simply takes for granted that there is a connection between Lincoln's equality and the modern Court's view of equal protection.[8]

Despite DiLorenzo's claim, the extent to which Wills is "obviously thrilled" with Lincoln's emphasis on equality is not so clear. In fact, DiLorenzo and Wills appear closer in their opinions on Lincoln than DiLorenzo might suggest. As Joseph Fornieri notes, "Wills' subtle ambiguity concerning his own approval or disapproval of Lincoln's words at Gettysburg can be misleading to the less than careful reader." In the prologue to his *Inventing America: Jefferson's Declaration of Independence,* Wills explicitly condemns Lincoln for reconstituting the American political tradition, creating the myth that the Declaration of Independence is a "founding document," and thereby turning our reverence away from the Constitution and the rule of law. Lincoln's rhetoric of equality, Wills suggests, dedicates the nation not only to an abstract proposition but to a unique mission to provide hope that all should have an equal chance in the race of life. Wills argues that Lincoln's words contribute to a desire in the American people and their political representatives to remake our nation, perhaps even to remake the world, in our nation's image, even if this means the redemptive shedding of American blood in the name of equality and democracy.[9]

Still others have criticized Lincoln's argument that the Declaration establishes equality as a binding national commitment. Take, for example, conservative political theorist Frank Meyer's claim that Lincoln the "champion of equality," Lincoln the "creator of concentrated national power," and Lincoln the "President who shattered the constitutional tension" between the federal and state governments are "one and the same man."[10] Meyer's argument is that Lincoln's actions as executive during the war were destructive of the federalism and separation of powers of the Founders' Constitution. Such actions, according to Meyer, were fundamentally tied to the pursuit of equality. The effort to enforce equality, Meyer claims, "so frequent in the twentieth century . . . leads inevitably to the restrictions and eventual destruction of freedom." The effort to enforce the "abstract, overarching, unmodified" idea of equality "upon men, always unequally endowed, is the primrose path to tyranny."[11] Meyer contends that Lincoln is partially responsible for the modern welfare state, of which he is quite critical. "Were it not for the wounds that Lincoln inflicted upon the

Constitution," Meyer writes, "it would have been infinitely more difficult for Franklin Roosevelt to carry through his revolution, for the coercive welfare state to come into being." According to Meyer, acting in the name of equality, Lincoln "undermined the constitutional safeguards of freedom as he opened the way to centralized government with all its attendant political evils."[12]

Similarly, traditionalist conservative M. E. Bradford has also condemned Lincoln as a usurper who smuggled the idea of equality into the American political tradition. "Equality as a moral or political imperative," notes Bradford, "pursued as an end in itself—Equality with the capital 'E'—is the antonym of every legitimate conservative principle."[13] Bradford contends that "Lincoln's 'second founding' is fraught with peril and carries with it the prospect of an endless series of turmoils and revolutions, all dedicated to freshly discovered meanings of equality as a 'proposition.'" Equality, for Bradford, is a mere abstraction. Like Wills, he argues that Lincoln's claim that the Declaration dedicates the nation to the proposition that all men are created equal injects a dangerous confusion and ambiguity into the American political tradition. "Trying to preserve property," Bradford writes, "secure tranquility, and promote equal rights, all at the same time, insures that none of these purposes will be accomplished; And insures also a terrible, unremitting tension, both among those in power and among those whose hopes are falsely raised."[14]

The conservative criticism of Lincoln's equality is also forcefully advanced by Willmoore Kendall and George W. Carey in *The Basic Symbols of the American Political Tradition*. According to Kendall and Carey, by treating the Declaration as a founding document and claiming that equality is a binding national commitment, Lincoln fostered the "derailment" of the American political tradition. Lincoln is said to have transformed a regime once dedicated to the symbol of a virtuous, self-governing people deliberating under God to one dedicated to the idea of equality. And this dedication to equality is deemed not just mistaken, but dangerous.[15] Elsewhere, Kendall warns against "a future made up of an endless series of Abraham Lincolns, each persuaded that he is superior in wisdom and virtue to the Fathers, each prepared to insist that those who oppose this or that new application of the equality standard are denying the possibility of self-government, each ultimately willing to plunge America into Civil War rather than concede his point." According to Kendall, Lincoln's words and deeds set a dangerous precedent for future presidents and other leaders, to speak and act in a manner destructive of American constitutional government. The end, Kendall claims, is the "cooperative commonwealth of men who will be so equal that no one will be able to tell them apart."[16]

We shall discuss Kendall's thesis in more detail later. For now we should note that Kendall particularly has in mind the pursuit of equality characteristic of modern plebiscitary presidents (including TR, Woodrow Wilson, and Franklin Roosevelt) and the modern Supreme Court, both of which to some degree, he argues, can be traced ultimately to Lincoln. Thus, some of Lincoln's most vocal critics fundamentally agree with some of his most enthusiastic defenders. The Lincoln we often encounter among those on the American political left is not really that dissimilar from the Lincoln we often encounter on the right. The modern liberals' version of Lincoln and the version of Lincoln offered by many conservatives are both indebted to the progressives' account of American political development and Lincoln's place in it. Both claim that Lincoln either participated in or was single-handedly responsible for the "derailment" of the American political tradition. They only disagree as to whether that tradition, as it supposedly stood before Lincoln, was superior or inferior to the tradition as it stood after Lincoln.

The Misuse of Lincoln

According to Carey, the publication of the 1995 paperback edition of *Basic Symbols* afforded the opportunity to write a new preface to elaborate on the derailment thesis and answer, "if only by indirection in some cases, those who have taken exception with one or more of its constituent elements."[17] While the new preface speaks to the debated question of the place of the Declaration and equality in the American political tradition, most of the discussion therein specifically concerns Lincoln. As Carey notes, perhaps the single most controversial claim in *Basic Symbols* is that Lincoln fostered the derailment of the American political tradition. According to Carey, the most forceful rejoinder to this contention consists of two fundamental propositions: first, Lincoln's account of the Declaration of Independence as a founding document and equality as a binding national commitment is simply correct.[18] As to this first proposition, Carey reasonably suggests that "there is a definite parting of the ways between *Basic Symbols* and its critics, with little left to be said."[19] Carey suggests that the second proposition is best stated by Steven Hayward, that the meaning of equality set forth in the Declaration and the Gettysburg Address is not to be confused with "those advanced by Progressivism or welfare statism, much less the radical egalitarianism that has emerged in recent decades."[20] Carey claims this second part of the rejoinder raises an interesting question that is a matter of ongoing debate, namely, "what is the relationship, if any, between Lincoln's position and that of later Progressives, egalitarians, 'reformers' and the like? In what sense, if any, can we say that Lincoln was the father of the modern, centralized, ever expanding, social welfare state that promotes egalitarianism?"[21]

Carey's answer to this question is interesting. On the one hand, he admits that there is reasonable support for the view, espoused by those he describes as "Lincoln's conservative defenders," that Lincoln subscribed to a specific and necessarily limited view of equality. Citing Lincoln's June 26, 1857, speech on the *Dred Scott* decision, Carey acknowledges that Lincoln "reveals a less than expansive conception of . . . the 'all men are created equal' clause." Lincoln claimed that, while the authors of the Declaration meant to include all men in the phrase "all men are created equal," they did not intend to declare men equal in "all respects" such as "color, size, intellect, moral developments, or social capacity." Rather, they understood men to be equal in "certain inalienable rights, among which are life, liberty, and the pursuit of happiness." This much is clear, but according to Carey, the "sentences that follow immediately upon these . . . convey a spirit and perspective that leave the door open to a more expansive view of equality, one that moves well beyond simply the slavery question." Carey refers here to Lincoln's famous statement that, in declaring that all men are created equal, the authors of the Declaration "meant to set up a standard maxim for free society . . . never perfectly attained" but "constantly approximated, and thereby constantly spreading and deepening its influence, and augmenting the happiness and value of life to all people of all colors everywhere."[22] Carey also reminds us of Lincoln's argument that the Declaration was of no "practical use in effecting our separation from Great Britain" but was rather intended for "future use," and of his claim that the purpose of the Civil War was to "lift artificial weights from all shoulders . . . to afford all, an unfettered start, and a fair chance in the race of life." Carey argues that such statements suggest it is "not unreasonable to associate Lincoln's words and thoughts with the egalitarianism that characterizes the modern, centralized welfare state." According to Carey, "Lincoln's words can be, and more frequently than not are, linked to a broad conception of equality that is considered to be central to our political tradition."[23]

We should wonder, however, why Lincoln's words can be so easily used, given that Lincoln himself held to a different notion of equality than many who would later invoke his name. Again, Carey's answer is interesting:

> [T]he argument over the degree to which Lincoln's substantive notions of equality—that is, the specific content of his equality—give rise to or square with modern egalitarian beliefs and policies is not central to the thesis advanced in *Basic Symbols*. Rather, it is other attributes of his notion of equality—namely, that it is both universal and a seemingly transcendent goal whose realization is constantly to be striven for—that render it so inviting for modern egalitarians to use as a justification of, or source for, the advancement of their policies. . . . [T]he concern over substance—that is, whether Lincoln would agree or not with this or that policy designed to fulfill our presumed commitment to equality—is really secondary to the fact that the character of his equality, particularly its open-endedness and universality, is so congenial to modern egalitarians.[24]

To suggest that Lincoln's words can be associated, and often are associated, with modern egalitarianism in no way suggests that they are rightly so associated. Carey seems to concede this much. That Lincoln's words are inviting appears to be true, but as Leo Paul S. de Alvarez has suggested, one wonders about Lincoln's supposed role in the derailment of the tradition if the substance or content of progressivism or modern egalitarianism can no longer be unqualifiedly traced to Lincoln. As de Alvarez rightly argues, "either Lincoln's thought brings about a fundamental break that ultimately results in a false interpretation of the American political tradition or it does not." Carey's thought seems to be that "Lincoln has to be attacked not because of his understanding of the American political order but because he has been misused."[25] As John Murley has suggested, the "flawed initial misstep of *Basic Symbols* is the failure to adequately distinguish Lincoln and the Declaration of Independence from the *misuse* of Lincoln and the Declaration of Independence in Progressive thought."[26]

Carey notes Lincoln's distinction between equality of rights and equality of personal attributes or talents. In doing so, he begins the work of distinguishing Lincoln's pursuit of equality from that of the progressives. But Carey does not go far enough here. For Lincoln, the principle that all men are created equal suggested that the pursuit of equality, rightly understood, is necessarily constrained by the fundamental principle of government by consent of the governed and tempered by other political and constitutional goods. Moreover, for Lincoln, the pursuit of equality was often necessarily subject to the practical restraints imposed by the varied circumstances of political life. Lincoln's equality should be distinguished further from progressive and modern liberal egalitarianism in both principle and practice.

Lincoln's Understanding of the Principle of Equality

Those who argue that there is an identifiable connection between Lincoln's equality and modern egalitarianism tend to focus on a few key passages in Lincoln's speeches and writings. Apart from the Gettysburg Address, perhaps none receives more attention than Lincoln's notion of the "standard maxim" mentioned above. This passage from Lincoln's speech on the *Dred Scott* decision is worth quoting at length for our purposes here. In his opinion on *Dred Scott,* Chief Justice Taney infamously argued that, given the existence and toleration of slavery at the Founding, the authors of the Declaration of Independence could not have intended the Negro to be included in the phrase "all men are created equal." Lincoln responded with the following:

> I think the authors of that notable instrument intended to include *all* men, but they did not intend to declare all men equal *in all respects*. They did not mean to say all were equal in color, size, intellect, moral developments, or social capacity. They defined with tolerable distinctness, in what respects they did consider all men created equal—equal in "certain inalienable rights, among which are life, liberty, and the pursuit of happiness." This they said, and this meant. They did not mean to assert the obvious untruth, that all were then actually enjoying that equality, nor yet, that they were about to confer it immediately upon them. In fact they had no power to confer such a boon. They meant simply to declare the *right,* so that the *enforcement* of it might follow as fast as circumstances should permit. They meant to set up a standard maxim for free society, which should be familiar to all, and revered by all; constantly looked to, constantly labored for, and even though never perfectly attained, constantly approximated, and thereby constantly spreading and deepening its influence, and augmenting the happiness and value of life to all people of all colors everywhere.[27]

To understand truly the idea of the standard maxim, one should note that Lincoln here drew a clear distinction between equality of rights, on the one hand, and equality of personal attributes, abilities, and talents, on the other. Following the political theory of the Declaration, Lincoln held that human beings possess natural equality. That is, according to the Laws of Nature and Nature's God, all human beings are equally endowed with natural and inalienable rights, among which are life, liberty, and the pursuit of happiness. In Lincoln's view, no human being has a claim by nature to rule over any other human being without his consent. Hence governments derive their just powers by the consent of the governed. "No man," Lincoln claimed, "is good enough to govern another man, *without that other's consent*. I say this is the leading principle—the sheet anchor of American republicanism." For Lincoln, the natural equality of all men in their inalienable rights was "the father of all moral principle" and the very essence of free government.[28] According to Lincoln, by denying the principle of natural equality, the Southern slave interest had undercut any principled, objective argument for government by consent of the governed.

While there is no clear indication that Lincoln had read Locke's *Second Treatise of Civil Government,* his understanding of natural equality and government by consent of the governed here had an arguably Lockean character.[29] While Lincoln argued for the equality of all men in their inalienable rights, he did not believe—as Locke did not believe, indeed as the Founders did not believe—that human beings are equal in all respects. Such a claim would be absurd. As Jaffa suggests, there is surely an inequality of particular characteristics and talents among human beings. No human being could claim that he has no superior in one respect or another, be it intelligence, physical prowess, moral capacity, or any other quality of this sort, nor would any one likely claim that he has no inferior in such things. But, for Lincoln, as for the Founders, this question had no bearing on the right to rule.[30] This understanding of the basis of self-government was the root of Lincoln's moral condemnation of slavery. Consider the following "Fragment on Slavery":

> If A. can prove, however conclusively, that he may, of right, enslave B.—why may not B. snatch the same argument, and prove equally, that he may enslave A?—You say A. is white, and B. is black. It is *color,* then; the lighter, having the right to enslave the darker? Take care. By this rule, you are to be slave to the first man you meet, with a fairer skin than your own. You do not mean *color* exactly?—You mean the whites are *intellectually* the superiors of the blacks, and, therefore have the right to enslave them? Take care again. By this rule, you are to be slave to the first man you meet, with an intellect superior to your own. But, say you, it is a question of *interest;* and, if you can make it your *interest,* you have the right to enslave another. Very well. And if he can make it his interest, he has the right to enslave you.[31]

In short, any argument that might be used to justify one man's enslavement of another human being can too easily be turned around to justify one's own enslavement. Some human beings may indeed be superior in "color, size, intellect, moral development, or social capacity," and this may allow them to fare better in pursuit of their interests than others. But no one can claim a right by nature to rule over another without that other's consent. For Lincoln, as for the Founders, the alleged superiority of one man over another is no justification for denying any man his rights to life, liberty, and the pursuit of happiness. This was the equality affirmed by the Declaration of Independence.[32]

According to Lincoln, this understanding of equality accords with our commonsense views of human nature. The simple injustice of slavery is so evident that anyone with "ordinary perceptions of right and wrong" can easily understand it. According to Lincoln, although "volume upon volume is written to prove slavery a very good thing, we never hear of the man who wishes to take the good of it, *by being a slave himself*" and even "the most dumb and stupid slave that ever toiled for a master, does constantly *know* he is wronged." In response to Stephen Douglas and the Kansas-Nebraska Act, Lincoln argued that it is contrary to "the law of nature" to allow the slaveholder to take his slaves to Kansas just as a freeman would take his hogs or horses. Slaves are not property as horses and dogs are property because slaves have "mind, feeling, souls, family affections, hopes, joys, sorrows—something that made them more than *hogs or horses*." According to Lincoln, the only internally consistent way for the slave interest to justify the rightness of slavery is ultimately to deny the humanity of the slave, that is, to do something that contradicts our commonsense understanding of nature.[33]

As James Ceaser explains, for the American Founders and Lincoln, nature referred to something timeless and unchanging that transcended history and circumstance and that could provide some standard of right discernible by human reason. In politics, the "primary substance or matter of nature" is "human nature, or the psychological makeup of individual human beings." According to Ceaser, "this 'substance' was then treated within a form of logical or hypothetical reasoning that was related to the question of how to put together a stable political order." Derived from reflection on nature, these first principles (what the Declaration of Independence referred to as the Laws of Nature and Nature's God) were thought to provide guidance about the legitimate ends of government. Yet, while nature might provide the ultimate standard regarding the ends of government, prudence or practical wisdom would ultimately help to determine the necessary means by which we might secure those ends in light of changing political and historical circumstances.[34] This understanding guided Lincoln's pursuit of equality.

For Lincoln, according to nature, individuals ought to have equal liberty to pursue their own interests. Lincoln's understanding of equal liberty is captured in his many statements on natural rights and free labor. Lincoln often presented this idea in Lockean terms, suggesting that a human being ought to be able to eat the bread that he has earned by the sweat of his own brow. Lincoln shared with Locke the view that the origin of private property consists in the natural and equal right that every human being has to his body, to the labor of that body, and to the fruits of his labor.[35] "Certainly," Lincoln claimed in his July 20, 1858, speech at Springfield, "the negro is not our equal in color—perhaps not in many other respects; still, in the right to put into his mouth the bread that his own hands have earned, he is the equal of every other man, white or black." Again, in the first debate with Douglas, Lincoln argued that "there is no reason in the world why the negro is not entitled to all the natural rights enumerated in the Declaration of Independence . . . he is as much entitled to these as the white man. I agree with Judge Douglas he is not my equal in many respects—certainly not in color, perhaps not in moral or intellectual endowment," but, Lincoln claimed, "in the right to eat the bread, without leave of anybody else, which his own hand earns, *he is my equal and the equal of Judge Douglas, and the equal of every living man.*" Again, in his March 5, 1860, speech at Hartford, Connecticut, Lincoln suggested that "every man, black, white or yellow, has a mouth to be fed and two hands with which to feed it—and that bread should be allowed to go to that mouth without controversy."[36]

This natural and equal right to eat the bread that one has earned is the basis of Lincoln's defense of equality of opportunity and free labor. In his March 6, 1860, speech at New Haven, Connecticut, Lincoln claimed that "we do wish to allow the humblest man an equal chance to get rich with everybody else. When one starts poor, as most do in the race of life, free society is such that he knows he can better his condition; he knows that there is no fixed condition of labor, for his whole life. . . . I want every man to have the chance."[37]

Some, such as James McPherson, have argued that Lincoln endorsed the idea of "positive liberty," understood as the exercise of government power in a way that anticipates twentieth-century welfare-state liberalism. However, others such as historian and Lincoln scholar Herman Belz suggest that Lincoln's use of government power to emancipate slaves and abolish slavery promoted "negative liberty," what Belz identifies as the classic nineteenth-century understanding of liberty. By removing the legal restraints of slavery (that is, removing artificial weights), emancipation and abolition were meant to secure liberty defined as a basic right of noninterference. "It consisted," Belz concludes, "in specific rights of person and property that created legal and moral space in which individuals were free to exercise their personal capacities and talents in pursuit of their interests."[38] But here terms can become rather sticky and sometimes misleading. Even Belz's account does imply a certain "positive" role in government, in the sense that government protects the rights of property and person, securing the conditions by which individuals may pursue their interests. Fornieri characterizes Lincoln's equality very well when he suggests that, politically speaking, equality of opportunity has both a *positive* and a *negative* aspect. Positively, equality of opportunity means that government must, at the very least, secure the *conditions* by which people can actualize their potential talents and compete productively for status, wealth, and honor within society. Negatively, it means that government should not impose arbitrary penalties or confer rewards on the basis of race, creed, or color.[39]

In this sense, the principle of equality is not the grounds for the leveling effect that concerns some of Lincoln's conservative critics but is, rather, the ground upon which the natural differences between human beings might be expressed. As Jaffa notes, there is a tendency among conservatives to associate equality with a kind of socialism, or in Kendall's words, a "cooperative commonwealth of men who will be so equal that no one will be able to tell them apart."[40] But in its Lockean sense, the principle of equality makes possible the expression of the natural *differences* among human beings. The principle of the natural equality of men in their inalienable rights is foundational to the institution of private property.[41] Far from mandating the kind of redistribution that some associate with the pursuit of modern egalitarianism, Lincoln's equality is best understood as an equality of rights or opportunity but not as an equality of rewards. Thus, Lincoln could declare to the New York Workingmen's Association during the Civil War that "[p]roperty is the fruit of labor—property is desirable—is a positive good in the world. That some should be rich, shows that others may become rich, and hence is just encouragement to industry and enterprise. Let not him who is houseless pull down the house of another; but let him labor diligently and build one for himself, thus by example assuring that his own shall be safe from violence when built."[42] Lincoln's views here were consistent with those of the American Founders. Madison famously offered this understanding of equality in the 10th *Federalist*. The first object of government, Madison argued, is the protection of the different and unequal faculties of acquiring and possessing property.[43] Lincoln's idea of the standard maxim of equality shared this assumption.

egalitarianism often rejects this idea of an unchanging human nature and thus rejects the idea that political life must necessarily cope with human imperfections. With their faith in human perfectibility through social planning, proponents of progressivism and modern liberalism will come to deny the natural right basis of the Founding and Lincoln's political thought. Progress rather than nature reveals what man is and what he is capable of. Historian Richard Hofstadter summarized the progressive view best when he stated that "No man who is well abreast of modern science as the Fathers were of eighteenth century science believes any longer in unchanging human nature. Modern humanistic thinkers who seek for a means by which society may transcend eternal conflict and rigid adherence to property rights as its integrating principles can expect no answer in the philosophy of balanced government as it was set down by the Constitution makers of 1787."[47] We might add here that no one wishing to "transcend eternal conflict and rigid adherence to property rights" will find an answer in Lincoln either.

With this faith in human perfectibility, modern egalitarianism thus implies a faith in the elimination of human inequality. Lincoln's pursuit of equality, however, did not pretend to conquer our nature but, rather, proceeded in a manner not only consistent with our imperfections but conducive to the cultivation and exercise of individuals' diverse and unequal faculties. And even in this most fundamental and limited formulation, in the right to pursue one's interests under the rule of law, Lincoln's pursuit of equality was subject to inherent limitations. If there is to be a sensible dedication to equality, certain qualifications and limitations on the pursuit of that equality must be acknowledged.[48]

Prudence and the Principle of Equality

Some see Lincoln's explanation of the "standard maxim" as the most open-ended of his statements about equality, but even here Lincoln admitted that the standard maxim is "constantly looked to" and "constantly labored for" but "never perfectly attained" and "constantly approximated." Likewise, in his call to lift "artificial weights" from the shoulders of all, Lincoln suggested this endeavor must yield to "partial and temporary departures, from necessity." According to Lincoln, the pursuit of equality had always "submitted patiently to whatever of inequality there seemed to be as matter of actual necessity." Lincoln continually reminded his audiences not only of the principled but also of the practical limitations

Lincoln expressed this sentiment most clearly in his metaphor of the race of life. As noted above, Carey rightly argues that Lincoln's call to secure individuals' equality in the race of life is inviting to modern egalitarians. We shall find that U.S. presidents, in pursuit of modern egalitarian policies, have often invoked Lincoln's words on the race of life. However, when we look at what Lincoln actually said about equality in the race of life, the real differences between Lincoln's equality and modern egalitarianism are clear. Lincoln's statement is worth our close consideration.

In making the case for Union in his July 4, 1861, message to Congress in special session, Lincoln declared:

> This is essentially a People's contest. On the side of the Union, it is a struggle for maintaining in the world, that form, and substance of government, whose leading object is, to elevate the condition of men—to lift artificial weights from all shoulders—to clear the paths of laudable pursuit for all—to afford all, an unfettered start, and a fair chance, in the race of life. Yielding to partial, and temporary departures, from necessity, this is the leading object of the government for whose existence we contend.[44]

Lincoln thus characterized the pursuit of equality as being an effort to secure individual equality of opportunity, under the rule of law, to exercise diverse and necessarily unequal talents and abilities. Lincoln's race of life metaphor implies a distinction between—and combination of—equality at the starting line, and liberty in the race. And this formulation assumes the justice of an unequal finish. In "lifting artificial weights" from all shoulders, Lincoln's metaphor suggests that a fair race is one in which no participant is saddled with artificial or arbitrary burdens, but the natural inequalities among the runners are allowed, indeed expected, to manifest themselves in the race, and these inequalities are expressed in the order of the finishers. The only equality we see in the end result, as Jaffa suggests, is the proportional equality of unequal prizes for unequal finishers. Rather than demanding an equality of results among individuals in this pursuit, Lincoln's metaphor assumes an inequality of results.[45]

Recognizing the imperfections of an unchanging human nature, Lincoln and the Founders' understanding of equality did not seek to eliminate the natural inequalities between human beings but, rather, sought to compromise with those inequalities in the best manner possible.[46] Lincoln's equality is distinguished from modern egalitarianism in its realistic view of the human condition. In following chapters, we shall find that modern of the standard maxim.[49] Lincoln is no doctrinaire, and this helps us to understand his pursuit of equality better.

In his seventh debate with Douglas, quoting Henry Clay, Lincoln suggested that the idea that all men are created equal is true as an abstract principle but cannot be practically applied in all cases. Yet, in any case, the principle of natural equality is to serve as the guiding fundamental principle of the regime.[50] Lincoln acknowledged a disjunction between theory and practice in the pursuit of equality and recognized that the political sometimes imposes restraints upon what we can achieve in that pursuit. As a very practical illustration of this line of reasoning, in his 1864 speech to the 164th Ohio Regiment, Lincoln claimed that we live in a free government wherein every man has a right to be equal with every other man. However, he continued, "there may be some irregularities in the practical application of our system."[51] For example, Lincoln suggested, "it is fair that each man shall pay taxes in exact proportion to the value of his property; but if we should wait before collecting a tax to adjust the taxes upon each man in exact proportion with every other man, we should never collect any tax at all."[52]

Lincoln used this same example in his September 14, 1863, "Opinion on the Draft." In this opinion, Lincoln answered objections to draft laws, particularly the controversial "three hundred dollar" provision, in which a man could buy his way out of the draft by paying three hundred dollars. This provision, Lincoln explained, was not generally objected to on the grounds that it is unconstitutional but, rather, "for inequality—for favoring the rich over the poor." There was a certain inequality in the money provision, Lincoln explained, yet there was another provision in place that permitted one man to substitute another man for himself. Of course, such a substitution probably involved a monetary incentive, and without the money provision, Lincoln argued, the price for buying substitutions would, most likely, greatly exceed three hundred dollars. According to Lincoln, the money provision actually benefited the poor man because it enlarged "the class of exempts from actual service simply by admitting poorer men into it." Lincoln claimed that, similar to tax laws, draft laws belong to a class "composed of those laws whose object is to distribute burthens or benefits on the principle of equality." No one of those laws, however, "can ever be practically administered with that exactness which can be conceived of in the mind."[53]

Lincoln understood statesmanship in light of the classical virtue of prudence, which is the unique ability to reconcile universal and timeless moral and theoretical truths with the variable circumstances of everyday practice. Prudence constitutes a kind of practical wisdom and allows a statesman to do the right thing, at the right time, according to the given circumstances at hand.⁵⁴ As Fornieri argues, prudence is best understood as a mean between political idealism on the one hand and political pragmatism on the other. Political idealism, in its doctrinairism and rigid inflexibility, fails to consider the varied circumstances and inherent limitations to political action. Dwelling solely in the realm of abstract principles, political idealism fundamentally misunderstands the political world and the limitations placed upon right political action. Pragmatism, on the other hand, fails to consider sufficiently the primacy of timeless and universal theoretical truths to practical political judgment. The pragmatist, Fornieri argues, "decides politics in the ethically relative terms of utility, expediency and/or self-interest. . . . [Pragmatism] suffers from an ethical myopia that is blind to the preeminence of moral claims in guiding public policy."⁵⁵ The prudent statesman must recognize and navigate the persistent disjunction between theory and practice in the pursuit of any good. As Lincoln once suggested:

> Inequality is certainly never to be embraced for its own sake; but is every good thing to be discarded, which may be inseparably connected with some degree of it? If so we must discard all government. . . . The true rule, in determining to embrace, or reject any thing, is not whether it have *any* evil in it; but whether it have more of evil than of good. There are few things *wholly* evil or *wholly* good. Almost every thing, especially of governmental policy, is an inseparable compound of the two; so that our best judgment of the preponderance between them is continually demanded.⁵⁶

For Lincoln, the pursuit of equality, no less than the pursuit of any other good, is often subject to the dictates of prudence.

There is perhaps no better example of Lincoln's understanding of prudence than his characterization of the Founders' handling of the slavery question at the Convention of 1787. Many, including Douglas and Roger Taney, argued that the Founders' toleration of slavery indicated they were not dedicated to the principle of natural equality. Lincoln routinely defended the Founders against this charge and always insisted that they handled the slavery problem with the greater good in mind. Lincoln's praise of the Founders rested not only upon the direction in which their words pointed (although his praise of the Declaration and his understanding of the standard maxim of equality certainly do this) but also upon the prudential application of those principles in light of extremely difficult political circumstances. Lincoln reasoned:

> It may be argued that there are certain conditions that make necessities and impose them upon us, and to the extent that a necessity is imposed upon a man he must submit to it. I think that was the condition in which we found ourselves when we established this government. We had slavery among us, we could not get our constitution unless we permitted them to remain in slavery, we could not secure the good we did secure if we grasped for more, and having by necessity submitted to that much, it does not destroy the principle that is the charter of our liberties. Let that charter stand as our standard.[57]

The "principle that is the charter of our liberties" was, of course, the principle that all men are created equal. The existence of slavery, in light of historical circumstance and political necessity, did not destroy the truth of the proposition that all men are created equal, nor did it disprove or cast doubt upon the Founders' dedication to that proposition. To say that practice disproves the theory, or the Founders' and Lincoln's dedication to that theory, is to misunderstand the disjunction between theory and practice that characterizes political life.

For Lincoln, the standard by which we deem the Founders worthy of national reverence resides *not only* in their profession of the proposition that all men are created equal but also in their *application* of that principle in light of political necessity, by their clear efforts to place slavery in the course of ultimate extinction (for example, prohibiting slavery in the Northwest Territory, giving Congress the power to abolish the international slave trade after 1808).[58] These observations apply no less to Lincoln's pursuit of equality. We have seen some claim that the universalism and supposed open-endedness of Lincoln's equality smacks of a certain utopianism. Yet, Lincoln's idea of equality was not only limited in principle but necessarily intertwined with a prudential appreciation for the limitations of political practice. Indeed, Lincoln's principled understanding of equality and his prudence in pursuit of equality are inseparable.

Take, for example, Lincoln's handling of the slavery problem both before and during the war. In this case, the pursuit of equality was necessarily inhibited by the constitutional structure established by the consent of the governed and by the practical limitations to emancipation. Lincoln's cautious, prudential approach to the slavery problem prompts some modern commentators to question his dedication to emancipation and equal rights.[59] But such views often fail to understand or appreciate Lincoln's reasoning on emancipation. Despite the fact that Lincoln believed slavery to be an affront to the principles of the Declaration, he rejected the notion that national authority could legitimately be used to abolish slavery in the states where it already existed. As Fornieri notes, Lincoln rightly understood that the slavery question was necessarily wrapped up in different jurisdictions of authority; that is, he distinguished legally between slavery as a local, state, and national institution. Lincoln believed that, constitutionally, the federal division of power prohibited the national government from interfering with slavery where it already existed. But the territories, being under federal authority, were a different matter. It had been assumed, at least as far back as the Northwest Ordinance, that Congress had the power to legislate with respect to slavery in the territories. Thus, the federal government could make a reasonable case for the restriction of slavery in the western territories. Prior to the Civil War and the passage of the Reconstruction Amendments, to have argued that the general government possessed the right to interfere with slavery where it already existed would have been understood as unconstitutional and seen as a usurpation of state and local authority.[60]

Lincoln's efforts to restrict the spread of slavery into the territories, and his ultimate handling of emancipation, illustrate both the principled limitations and the practical limitations of his pursuit of equality. In his attempt to approximate the standard maxim, Lincoln sought to return slavery to the path of ultimate extinction through established political and constitutional means. Given his constitutional reservations about the power of the federal government to interfere with slavery where it already existed, he believed that emancipation was constitutionally defensible only as a war measure. Emancipation was a necessary means to impair the South's war effort by confiscating slave property, under the commander-in-chief power accorded to the president under Article II of the U.S. Constitution. But emancipation of course would be incomplete without an amendment to the Constitution itself; that is, emancipation in its fullest sense could be accomplished only through the constitutionally structured consent of the governed.

Many wonder why Lincoln did not free slaves in states that were not in open rebellion against the U.S. government. Yet one must understand this decision in light of the requirement of consent that guides his pursuit of equality. According to Lincoln's reasoning, it would have been unconstitutional to free slaves in states not in open rebellion against the United States without the consent of those states. And one must not forget that, as was the case in the Preliminary Emancipation Proclamation, Lincoln offered the border states compensated, consensual emancipation, while Southern states were offered compensated emancipation should they return to the Union. Lincoln's refusal to free slaves in the border states with the Emancipation Proclamation only reinforces the fact that he understood the pursuit of the standard maxim to flow through the constitutionally structured means of government by consent of the governed.[61]

This union of principle and prudential judgment applied no less to Lincoln's thoughts on extending civil and political rights to freed slaves. Lincoln is often remembered for his October 16, 1854, speech at Peoria, where he discussed various solutions to the slavery problem. Among the options he surveyed was this: "Free them, and make them politically and socially, our equals? My own feelings will not admit of this; and if mine would, we well know that those of the great mass of white people will not. Whether this feeling accords with justice and sound judgment, is not the sole question, if indeed, it is any part of it." A "universal feeling," Lincoln suggested, "whether well or ill-founded, can not be safely disregarded. We can not, then, make them equals."[62] As Fornieri has observed, Lincoln must attempt to secure the good that he can get, without destroying the possibility of securing good in the future. Politically speaking, to have advocated emancipation, black citizenship, and suffrage unqualifiedly, when majority opinion not did support these things, would have endangered Lincoln's early efforts to stop the spread of slavery into the territories. There is prudence in recognizing the limitations of what one can hope to achieve at a given time, under given circumstances. In popular government a universal feeling, even if ill-founded, cannot safely be ignored. In a free government this must always include an appreciation of the limitations imposed upon the statesman by the opinion of the governed and, above all, the requirement of consent.[63] Yet the demands of practice do not invalidate or disprove the truth of the theory. Indeed, Lincoln's prudential approach to slavery only makes sense in light of his principled understanding of natural equality and government by consent. Whatever we might concede to the disjunction between theory and practice, natural right remains the theoretical foundation of Lincoln's defense of free government. We shall find that this ultimately distinguishes Lincoln's understanding of equality from that of the progressives and modern liberals who will invoke his name.

Conclusion

We have seen that critics and defenders of Lincoln's pursuit of equality may have more in common than we might first expect. Many share the fundamental assumption that Lincoln was responsible for refounding the

American political order on the basis of equality. Such observers agree that this push toward greater equality is responsible, at least in part, for the modern egalitarianism that characterizes much of modern American political discourse. For some, Lincoln is to be praised for this contribution to the march of equality. For others, Lincoln is to be blamed for introducing a dangerous abstraction into our political discourse, fundamentally and negatively altering the nature and scope of American democracy.

Some of Lincoln's conservative critics might look to *Democracy in America* and Alexis de Tocqueville's not unreasonable fears about the dangers and excesses of equality in American popular government. According to Tocqueville, the passion for equality leads individuals to sacrifice true self-government for equality in nearly every aspect of life, an equality secured only by an increasingly centralized national government with soft despotic power.[64] But Lincoln, too, understood and appreciated the dangers of equality, as evidenced by his thoughtful commentary on the excesses of Jacksonian democracy in his famed "Lyceum Address." Here Lincoln denounced the mob rule that was sweeping the country in the 1830s as being a threat not only to the lives and liberties of citizens but to the very preservation of our political institutions. For Lincoln, the effect of mob rule is to alienate citizens from the government and the laws, rendering them more susceptible to the charms of ambitious demagogues and would-be tyrants who seek to tear those institutions down. Only through a reverence for the Constitution and the laws, claimed Lincoln, could we guard against this danger.[65]

Tocqueville, as a commentator, seemed to think it necessary to distract attention away from the Declaration, perhaps fearing its appeal to what some might regard as an overly philosophic and potentially doctrinaire statement of natural equality.[66] Lincoln, however, as a statesman, did not attempt to turn our eyes away from the Declaration. Indeed, circumstances required that Lincoln confront the Declaration, the problem of slavery, and the idea of equality squarely. Proponents of the slave interest denied the natural equality of all human beings in their inalienable rights and thus denied the very basis of government by consent of the governed. It is wrong to suggest that Lincoln somehow did not see equality as problematic, for Lincoln seems to have understood that equality is prone to be misunderstood. And any student of Tocqueville understands that this problem is particularly acute in democracies. Yet, in a sense, both Tocqueville and Lincoln were engaged in the same pursuit, each in his own fashion. That is, they both attempted to moderate the excesses of democracy. Lincoln's understanding of equality as equal liberty under the rule of law exalted the rights of property and accepted unequal results among citizens in the pursuit of their interests. All of these qualities help to temper the leveling effects of the debased taste for equality.[67] Even when forced to rearticulate the central idea of equality in the face of those who would deny the fundamental principles of free government, Lincoln took care to acknowledge both the principled and the practical limits inherent in the pursuit of equality.

Lincoln's understanding of equality would come under attack in American political discourse in the twentieth century. Many of those who would criticize the notion of equality espoused by Lincoln, however, would nevertheless invoke his authority in attempting to articulate and defend non-Lincolnian ideas. This requires the rhetorical use and abuse of Abraham Lincoln. While the Lincoln image has sometimes been abused, the mere fact that later actors looked to him to justify their claims does not detract from the importance of trying to understand Lincoln as he understood himself.[68] The effort to understand American political development cannot rest content with merely drawing a line from the Gettysburg Address or the standard maxim to modern variants of egalitarianism. Rather, one ought to note the differences between Lincoln's equality and later egalitarianism, differences that are most definitely there to be seen.

Following the Civil War, with the rise of progressivism, political pragmatism, and the widespread rejection of natural right thinking, those who would come to call on Lincoln in the name of equality often embraced a decidedly non-Lincolnian understanding of equality. His idea of equality was rooted in the natural rights principles informing the Declaration of Independence. Carey claims that, despite the variations among the political thought of the progressives, one constant has always been that "the Declaration has always been on the 'angelic' side of a great divide that separates it from the Constitution." That is, while the Declaration of Independence is consistently portrayed as the ultimate and authoritative expression of egalitarianism, majority rule, and human rights, the Constitution is generally seen as a reactionary, antidemocratic, oligarchic document. This progressive understanding, Carey suggests, is at least partially attributable to Lincoln's exaltation of the Declaration as a founding document.[69]

However, for the progressives, the theoretical basis of man's equality did not reside in the self-evident truth that we are equally endowed with natural and inalienable rights. The progressives preferred a "denatured" Declaration of Independence, wherein our rights were defined by reference to history and economic forces rather than nature. As Murley notes, the progressives denied the natural rights foundation of the Declaration, but they nevertheless advocated the goal of social, political, and economic equality. "Once stripped of any foundation in nature," Murley explains, the progressives championed a "denatured Declaration" as the "real and legitimate source of the American democratic and egalitarian tradition."[70] This reading of the Declaration is fundamentally at odds with Lincoln's reading. We shall find that this has significant consequences, both for how we understand equality as a goal to be secured and for our understanding of the legitimate means by which we should pursue that goal.

As an intellectual and political movement, progressivism sought to give the people greater control over government and to give government greater control over the economy, often in the name of egalitarian reform. The progressives' rhetorical appeal to the Lincoln image became central to this effort.[71] In their use and abuse of Lincoln, the progressives adopted a different understanding of the ends of government, an understanding that, consequently, demanded a different understanding of the means to pursue those ends. As Thomas Krannawitter has recently argued, many progressives "simply ignored Lincoln's manifest defense of natural rights and insisted that the progressive reform movements of the late nineteenth and early twentieth centuries represented a continuation of the same fight against oppression that Lincoln fought."[72] While the progressives would elevate and rhetorically appeal to Lincoln's legacy of equality, they would reject its defining principles. The fact that the distance between the progressives and Lincoln is so rarely noted, particularly with respect to equality, is a testament to their appropriation of the Lincoln image.

TWO

Theodore Roosevelt's Lincoln

ON THE EVE OF HIS SECOND PRESIDENTIAL inauguration, Theodore Roosevelt received a gift from his friend and former Lincoln secretary, John Hay. While taking the oath of office the next day, Roosevelt wore this gift upon his finger—a ring holding a lock of hair snipped from the head of Abraham Lincoln shortly after his assassination. Several years later, in his *Autobiography*, Roosevelt recalled the significance of the event, claiming that "The ring was on my finger when the Chief Justice administered to me the oath of allegiance to the United States; I often thereafter told John Hay that when I wore such a ring on such an occasion I bound myself more than ever to treat the Constitution, after the manner of Abraham Lincoln, as a document which put human rights above property rights when the two conflicted."[1] Roosevelt was a lifelong admirer of Lincoln, and he consistently invoked Lincoln's name throughout his political career. By the time of his 1912 bid for president with the newly formed Bull Moose Progressive Party, Roosevelt would endeavor to wrest the Lincoln image from his former Republican Party, claiming that the Progressives, and only the Progressives, were the rightful heirs of Abraham Lincoln.[2]

In his political rhetoric, Roosevelt appealed to Lincoln as a "pure democrat" who foreshadowed progressive political reforms such as the initiative and referendum, the recall of judges and judicial decisions, and increased national legislation aimed at securing social and industrial justice.[3] If Lincoln had been alive at the dawn of the twentieth century,

Roosevelt claimed, he would have understood and endorsed democratizing political reforms to address social and economic inequality, above all, on the principle that the people are the rightful masters of their public servants and the Constitution. However, that Roosevelt frequently appealed to Lincoln does not mean that he rightly understood, or rightly represented Lincoln's political thought. Roosevelt often redefined and reinterpreted Lincoln to fit the needs of progressive political rhetoric. His appeal to Lincoln was often misleading, hinging on highly selective or incomplete accounts of Lincoln's speeches. The effect is that Roosevelt often divorced his Lincoln from the principles that guided Lincoln's actual understanding of the ends and means of American democracy. Despite his repeated claims to follow Lincoln's example, Roosevelt departed from Lincoln's principles.

Roosevelt's Many Claims to the Lincoln Inheritance

Perhaps more than any other American politician, Teddy Roosevelt frequently invoked Lincoln's name in support of his political opinions and policies. Roosevelt's speeches and writings abound with references to Lincoln. His most famous appeal to Lincoln was probably his Jackson-Lincoln theory, or "stewardship theory" of the executive, which deserves brief mention here. According to Roosevelt, as "steward of the people," the president possessed both the right and the duty to take any action he deemed necessary for the nation, unless such an action was explicitly denied by the Constitution and the laws.[4] Roosevelt saw precedent for this view in the presidencies of both Jackson and Lincoln. However, one should be cautious in simply equating Jackson, Lincoln, and Roosevelt on their theories of executive power. In his famous veto of the National Bank Bill, Jackson had proclaimed "stewardship" to *limit* the scope of the general government. Roosevelt, however, used the idea of stewardship to pursue domestic policy agendas that would broaden the scope of the general government.[5] And while Roosevelt was correct to recognize the executive powers Lincoln assumed during the Civil War, Lincoln did not exercise the broad executive powers often attributed to him. Concerned primarily with fighting the war, Lincoln took little part in the domestic legislation of his day, rarely used the presidential veto power, and played little role in foreign policy.[6] Moreover, Lincoln's claims to executive prerogative were justified primarily in light of the crisis of war. Roosevelt took his bearings from this extreme case and extended war or crisis powers to the normal politics of the executive.[7]

Roosevelt's appeal to Lincoln in support of his stewardship theory is well-known among students of the American presidency.

However, when Roosevelt broke with the Republicans he would take his use of Lincoln in another and perhaps less well-known direction. Roosevelt claimed that, like Lincoln, he believed the purpose of American democracy was to secure equality of opportunity for all Americans.[8] Roosevelt claimed that there can be no "genuine" democracy without "economic democracy," wherein men are given the equal opportunity to become intellectually, morally, and materially fit to be their own masters.[9] Roosevelt argued that, in modern industrial America, the national government must increase its efforts to secure this opportunity by reining in special interests. This would not happen, Roosevelt believed, unless the people were given increased and more direct control over their elected representatives, court decisions at both state and federal levels, and the Constitution.

The importance of the Lincoln image to Roosevelt and the progressive movement, as Barry Schwartz observes, was summed up in the *Chicago Tribune*'s February 1909 centennial editorial: "Our political institutions are being retested from the standpoint of their effectiveness and responsiveness as instruments of the popular will. The demand for popularization of the senate, for the democratization of party organization through direct primaries, for the initiative and referendum and even the recall," resulted in a "tide of democracy." In this "ripe hour the American people turn to their noblest memory.... For Lincoln's life and Lincoln's character illustrate more perfectly than that of any other of America's great men the essential rightness and practicability of democracy." And if Lincoln's presidency was understood as the first phase of the progressive movement, then, as Schwartz suggests, the Gettysburg Address was its manifesto. Yet the progressive claim to Lincoln was a matter of dispute, and Schwartz notes that, by 1913, *The Nation* would suggest that "Nobody knows, and there is nothing in Lincoln's acts or words, to tell, whether or not he would have been for the initiative and referendum, for endowment of motherhood, or for single tax; yet enthusiastic advocates of almost any 'advanced' proposal of our day find little difficulty in persuading themselves that it is a corollary of the Gettysburg Address."[10]

At a 1913 Lincoln Day banquet in New York City, Roosevelt summed up his claim to the Lincoln legacy by dedicating a single powerful speech to this theme—"The Heirs of Abraham Lincoln." Here we see clearly the sort of claims that Schwartz describes above. Roosevelt suggested in this speech that Lincoln's political thought contained a "curious applicability" to the questions of the present day. According to Roosevelt, Lincoln and his supporters were in fact the "progressives of their day," and the current Republican Party machinery was comprised of reactionaries comparable to "Bourbon Democrats and Cotton Whigs." According to Roosevelt, critics of the Progressive Party were the spiritual heirs of those who once accused Lincoln of being a "revolutionist," who "denounced the Supreme Court." They were comparable to those who labeled Lincoln a "radical," an "innovator," an "opponent of the Constitution," and an "enemy of property." Roosevelt argued that, even though Lincoln's thoughts and actions were concerned largely with slavery and Union, it was "curious to note the exact parallelism of [Lincoln's] general attitude with the attitude that the Progressive party has now taken."[11]

Roosevelt attempted to illustrate this "exact parallelism" between Lincoln and the Progressive Party by making several interrelated arguments. First, he argued that the purpose of progressive political and economic reform at the turn of the century was to "establish in this world the rights of man, the right not only to religious and political but to economic freedom; and to make these rights real and living." Insofar as we are to see Lincoln as the intellectual and political progenitor of the Progressive Party, we should infer that this too was Lincoln's purpose in his own day. Second, Roosevelt claimed that, like the new Progressive Party, Lincoln understood the "right and the duty of the citizens to form a new party when the old parties prove incompetent to help the people." Born in the controversy surrounding the Kansas-Nebraska Act, Lincoln and the Republicans formed a new party when existing parties proved incapable of preventing the spread of slavery into the West, filling the political space left by the collapse of the Whigs and a bitterly divided Democratic Party. According to Roosevelt, the Progressives followed the same spirit. They formed a new party when existing parties proved incompetent to protect the people from exploitive special interests, corrupt politicians, and irresponsible judges who blocked the advancement of social and industrial justice.[12]

Third, according to Roosevelt, in warring against special privilege and for equal opportunity in the race of life, "the Progressive platform of to-day is but an amplification" of Lincoln's denunciation of the tyrannical principle that "it is one man's duty to toil, and work and earn bread and the right of another man to eat it when earned."[13] Roosevelt claimed that, like Lincoln, the Progressives understood that labor is superior to capital and that human rights should take precedence over property rights if the two should come into conflict. Lincoln's support of free labor and the Progressive demand for "economic democracy" and "industrial representation" are asserted to rest on the same fundamental principles.

Fourth, Roosevelt supported democratizing reforms such as the initiative, referendum, and recall, and he used Lincoln to argue for these measures. According to Roosevelt, like Lincoln, the Progressives believed in the right of the people to "control all their public servants, judicial, executive, and legislative alike." Lincoln had publicly condemned the secessionists for denying that the people have the right to participate in the selection of public officers "except the legislative" and for wrongly holding that large control of the people in government is the "source of all political evil." These words, Roosevelt argued, apply "without the change of a word" to those who assail the Progressive demand for increased and more direct popular control over government.[14]

Finally, Roosevelt claimed that, in criticizing the *Dred Scott* decision, Lincoln laid the foundation for the idea that the people should have a right to recall erroneous or unjust judicial decisions by referendum. Roosevelt pursued this argument in "The Heirs of Abraham Lincoln," yet it ran throughout his speeches and writings on the judiciary. In his Charter of Democracy Address, before the Ohio Constitutional Convention in 1912, Roosevelt suggested that the word *recall* was unknown to Lincoln, but by appealing to the people "against the judges when the judges went wrong," he helped to secure the "practical recall" of *Dred Scott*.[15] Let us consider each of Roosevelt's arguments in turn.

The Redefinition of Rights

According to Roosevelt, the Progressive Party was the direct political and intellectual descendent of Abraham Lincoln. "We Progressives and we alone," Roosevelt proclaimed, "are to-day the representatives of the men of Lincoln's day who upheld the hands of Lincoln. . . . Lincoln and Lincoln's supporters were emphatically the progressives of their day."[16] Yet, immediately, the opening lines of his "Heirs of Abraham Lincoln" suggest an incongruence between Roosevelt's argument and Lincoln's political thought. Consider the following:

> The Progressive movement which culminated last August in the creation of the Progressive party is no mere sign of temporary political discontent, it is a manifestation of the eternal forces of human growth, a manifestation of the

God-given impulse implanted in mankind to make a better race and a better earth. Its purpose is to establish in this world the rights of man, the right not only to religious and political but to economic freedom; and to *make these rights real and living.*[17]

Roosevelt frequently referred to the rights of man in his speeches and writings, yet he rarely referred to the "natural" or "inalienable" rights of man. This merits our attention. He often asserted that the purpose of government is to secure the individual rights to life, liberty, and the pursuit of happiness, but it is important to note that he believed those rights had changed (and would continue to change) in light of historical and economic conditions.[18] Roosevelt consistently redefined the rights to life, liberty, and the pursuit of happiness, "as we may restate them in these later days, [as] the rights of the worker to a living wage, to reasonable hours of labor, to decent working and living conditions, to freedom of thought and speech and industrial representation—in short, to a measure of industrial democracy and, in return for his arduous toil, to a worthy and decent life according to American standards."[19]

We observe that Roosevelt asserted that the purpose of the Progressive Party is "to establish in this world the rights of man . . . and to make these rights *real and living.*"[20] Roosevelt suggested, it appears, that if the rights of man are to be established in this world, if they are to be *real* and *living*, they must be actively enjoyed by individuals. Yet if this sentiment is somehow part of Roosevelt's claim to Lincoln's inheritance, then Roosevelt's thinking runs into trouble.

We recall that Lincoln declared that the American Founders "defined with tolerable distinctness, in what respects they did consider all men created equal—equal in 'certain inalienable rights, among which are life, liberty, and the pursuit of happiness' . . . *they did not mean to assert the obvious untruth, that all were then actually enjoying that equality,* nor yet, that they were about to confer it immediately upon them."[21] As we have seen, Lincoln understood the natural and inalienable rights of men as timeless, self-evident truths rooted in the Laws of Nature and Nature's God. That some men are not currently enjoying their equal rights to life, liberty, and the pursuit of happiness is no indication that those rights, forever rooted in nature, are not "real" or "living." Indeed, this is fundamental to Lincoln's moral condemnation of slavery. The slave's right to eat the bread he has earned by the sweat of his brow is just as real as the free man's right to do the same. While Roosevelt often referred to the rights of the individual, his supposed kinship to Lincoln in this respect is not convincing. For Lincoln these rights were transhistorical, true everywhere and always. For Roosevelt, rights could not be real and living unless they were continually redefined in light of history or economic circumstances. We shall find that this has consequences. By disagreeing about the nature and basis of rights, Roosevelt and Lincoln necessarily disagree about the legitimate ends and means of American government. Nevertheless, despite these fundamental differences, Roosevelt asserted that the Progressive platform was nothing more than a modern-day application of Lincolnian principles.

The Right to Form New Parties

Roosevelt reminded his audience that the great phase of Lincoln's political career began after the collapse of the Whigs, when he took part in helping to form the new Republican Party, "the Progressive party of that day." Roosevelt claimed that the 1854 Republican Party platform "contains the absolute justification for the actions of the Progressives to-day, and shows how fundamentally and basically alike the Progressive movement of to-day and the Republican movement of 1854 are."[22] The 1854 Republican platform began by adopting the language of the Declaration of Independence, suggesting that, whenever political parties become destructive of the ends for which they are established, the people have both the right and the duty to organize new parties:

> I. Resolved. That we believe this truth to be self-evident, that when parties become subversive of the ends for which they are established, or incapable of restoring the government to the true principles of the Constitution, it is the right and duty of the people to dissolve the political bands by which they have been connected therewith, and to organize new parties upon such principles and with such views as the circumstances and the exigencies of the nation may demand.[23]

Roosevelt initially quoted the 1854 Republican platform directly and accurately. But soon after, in his recapitulation of the platform's principles, he offered a rather selective summary. "When parties become subversive of the ends for which they are established," Roosevelt claimed, "it is the right and the duty of the people to dissolve the bands by which they have been connected therewith, and to organize new parties."[24] Noticeably absent from

Roosevelt's statement is the right and the duty of the people to organize new parties when old parties prove "incapable of restoring the government to the true principles of the Constitution." The express end of the new Republican Party was to "*restore* the government to the *true principles of the Constitution*" and to "organize new parties *upon such principles* and with such views as the circumstances and the exigencies of the nation may demand." The repeal of the Missouri Compromise in the form of the Kansas-Nebraska Act was seen as an affront to the principles of the Declaration and the Constitution, as well as a reversal of years of established legislative practice. The stated purpose of the Republican Party was a return to fundamental principles.[25]

We should question the supposed parallelism between Lincoln and the Progressive Party here. Roosevelt and the progressive movement assumed that the principles of the Founders' Constitution (the protection of inalienable rights and various institutional arrangements meant to secure this end, such as separation of powers, limited government, and federalism) had been rendered obsolete by changing economic and historical circumstances. The Progressives, rather than looking to the past and the restoration of those principles, looked only toward the future and the historical overcoming of those principles.[26] Thus, Roosevelt's claim that the 1854 platform "contains the absolute justification for the actions of the Progressives to-day" should be regarded with suspicion. However, as important as the right and duty to form new parties may be to the "exact parallelism" between Lincoln and the Progressives, Roosevelt made clear that parties are but vehicles for securing the ends of government. For Roosevelt, the exact parallelism between Lincoln and the Progressives was illustrated, more fundamentally, in the "issues which underlie the need of parties."[27]

Roosevelt's "Practical Equality of Opportunity"

In his debates with Douglas, Lincoln claimed that the slavery question was a manifestation of "the eternal struggle between . . . two principles—right and wrong—throughout the world." According to Lincoln, these two principles "have stood face to face from the beginning of time; and will ever continue to struggle." One principle "is the common right of humanity." The "other is the divine right of kings. It is the same principle in whatever shape it develops itself. It is the same spirit that says: 'You toil and work and earn bread, and I'll eat it.' No matter in what shape it comes, whether from the mouth of a king who seeks to bestride the people of his own nation and live by the fruit of their labors, or from one race of men as an apology for enslaving another man, it is the same tyrannical principle." Surely, Roosevelt concluded, "the Progressive platform is but an amplification of this statement of Lincoln's." According to Roosevelt, the Progressives stood for the common right of humanity and against the idea "whether enunciated by political kings or by money kings, whether championed from a throne, or by a judge from the bench" that it is one man's duty to work and earn bread and another man's right to eat it.[28]

Roosevelt held that, similar to Lincoln, the Progressives had been criticized by their political opponents for asserting that the rights of labor are to be preferred to the rights of capital, and that human rights ought to take precedence over property rights if ever the two conflicted. Employing language familiar to us, Roosevelt claimed the Progressives sought "to elevate the condition of men—to lift artificial weights from all shoulders—to clear the paths of laudable pursuit for all—to afford all, an unfettered start, and a fair chance, in the race of life." Roosevelt asked whether there could possibly be a better statement of the purpose of the Progressive Party—"to war against privilege and for an equal opportunity."[29] One should immediately note that Roosevelt injected new language into Lincoln's statement by speaking not only of a war for equal opportunity but of a war "against privilege."

Roosevelt repeatedly claimed in "The Heirs of Abraham Lincoln" and elsewhere that the purpose of the Progressive Party was to foster the triumph of real or genuine democracy. In his famous "New Nationalism" speech in Osawatomie, Kansas, speaking before a crowd that included veterans of the Civil War, Roosevelt described this real democracy as including an economic system that guaranteed the opportunity for men to show what is best in them. "In every wise struggle for human betterment," Roosevelt suggested, "one of the main objects, and often the only object, has been to achieve in large measure equality of opportunity." At every stage of development, and under all circumstances, "the essence of the struggle is to equalize opportunity, destroy privilege, and give to the life and citizenship of every individual the highest possible value both to himself and to the commonwealth. That is nothing new. All I ask in civil life is what you fought for in the Civil War."[30] Again, we observe that Roosevelt characterized the Civil War as a war against privilege, in this instance, as a war to "destroy privilege."

Although Roosevelt conceded that perfect equality in this struggle was impossible, he urged that we could secure a "practical equality of opportunity."[31] According to Roosevelt, this equality would have two great results:

> First, every man will have a fair chance to make of himself all that in him lies; to reach the highest point to which his capacities, unassisted by special privilege of his own and unhampered by the special privilege of others, can carry him, and to get for himself and his family substantially what he has earned. Second, equality of opportunity means that the commonwealth will get from every citizen the highest service of which he is capable. No man who carries the burden of the special privileges of another can give to the commonwealth that service to which it is fairly entitled.[32]

At first glance, Roosevelt's "practical equality of opportunity" might sound like Lincoln's understanding of equal liberty. Roosevelt appeared to suggest that individuals should have the equal right to pursue their interests by exercising their own talents and abilities. Thus, Roosevelt could urge that government must give a man "a chance, not push him up if he will not be pushed. Help any man who stumbles; if he lies down it is a poor job to try to carry him; but if he is a worthy man, try your best to see that he gets a chance to show the worth that is in him."[33] However, before we can assume the "exact parallelism" between Lincoln's views and Roosevelt's argument for "practical equality of opportunity," we must note a difference between the two. Roosevelt was careful to admit that "Lincoln's principles were actively applied to the great questions of union and slavery," both of which had been solved.[34] For Lincoln, the artificial weights in question were primarily the shackles of slavery. For Roosevelt, the artificial weights manifested themselves in the form of "wage slavery" created by modern industry. But Roosevelt argued that the Progressive Party faced the same basic issue that confronted Lincoln, that is, the struggle between the rights of man and the tyrannical principle that it is one man's duty to labor and another man's right to enjoy the fruits of that labor.[35] While this was a key theme in "The Heirs of Abraham Lincoln," it ran throughout Roosevelt's writings and speeches during the Progressive campaign.

He developed this argument in greater detail in his essay "Washington and Lincoln: The Great Examples," where he wrote that Lincoln's argument for the man over the dollar "applied to black slavery then. It applies now to any wealthy corporation which fails to respect and preserve and encourage all the manhood rights of its workers and to treat them as partners; and it no less applies to any powerful labor-union which shows brutality or insolent disregard for equity in dealing with the rights of any of our citizens." Lincoln, Roosevelt claimed, "had a seriously thought-out philosophy about the rights of capital and the rights of labor," and "his radicalism had not a touch of Marxian Socialism." Rather, like the Progressive Party, Lincoln believed that a "certain relation" between labor and capital "rightly existed."[36] According to Roosevelt, like Lincoln, the Progressives made no war upon capital. Roosevelt pointed to Lincoln's March 6, 1860, speech at New Haven, Connecticut. "It is best for all," Lincoln argued, "to leave each man free to acquire property as fast as he can. Some will get wealthy. I do not believe in a law to prevent men from getting rich: it would do more harm than good. So while we do not propose any war upon capital, we do wish to allow the humblest man an equal chance to get rich with everyone else." Just following these words, we recall how Lincoln declared that when one starts poor, "as most do in the race of life, free society is such that he knows he can better his condition; he knows that there is no fixed condition of labor for his whole life." But it is here that Roosevelt admitted, in his opinion, Lincoln's understanding of free labor was not wholly applicable to twentieth-century America.[37]

Lincoln had always argued, as he did in his December 1861 annual message to Congress, that "labor is prior to and independent of capital. Capital is only the fruit of labor, and could never have existed if labor had not first existed. Labor is the superior of capital, and deserves much the higher consideration." When Lincoln looked out at the America in front of him, he saw that most people were neither wage-laborers nor capitalists. Rather, most "work for themselves, on their farms, in their houses, and in their shops, taking the whole product to themselves, and asking no favors of capital on the one hand, nor of hired laborers on the other." As a response to the pro-slavery arguments of those such as George Fitzhugh and South Carolina senator James Hammond, Lincoln argued that "there is not, of necessity, any such thing as the free hired laborer being fixed to that condition for life."[38] Hammond and Fitzhugh believed that there was no genuine social mobility in Northern society. In Hammond's words, there would always be a "mud-sill" in all societies, a class of laborers to perform the meanest tasks in life. Lifetime wage-earners, Fitzhugh argued, were equivalent to slaves.[39] Lincoln denied this theory, suggesting that "[t]he prudent, penniless beginner in the world, labors for wage awhile, saves a surplus with which to buy tools or land for himself; then labors on his own account another while, and at length hires another new beginner to help him. This [free labor] is the just, and generous, and prosperous system, which opens the way to all—gives hope to all, and consequent energy, and progress, and improvement of condition to all."[40] As we have seen, Lincoln identified free labor as *the* system of equal liberty, that is, a system in which men may labor diligently without artificial restraints, exercising diverse and unequal talents in acquiring and possessing property.

But Roosevelt argued that, after the Civil War, the modern industrialized economy threw a wrench into Lincoln's understanding of free labor and equality of opportunity. In "Washington and Lincoln," Roosevelt suggested that, in a sense, Lincoln remained a man of his times:

> The kind of democracy with which Lincoln was familiar was the democracy of a farming country where the conditions were akin to those of pioneer days, and of "cities" which were hustling, overgrown villages, where there was little stratification of either the raw social or the raw industrial life. In consequence what he says has no direct bearing in detail on a community life of great capitalists and masses of wage-workers, where the social conditions are far more static than in the early decades of the statehood of Illinois. His experience on the prairies had not enabled him to think out either the indispensable necessity of capitalism in great industrial achievements, or the need of a complex system of safeguards for labor under the very conditions necessary for such achievements. But the principles apply; and he carefully guarded his statements, so that they should not be too sweeping.[41]

In order to live up to the "spirit" of Lincoln's teaching, Roosevelt suggested, we must refuse to be bound by the "letter" of that teaching. According to Roosevelt, in Lincoln's simple world, labor could "maintain its rights under a system of primitive individualism" without being organized, and capital itself was of far smaller importance. What Lincoln *saw* was that most men were neither employers nor wage-earners but, rather, owned the tools with which and on which they worked. But, Roosevelt contended that what Lincoln "upheld as a *desirable principle*" was that "the average man—who can never be the man of large means—should himself own a piece of the world." What "Lincoln saw" had changed. "What he upheld as the desirable principle" had not changed.[42]

Of course, Lincoln did live prior to the great industrialization of the late nineteenth and early twentieth centuries, and one would be foolish to deny the effects of this development on American society. To some, Lincoln's economic individualism might seem, if nothing else, rather antiquated.[43] Gabor S. Boritt addresses this concern in his influential study on Lincoln's economic thought, *Lincoln and the Economics of the American Dream*. Boritt identifies Lincoln's belief in the right to rise in society as the central orienting feature of his economic, moral, and political thought. He generally exalts Lincoln's principles, but he also suggests that some might fault Lincoln for being "too simplistic in emphasizing prudence, industry, sobriety, and honesty as the keys to success."[44] Lincoln claimed not only that free laborers are not fixed to their condition for life but also that, if one should remain a hired laborer, "it is not the fault of the system, but because of either a dependent nature which prefers it, or improvidence, folly or singular misfortune." Boritt claims that such "self-righteous" utterances represented an "extreme stance" in Lincoln's career, temporarily called forth by the equally extreme pro-slavery proponents such as Fitzhugh.[45]

According to Boritt, Lincoln summarized his true views on the subject in his 1862 address on colonization to a deputation of Negroes. "Success," Lincoln claimed, "does not *as much* depend on external help as self-reliance."[46] For Boritt, this means Lincoln understood that external (that is, governmental) help might sometimes be necessary to aid the individual. One might be reminded here of Lincoln's frequently cited Fragments on Government. These fragments suggest that Lincoln believed "government ought not to interfere" in all things that "the people can individually do as well for themselves." But certain things do sometimes require "combined action [such as], public roads and highways, public schools, charities, pauperism, orphanage, estates of the deceased, and the machinery of government itself."[47] At the heart of Lincoln's Whiggery, Boritt argues, was the belief that government should afford to the people, as far as it is possible, such "external help." But we should note that, however "self-righteous" some might find Lincoln's statements praising industriousness and blaming dependency and folly, these statements reflect Lincoln's understanding that the free labor system demands a certain cultivation of the *incentive* to labor.[48] But Boritt does remind us of the *overriding* fact that most of Lincoln's statements on labor and equal opportunity were intricately bound up with the slavery problem, which sometimes makes it difficult to tease out just how Lincoln might have responded to the problems created by industrialization.[49]

We can thus understand why Roosevelt might suggest that Lincoln's views on equal opportunity and the superiority of labor to capital have little *direct* bearing on the modern relationship between labor and capital. And it is not unreasonable for Lincoln's successors to claim that he believed government must sometimes address public problems in order to secure legitimate public goods. While Roosevelt conceded that Lincoln's principles were applied largely to the artificial weights of slavery, and that any broader views on labor as such were usually expressed incidentally, Roosevelt claimed that Lincoln's *principles* still applied.[50] According to Roosevelt, his own call for "practical equality of opportunity" was nothing more than a new, modern manifestation of Lincoln's pursuit of equality. But was this really the case?

Those familiar with the "New Nationalism" speech at Osawatomie should seriously question Roosevelt's claim to be led by Lincoln's principles. Despite Roosevelt's assertions that the Progressives declared no war upon capital, and no war upon the institution of private property, the New Nationalism conveyed a rather different view. At Osawatomie, Roosevelt very bluntly explained what the pursuit of his "practical equality of opportunity" entailed for property rights:

> We grudge no man a fortune in civil life if it is honorably obtained and well used. It is not even enough that it should have been gained without doing damage to the community. We should permit it to be gained only so long as the gaining represents benefit to the community. This, I know, implies a policy of a far more active governmental interference with social and economic conditions in this country than we have yet had, but I think we have got to face the fact that such an increase in governmental control is now necessary.[51]

Note that, for Roosevelt, a man's right to his fortune was to be respected only if his gaining that fortune somehow benefited the entire community. It was not enough that a man's fortune was honorably attained. Nor was it enough that a man's fortune was made without harming the common good. According to Roosevelt, we should permit a man to gain his fortune only if it actively benefits the entire community. In short, the general government must be empowered to determine the acceptable use of property, and it must respect property rights only insofar as it is socially useful to do so. Such a system, as Yarbrough notes, is "frankly redistributionist." Roosevelt held nothing back in explaining the implications of this policy. According to Roosevelt, the "central condition of progress" is to "take from some one man or class of men the right to enjoy power, or wealth, or position, or immunity, which has not been earned by service to his or their fellows" and redistribute these goods to "men who have earned more than they possess."[52] This seems a far cry from Lincoln who, along with the American Founders, placed the origin of private property in the self-ownership and labor of the individual and sought to protect the diverse and unequal faculties of acquiring property. While Roosevelt claimed to prefer human rights to property rights if ever the two conflicted, note that for Lincoln and the Founders the right of property itself was rightly understood as a "human right," belonging by nature to all human beings as such.[53]

We are now in a better position to understand Roosevelt's explanation of the "two great results" of his practical equality of opportunity. Roosevelt had suggested that practical equality of opportunity would allow "every man to have a fair chance to make of himself all that in him lies . . . unassisted by special privilege of his own." Clearly among such special privileges is property deemed useless to the community if left in private hands. Roosevelt claimed his practical equality of opportunity would not push up those who would not be pushed. But, in principle, it seems, there was no problem in pulling down those who would not be pulled. I am aware of nothing in Lincoln's speeches and writings to suggest that he understood the pursuit of equality as a "war against privilege" in the sense that Roosevelt suggests. Despite his attempts to claim the Lincoln inheritance, Roosevelt's "practical equality of opportunity" rested on non-Lincolnian ground. Above all, Roosevelt denied the very foundation of Lincoln's notion of equality—that by nature, nothing should come between a man's hand and his mouth. For Lincoln, this meant that, insofar as it is possible, government should exalt and protect the rights of private property. This is not to deny, of course, that government must sometimes enact legislation to address legitimate public problems, or that the people might be taxed. But Roosevelt's theory went far beyond this because it started from a very different place.

Lincoln began his reasoning from the position that, by nature, a man is rightfully entitled to the fruits of his labor. Roosevelt reminded us that Lincoln believed it wrong that an individual must "toil and work and earn bread" while another eats that bread. According to Lincoln this is a tyrannical principle, and Roosevelt often claimed to act in light of this understanding. But at the same time, Roosevelt argued that a man should not enjoy the fruits of his labor unless that man could first justify to the community why he should be permitted to do so. For Roosevelt, the idea that an individual should toil and work and earn bread while another eats that bread is *not* a tyrannical principle as long as it comes in the shape of the redistribution of wealth, as long as it is the *community* that gets to eat the bread. In short, the unstated premise beneath his redistributionism is that majority tyranny is impossible. Roosevelt once wrote that there "are sincere and well-meaning men of timid nature who are frightened by the talk of tyranny of the majority. These worthy gentlemen are nearly a century behind the times. It is true that De Tocqueville, writing about eighty years ago, said that in this country there was great tyranny by the majority. His statement may have been true then, although certainly not to the degree he insisted, but it is not true now."⁵⁴ For Roosevelt, the problem of majority tyranny had been relegated to the dustbin of history.

Roosevelt's "practical equality of opportunity" thus rests upon very different foundations than Lincoln's equality, and it implies different and expanded means to secure its end. Roosevelt's pursuit of equality necessitates an overcoming of the very institutions that Lincoln believed fostered a healthy republican government. For Lincoln, the pursuit of equality, rightly understood, would recognize the worth of the constitutional forms and institutions that help to structure and shape a measured and sober popular government. The means we use to pursue equality must not in the process destroy these goods. Part of the task of democratic statesmanship is to ennoble the pursuit of equality so characteristic of democratic regimes, to foster a sober and moderate love of equality, and to remind us of its tendency, when wrongly understood, to threaten the very institutions that help make free government possible.⁵⁵

Initiative, Referendum, and the Recall of Public Servants

For Roosevelt, if the people were to achieve "practical equality of opportunity," they needed increased and more direct means of controlling their government. In "The Heirs of Abraham Lincoln," he reminded his audience that his political opponents criticized the Progressives for trying to substitute pure democracy for representative government. As a defense against this charge, he suggested:

> Our opponents have especially objected to our doctrine that the people have the right to control all their servants, judicial, executive, and legislative alike. Well, listen to Abraham Lincoln. He assailed his opponents because they "made war upon the first principle of popular government, the rights of the people," because they "boldly advocated" "the denial to the people of the right to participate in the selection of public officers except the legislative," and because they argued "that large control by the people in government" is the "source of all political evil." Mind you, I am quoting from Lincoln's words uttered over fifty years ago. They are applicable in letter and in spirit to our opponents to-day. They apply without the change of a word to those critics who assail us because we advocate the initiative and the referendum and, where necessary, the recall, and because we stand for the right of the people to control all their public servants, including the judges when the judges exercise a legislative function.⁵⁶

We note that Roosevelt did nothing to deny explicitly the charge that the Progressives wanted to substitute pure democracy for representative government. Rather, he appealed to the authority of Lincoln to defend initiative, referendum, and recall. It was not unreasonable for Roosevelt's opponents to identify these measures with "pure" or direct democracy. However, it is surely an overstatement to suggest that Roosevelt wished to *substitute* pure democracy for representative government. It might be more precise to say that Roosevelt sought to inject more "purely" or directly democratic elements into representative government, seeking to get around what he believed were unnecessary limitations on the power of the people to control their government. But Roosevelt, in part, brought this charge that progressives wanted to substitute pure democracy for representative government upon himself.

Just one year prior to his speech "The Heirs of Abraham Lincoln," Roosevelt delivered his controversial "Charter of Democracy" speech before the Ohio Constitutional Convention. In this speech he drew heavy criticism for proposing the recall of judicial decisions by referendum. Moments into the speech, he declared, "I believe in *pure democracy*. With Lincoln, I hold that 'this country, with its institutions, belongs to the people who inhabit it. Whenever they shall grow weary of the existing government, they can exercise their constitutional right of amending it.'"[57] Thus, Roosevelt appeared to suggest that, in order to believe in "pure" democracy, one must believe with Lincoln that the people are sovereign over their own government and that they have the right to amend their constitution. But this is hardly unique to "pure" democracy and belongs rather to the broader category of popular government, which the American Founders, we recall, divided into pure democracies and democratic republics.[58] The people, of course, are sovereign in a democratic republic and may have the right to amend their constitution. Roosevelt claimed to be a "pure" democrat, in order to imply that his opponents were not democrats at all but, rather, oligarchs who held to the idea of "government of the people, not 'by the people,' but by a 'representative part' of the people."[59] Roosevelt ultimately suggested that "unless representative government does absolutely represent the people it is not representative government at all . . . we advocate, not as ends in themselves, but as weapons in the hands of the people, all governmental devices which will make the representatives of the people more easily and certainly responsible to the people's will."[60] For Roosevelt, these "weapons in the hands of the people" were all necessary to achieve a "real" or "genuine" democracy that would secure the "practical equality of opportunity" he attributed to the Lincolnian tradition.

In "Heirs of Abraham Lincoln," Roosevelt turned our attention toward Lincoln's December 1861 annual message to Congress. Lincoln did indeed criticize his "opponents" (that is, the Southern secessionists) for making war upon the "rights of the people." But we should consider Lincoln's words in their fuller context:

> It continues to develop that the insurrection is largely, if not exclusively, a war upon the first principle of popular government—the rights of the people. Conclusive evidence of this is found in the most grave and maturely considered public documents, as well as in the general tone of the insurgents. In those documents we find the abridgment of the existing right of suffrage and the denial to the people of all right to participate in the selection of public officers, except the legislative boldly advocated, with labored arguments to prove large control of the people in government, is the source of all political evil. Monarchy itself is sometimes hinted at as a possible refuge from the power of the people.[61]

Lincoln's remarks (unedited by Roosevelt) show that he was speaking here only of elections. Lincoln did not argue for initiative, referendum, or the recall of public servants, nor did he say anything to suggest that his support for the sovereignty of the people might require such devices. Lincoln did support the right of the people to control all their public servants, but he thought they must do so through established, constitutionally structured modes of consent.

Roosevelt's association of Lincoln with the recall of public officials is particularly problematic. Far from advocating the removal of officers by direct popular decision, it seems Lincoln held that established means of removing officials were sufficient, and indeed, prudent. While Roosevelt frequently cited passages from Lincoln's First Inaugural, for example, he neglected to mention the following passage from that same address. According to Lincoln, "By the frame of the Government under which we live ... [the] people have wisely given their public servants but little power for mischief; and have, with equal wisdom, provided for the return of that little to their hands at very short intervals. While the people retain their virtue and vigilance, no administration, by any extreme of wickedness or folly, can very seriously injure the Government in the short space of four years." Lincoln's words here about the executive office could no doubt be applied to all elected offices. According to Lincoln, elected officials were to be removed through established constitutional means, that is, through regular elections. This was Lincoln's notion of "recall," if we may use the term loosely.⁶²

Roosevelt obscured this fact, and his selective appeal to Lincoln became all the more misleading when he called our attention to the 1861 annual message to Congress and Lincoln's condemnation of the South's "denial to the people of the right to participate in the selection of public officers except the legislative."⁶³ This statement, Roosevelt contended, shows that Lincoln would have supported the people's right to recall all public servants, including judges, by direct popular vote. Given that Roosevelt seemed careful in his editing of Lincoln's remarks to suit his own rhetorical needs, the words he chose to keep probably remained there for a reason. Roosevelt probably drew attention to the phrase "except the legislative" in order to imply that Lincoln thought not only the executive but also the judicial power ought to be under more direct popular control. But Lincoln condemned the idea that the people would be prohibited from *participating* in the *selection* of public officers. As Madison explained in the *Federalist*, it is *essential* that a republican form of government "be derived from the great body of the society ... it is *sufficient* for such government, that the persons administering it be appointed, either directly or indirectly, by the people. ... Even the judges, with all other public officers of the Union, will, as in the several States, be the choice, though a remote choice, of the people themselves."⁶⁴ Roosevelt downplayed the obvious difference between "participating" in the "selection" of public officers and the popular "recall" of those officers. Only in this way could he attempt to apply Lincoln's words to the issue at hand. Roosevelt enlisted the Lincoln example to argue that more direct popular control over government was necessary to secure equality of opportunity. While Lincoln did believe that government should promote equality, nothing suggests he believed this to require more direct popular control over public servants. Roosevelt claimed that Lincoln's statements applied—without a change of word—to the current debate over recall. Indeed, Lincoln's words were not changed. But the application was incorrect.

The Recall of Judicial Decisions

Critics of the Progressive Party, Roosevelt claimed, were "especially fond of denouncing our attitude toward the courts, and above all, our demand that the people shall be made the masters of the courts as regards constitutional questions." Again, Roosevelt appealed to the authority of Lincoln to defend the Progressive position. In this instance, he used Lincoln to argue for the popular recall of judicial decisions. Roosevelt reminded his audience that Lincoln had once suggested, in an 1859 Speech at Cincinnati, that the "people of these United States are the rightful masters both of Congresses and courts, not to overthrow the Constitution, but to overthrow the men who pervert the Constitution." How is it "better possible," Roosevelt asked, "to state the progressive position to-day?"[65]

Lincoln did claim in Cincinnati that the people are the rightful masters of both congresses and courts. However, Roosevelt's rhetoric is misleading here. Despite the many differences between progressivism and its critics, most would probably agree that the people are the rightful masters of both congresses and courts. Roosevelt created a false dilemma by suggesting that, unless one is committed to more direct forms of popular control over representatives, the courts, and the Constitution itself, one does not believe the people are sovereign. The disagreement is not whether the people are the rightful masters of congresses and courts but, rather, about the means by which the will of the people shall be expressed in the safest and most deliberate manner. Moreover, if we consider Lincoln's Cincinnati remarks in context, we find that Roosevelt once again failed to convey Lincoln's position accurately:

> I say that we must not interfere with the institution of slavery in the states where it exists, because the constitution forbids it, and the general welfare does not require us to do so. We must not withhold an efficient fugitive slave law because the constitution requires us, as I understand it, not to withhold such a law. But we must prevent the outspreading of the institution, because neither the constitution nor general welfare requires us to extend it. We must prevent the revival of the African slave trade and the enacting by Congress of a territorial slave code. We must prevent each of these things being done by either Congresses or courts. The people of these United States are the rightful masters of both Congresses and courts not to overthrow the constitution, but to overthrow the men who pervert that constitution. To do these things we must employ instrumentalities. We must hold conventions; we must adopt platforms if we conform to ordinary custom; we must nominate candidates, and we must carry elections. In all these things, I think that we ought to keep in view our real purpose, and in none do anything that stands adverse to our purpose.[66]

Compare Roosevelt's edited version of Lincoln's remarks: "We must prevent these things [which are wrong] being done by either congresses or courts. The people of these United States are the rightful masters both of congresses and courts, not to overthrow the Constitution, but to overthrow the men who pervert the Constitution."[67] Roosevelt neglected to identify the things Lincoln wanted to prevent. This would only highlight the fact that Lincoln spoke of slavery extension and not Roosevelt's issues of social and industrial justice. More important, however, Roosevelt did not identify the means by which Lincoln proposed to address slavery extension. By offering just two sentences from Lincoln's speech, and by neglecting to follow Lincoln's thought through to its conclusion, Roosevelt obscured the unavoidable fact that Lincoln sought to address the slavery problem through established constitutional and political channels. There is nothing in Lincoln's remarks about the recall of judicial decisions by referendum. Rather, Lincoln urged that the people must hold conventions, adopt platforms, nominate candidates, and carry elections. In other words, to demonstrate that they are the rightful masters of both congresses and courts, the people must speak through the established electoral process and the established representative institutions.

Nevertheless, Roosevelt consistently argued that the recall of judicial decisions was a modern-day application of Lincoln's principles. This argument was not limited to his speech "The Heirs of Abraham Lincoln." In his 1912 address "The Recall of Judicial Decisions," Roosevelt explained his opposition to several New York State court decisions that he believed stood in the way of social and industrial justice. Roosevelt proposed his remedy: "My proposal is for the exercise of the referendum by the people themselves in a certain class of decisions of constitutional questions in which the courts decide against the power of the people to do elementary justice." Roosevelt limited most of his discussion of judicial recall to state court decisions. In "The Recall of Judicial Decisions," he argued that, "because of the peculiar features of our Constitution," the federal courts "must be treated by themselves."[68] But Roosevelt did not say that the federal courts would not—or should not—be treated.

In "The Heirs of Abraham Lincoln," given that he generally appealed to Lincoln's handling of an erroneous U.S. Supreme Court decision, Roosevelt's rhetoric sometimes made it difficult to determine just what level of government he was attempting to correct. Although he discussed a list of state court decisions, Roosevelt added *United States v. E. C. Knight Co.*, an 1895 case in which the Supreme Court had argued that Congress had no power under the Sherman Antitrust Act to regulate monopolies of manufacturing. Roosevelt also claimed that, although Justice Marshall performed a noble service in placing the Supreme Court "behind the national ideal[,] ... such a practice as he inaugurated could be maintained permanently only if it was exercised with the greatest moderation," thus drawing our attention once again to the Supreme Court.[69] And Roosevelt clearly had the Supreme Court in mind when he professed his support for Senator Joseph Bristow's proposed amendments to the U.S. Constitution in late 1912 and early 1913. Bristow's amendments would have allowed the president to submit for national referendum any measure he recommended to Congress that had not been acted upon for six months. The proposed amendments would also have given the people the right to recall Supreme Court decisions by national referendum. Roosevelt's support of judicial recall was thus not limited to state court decisions.[70]

In his characteristic attempt to appropriate the Lincoln inheritance, Roosevelt suggested in "The Heirs of Abraham Lincoln" that "Senator Bristow's recently introduced amendments to give to the people the right themselves to decide the policy of the government upon vital questions in cases where they do not agree with decisions rendered by the Supreme Court is but carrying out the principles set forth by Lincoln in . . . his first Inaugural Address." Calling upon Lincoln's legacy in "The Recall of Judicial Decisions," Roosevelt asserted that the recall of judicial decisions by popular vote was "precisely and exactly in line with Lincoln's attitude toward the Supreme Court in the Dred Scott case, and with the doctrines he laid down for the rule of the people in his first inaugural as President." According to Roosevelt, his own position differed "in no essential way . . . from the principles laid down and acted upon by Abraham Lincoln in this matter."[71]

True, Lincoln and Roosevelt both held that the judiciary is not the only legitimate interpreter of the Constitution. They also agreed that erroneous judicial decisions must not be regarded as the final determinant of general policy. But, despite Roosevelt's claim to the contrary, he and Lincoln fundamentally disagreed about the means by which erroneous judicial decisions should be addressed. It is not enough for Roosevelt to suggest that his "exact parallelism" consists in the singular fact that both he and Lincoln opposed erroneous judicial decisions. The means by which this opposition was effectively expressed helps reveal the fundamental differences between them.

Roosevelt sometimes compared his contemporary opponents to Douglas, who had attempted to paint Lincoln as a radical for having "resisted" the Court by publicly disagreeing with the *Dred Scott* decision. Roosevelt claimed his opponents had done the same to the Progressives for criticizing courts that struck down legislation aimed at social and industrial justice. In his debates with Lincoln, Douglas had claimed that he knew of "but one mode of reversing judicial decisions . . . by appealing from the inferior court to the superior court." But Douglas suggested that it was hard to see how one could appeal a decision of the Supreme Court, the highest court in the land.[72] Douglas did not mention the possibility of constitutional amendment. Nor did he mention that the Court could possibly overrule its own decision in a subsequent case. Lincoln supported such options as legitimate methods of handling erroneous Supreme Court decisions. Roosevelt, too, failed to mention these methods, probably because they were slow and "inefficient."[73] By neglecting to mention these options, Roosevelt also detracted attention from the fact that, in disagreeing with the Taney Court, Lincoln said nothing of a right of the people to decide constitutional questions by referenda.

Yet Roosevelt seems to have understood that his claim to Lincoln on this matter was not self-evident. This may be one reason why he emphasized Lincoln's "attitude" toward the Court, rather than the substance of his approach to the *Dred Scott* case. Roosevelt did correctly suggest that Lincoln "would not have the citizen conform his vote to this decision of the Supreme Court [*Dred Scott*] nor the member of Congress his," and that Lincoln opposed making it a "rule of political action for the people." However, as Roosevelt understood, this is not the same thing as judicial recall. In "The Heirs of Abraham Lincoln," Roosevelt was thus forced to argue that Lincoln advocated the current Progressive position *in principle*.[74] Roosevelt struggled with this problem in a different way in his 1912 speech to the Ohio Constitutional Convention:

> Lincoln actually applied in successful fashion the principle of the recall in the Dred Scott case. He denounced the Supreme Court for that iniquitous decision in language much stronger than I have ever used in criticizing any court, and appealed to the people to recall the decision—the word "recall" in this connection was not then known, but the phrase exactly describes what he advocated. He was successful, the people took his view, and the decision was practically recalled. It became a dead letter without the need of any constitutional amendment.[75]

In this same address, Roosevelt claimed that Lincoln "appealed to the people against the judges when the judges went wrong" and that he "advocated and secured what was *practically* the recall of the Dred Scott decision."[76] Such statements illustrate the difficulty inherent in Roosevelt's appeal to Lincoln as the forbearer of judicial recall. On the one hand, Roosevelt suggested that even though the term *recall* did not exist then, the *Dred Scott* decision was *practically* (that is, not exactly or precisely) recalled. On the other hand, in the same breath, Roosevelt argued that the word *recall* "exactly describes" what Lincoln advocated. It seems Roosevelt himself was struggling with his appeal to Lincoln here.

Roosevelt claimed that Lincoln secured the "practical recall" of *Dred Scott* without the need of any constitutional amendment. This is an odd claim given that, politically, the decision became a "dead letter" with the passage of the Reconstruction Amendments. Roosevelt did not mention how Lincoln always thought that, constitutionally, emancipation required constitutional amendment. Roosevelt implied that judicial recall was a more efficient mode of dealing with erroneous court decisions and, in particular, was more efficient than constitutional amendment. Roosevelt frequently claimed that the people needed more direct power over the Constitution itself. In his review of Herbert Croly's 1914 *Progressive Democracy,* Roosevelt praised Croly for showing that "the chief obstacles" to securing "a juster [sic] economic and social life" are "found in the legalism with which we have permitted our whole government to be affected, and in the extreme difficulty of amending the Constitution."[77] Roosevelt argued:

> Objection to an easier method of amending the Constitution can be reasonably advanced only by those who sincerely and frankly disbelieve in the fitness of the people for self-government.... As Mr. Croly says, what is needed is not to increase the power of Congress at the expense of the judiciary, or to conserve the power of the judiciary at the expense of Congress or of the Executive, but to increase popular control over all the organs of government; and this can be accomplished only by the increase of direct popular power over the Constitution.[78]

Thus, devices such as initiative, referendum, or the recall of public servants and judicial decisions must be accompanied by an easier method of amending the Constitution. Anyone who believed differently, Roosevelt claimed, disbelieved in the people's capacity for self-government. He held that the problem of majority tyranny had been overcome by historical and economic circumstances. For Roosevelt, new times required that we embrace new devices to control the minority tyranny of special interests that had managed to co-opt the federal judiciary. Since the Civil War, Roosevelt claimed, federal judicial power had "come to be exercised in utterly reckless fashion." Thus, new means such as the recall of judges and judicial decisions were necessary to defend the people against the courts.[79] He was rightly concerned with the courts' potential to abuse power, and he was correct to suggest that Lincoln stood against judges when the judges went wrong. But, arguably, no one "went wrong," no one offered a single decision in such an "utterly reckless fashion" as Justice Taney in *Dred Scott*. And still Lincoln did not "appeal to the people," in the sense that the people would directly decide the constitutional controversies of *Dred Scott* by popular vote.

Nevertheless, Roosevelt repeatedly insisted that judicial recall was a fulfillment of the principles of Lincoln's First Inaugural Address. In support of recall, Roosevelt quoted Lincoln as follows: "'If the policy of the government on vital questions affecting the whole people is to be irrevocably fixed by decisions of the Supreme Court' then 'the people will have ceased to be their own rulers, having to that extent resigned the government into the hands of that eminent tribunal.'"[80] Lincoln did, of course, utter these famous words. But Roosevelt again appealed to the First Inaugural only to rip Lincoln's words out of their immediate context. Lincoln argued that Supreme Court decisions must be binding on the individual parties in the case, and that such decisions ought to be accorded respect and consideration by other departments of government in all similar cases. Should the decision be erroneous, given that it is limited to particular individuals in a particular case, this procedure is comparatively better than any other practice because there is a chance the Court might overrule its own decision. If such questions are fixed by decisions of the Court, then immediately the people will have ceased to be their own rulers. The idea here is that if Supreme Court decisions are instantly and irrevocably fixed, with no chance of being overturned in a subsequent decision or by constitutional amendment, then the people will have resigned their government to the Court. Roosevelt would have us forget that Lincoln sought to deal with an erroneous Court decision through established constitutional and political means.

Roosevelt also referred his audience to Lincoln's July 10, 1858, speech at Chicago, but again he stopped short of giving a full representation of Lincoln's thoughts on *Dred Scott*. Roosevelt compared the Progressive response to erroneous judicial decisions to Lincoln's famous statement on *Dred Scott*—"somebody has to reverse that decision since it is made, and we mean to reverse it, and we mean to do it peaceably."[81] Once again, we should consider Lincoln's remarks in their fuller context:

> Somebody has to reverse that decision [Dred Scott], since it is made, and we mean to reverse it, and we mean to do it peaceably. What are the uses of decisions of courts? They have two uses. As to rules of property they have two uses. First—they decide upon the question before the court. They decide in this case that Dred Scott is a slave. Nobody resists that. Not only that, but they

say to everybody else, that persons standing just as Dred Scott stands is [sic] as he is. That is, they say that when a question comes up upon another person it will be so decided again, unless the court decides it another way, unless the court overrules its decision. Well, we mean to do what we can to have the court decide the other way. That is one thing we mean to try to do.[82]

Lincoln sought to have the Court overrule its own decision by carrying elections, by changing the makeup of the Court, and by bringing new cases in hopes that the Court would reverse its own decision. But Roosevelt remained silent on the actual details of Lincoln's reaction to *Dred Scott*. Again, he focused only on Lincoln's "attitude" toward the Court. It seems difficult to understand Lincoln's "attitude" fully, however, when it is taken in isolation from the specific content of his thoughts and deeds. The character of Lincoln's statesmanship is revealed in his means as well as in his ends. Roosevelt attempted to characterize Lincoln as a "tempered radical" who laid the foundations for progressive reforms such as the recall of judicial decisions. In actuality, Lincoln consistently held that his actions regarding *Dred Scott* were not the result of a desire for radical innovation but, rather, a defense of the principles of the American Founding and years of constitutional interpretation and political practice.

Herbert Croly's Lincoln and Human Brotherhood

Roosevelt's efforts to invoke Lincoln in support of direct popular controls over public servants, judicial decisions, the Constitution, and the laws were in the service of a higher end. By the end of "The Heirs of Abraham Lincoln," Roosevelt explained just what the Progressive Party sought through such political reform. Roosevelt revealed his understanding of the true purpose of government. "We must make this nation," he urged, "a real democracy; an economic as well as a political democracy free from every taint of either sectional or sectarian hatred; a democracy of *true brotherhood*." Roosevelt's emphasis on human brotherhood as the end of politics and the relevance of Lincoln to this notion owe much to Herbert Croly's *The Promise of American Life*, which deserves brief discussion here.[83]

Croly's profound influence on Roosevelt's thinking is well-known. As founder and editor of the *New Republic*, Croly was one of the most influential intellectuals of the Progressive Era. After reading Croly, Roosevelt was persuaded that American democracy should not be directed toward securing the natural and inalienable rights of citizens. History had demonstrated that the Founders' limited government constitutionalism was incapable of securing the ends of "real" or "genuine" democracy. Rather, in light of historical progress, American democracy must now strive to ensure the spiritual and material well-being of the entire nation.[84] Like Croly, Roosevelt saw progressive political reform as a means to this end.

In *The Promise of American Life,* Croly had offered an account of American political development organized around what he identified as the "formative constituents" of American political thought—the Jeffersonian and the Hamiltonian traditions. For Croly, the "democratic" Jeffersonian element was a tradition of individualism, equal rights, and local self-government. The "national" Hamiltonian element was a tradition of strong, efficient, central government directed toward securing the common interest. Croly contended that American democracy was defined by the antagonism between these two poles of political thought. The key problem in American politics had always been the failure to synthesize these principles.[85] Historically, both the average citizen and the political reformer had leaned too far toward the Jeffersonian side of this tension. According to Croly, individual effort was more likely to reward one with prosperity in a predominantly agrarian economy. Before industrialization, the common interest and the individual interest often coincided. But with the closing of the frontier, the rise of modern industry, and increasing economic specialization, the Jeffersonian tradition of individual rights and local self-government became inadequate to secure the material and spiritual well-being of average Americans. According to Croly, only a stronger, more focused, more efficient national democracy could secure the promise of American life.[86]

Croly suggested that, rightly understood, a genuinely national democracy must not attempt to secure the abstract individual rights of the Jeffersonian tradition. Rather, genuine democracy must be dedicated "to liberty and equality, in so far as they made for human brotherhood." He believed that democracy "must stand or fall on a platform of possible human perfectibility." The pursuit of human brotherhood presupposed a malleable human nature that could be perfected through the social planning of administrative experts. Through a "new nationalism," fulfilling our highest longings becomes the explicit purpose of government. Statesmanship toward this end would require the art of popular leadership to remind America of its true national purpose. Here we find Croly's ideal statesman in Lincoln. According to Croly, reformers could look to Lincoln as an enduring model for progressive leadership for the twentieth century.[87]

Croly claimed that by leading the nation through the Civil War, Lincoln reminded Americans that the union was a living principle rather than a merely legal bond. More than anything else, he claimed, Lincoln's character offered us a vision of the truly national man. Lincoln always believed in man's capacity for self-improvement. All of his thoughts and actions "looked in the direction of a higher level of human association." For Croly, Lincoln's thoughts and actions "looked towards the realization of the highest and most edifying democratic ideal. *Whatever his theories were,* he showed by his *general outlook and behavior* that democracy meant to him more than anything else the *spirit and principle of brotherhood.*"[88]

Roosevelt followed Croly in his attempt to connect the Lincoln image to the idea of human brotherhood as the end of American democracy. However, while Lincoln did sometimes speak of the idea of brotherhood, it seems difficult to attribute to him anything like Croly and Roosevelt's idea of human brotherhood as a national goal. Take, for example, Lincoln's October 16, 1854, speech at Peoria. In criticizing the Kansas-Nebraska Act, Lincoln claimed that restoring the Missouri Compromise would "restore the national faith, the national confidence, the national feeling of brotherhood."[89] Lincoln assumed that this national "feeling" of brotherhood had existed *previously.* This "feeling" of brotherhood had become threatened and was to be restored through a rededication to the principles of the Declaration. Yet, like Croly, in "The Heirs of Abraham Lincoln" Roosevelt identified "true" brotherhood as a *future* goal yet to be achieved, and it must consist in something other than a dedication to the principles of the Declaration.

Lincoln consistently offered an understanding of human nature that also distinguishes his views from those of Croly and Roosevelt. Commenting on the problem of slavery, he said:

> Slavery is founded in the selfishness of man's nature—opposition to it, is [in?] his love of justice. These principles are an eternal antagonism; and when brought into collision so fiercely, as slavery extension brings them, shocks, and throes, and convulsions must ceaselessly follow. Repeal the Missouri compromise—repeal all compromises—repeal the declaration of independence—repeal all past history, you still can not repeal human nature.[90]

While Lincoln chose to emphasize that opposition to the extension of slavery is rooted in our natural love of justice, we note that man is not *simply* defined by this other-regarding sentiment. In opposition to this sentiment, in *eternal antagonism* with this sentiment, is man's natural selfishness. We cannot repeal human nature so as to extinguish our natural love of justice. We cannot, for the same reason, extinguish man's natural selfishness. Lincoln's understanding of human nature is perhaps best expressed in his November 10, 1864, "Response to Serenade." Commenting on the difficulty of holding the 1864 elections during wartime, he suggested:

> The strife of the election is but human-nature practically applied to the facts of the case. What has occurred in this case, must ever recur in similar cases. Human-nature will not change. In any future great national trial, compared with the men of this, we shall have as weak, and as strong; as silly and as wise; as bad and good. Let us, therefore, study the incidents of this, as philosophy to learn wisdom from, and none of them as wrongs to be revenged.[91]

In contradistinction to Croly and Roosevelt, in Lincoln's thinking here there is no faith that history or progress will culminate in the perfection of human nature through social planning. There is no overcoming of man's nature in order to advance to new heights of civic association. But this is not a problem for Croly. Despite what Lincoln might have identified as his own moral and political principles (that is, "whatever his theories were"), Croly can somehow divine, in light of historical progress, what Lincoln revealed only through his general outlook and behavior.[92] We shall find that Croly's historicist appropriation of Lincoln is characteristic of the progressive and modern liberal appeal to the Lincoln image. In light of historical progress, Croly claimed to understand Lincoln better than Lincoln understood himself. He can thus enlist Lincoln in support of new and expanded ends for American democracy. Like Croly, Theodore Roosevelt's political thought rested upon a faith in human perfectibility, a faith in a "better race and a better earth" that would transcend the mere improvement of the human condition to achieve true human brotherhood through the political. The "genuine" or "real" democracy that Croly and Roosevelt sought to create had never yet existed on earth, but like Croly, Roosevelt argued the historical path toward genuine democracy had been cleared by Abraham Lincoln.

Conclusion

Drawing on Croly's Hamilton–Jefferson dichotomy, Roosevelt and other progressives sometimes referred to their vision of reform as "Hamiltonian means for Jeffersonian ends." Roosevelt sought to incorporate Lincoln into this vision, but his formulation is misleading. While Hamilton and Jefferson often disagreed about the preferable means of American government, both agreed as to the first principles and legitimate ends of that government. Both agreed as to the natural rights foundation of popular government as expressed in the Declaration of Independence.[93] As Ronald Pestritto notes, the Hamilton–Jefferson dichotomy directs our attention away from "the far more fundamental difference between progressive liberalism, which is grounded in historicism, and founding-era liberalism, which is grounded in transhistorical natural-rights theory... to which Hamilton and Jefferson were both primary adherents." Like Lincoln, Hamilton and Jefferson both believed that the proper end of government is to secure our natural and inalienable rights. The Founders understood, as Lincoln understood, that the key difficulty for republican government lay in combining an energetic government with a due respect for the liberty of the citizens.[94] But once this end is deemed obsolete by progress, and the concern with efficiency in government is divorced from the concern for natural and inalienable rights, there is no objective limit placed upon the objects to which the people might consent. The paramount political problem of combining energy and efficiency with the security of natural and inalienable rights simply disappears. The focus turns to achieving energy and efficiency in getting results, and the desirability of those results is not related to any ground in nature. Lincoln understood that only through the belief in natural and inalienable rights could there be a principled defense of limited government by consent of the governed.

The Founders' political science was rooted in their belief in an unchanging human nature, capable of both the greatest goods and the greatest ills. Accordingly, they sought to control the effects of faction by constructing political institutions in such a way as to moderate the political demands of majority faction.[95] Representation, separation of powers, and other supposedly antidemocratic devices like the amendment process were designed to allow the "cool and deliberate sense" of the community to find expression—as opposed to "every sudden breeze of passion" or "transient impulse" of the moment.[96] However, for Roosevelt, the problem of majority tyranny had ceased to exist in modern America, if it had ever existed. Roosevelt's embrace of direct democracy and redistributionism illustrates how far he really strayed from Lincoln and the Founders' understanding of American government. We have seen that Roosevelt sometimes compared his opponents to Douglas, but it is actually Roosevelt who resembles Douglas. Lincoln vehemently opposed Douglas's "Popular Sovereignty" because it placed no objective moral or constitutional limits on the will of the majority. Like Douglas, Roosevelt denied the very possibility of majority tyranny. Any reading of the Lincoln-Douglas debates would demonstrate that there was surely no better critic of Roosevelt's dismissal of majority tyranny than was Lincoln himself.

Despite his rhetorical claims to the Lincoln legacy, Roosevelt rejected Lincoln's principles. Following Croly, Roosevelt's New Nationalism demanded that interest be transcended in favor of a higher standard of morality to achieve nothing short of human brotherhood. In Roosevelt's view, any interest that did not actively and consciously serve the public good was a "special interest" and must be "driven out of politics."[97] Lincoln surely believed that self-interest could not serve as the sole standard of right action, but he understood that self-interest could not be expunged from the human soul and, hence, could not be driven out of the political. Just as the Founders believed that the latent causes of faction are sown in the nature of man, Lincoln too held that human nature will not change. For Lincoln, we shall always have men "as weak, and as strong; as silly and as wise; as bad and good"; thus the danger of majority tyranny cannot be transcended. Lincoln appreciated that our selfishness and our love of justice stand in "eternal antagonism."[98] According to Lincoln, the task of statesmanship and institutions was to mitigate that antagonism as far as possible. But to contend that either side of this fundamental tension could be abolished from the human condition was to expect the impossible.[99]

THREE

Woodrow Wilson's Lincoln

BY THE TIME OF THE 1912 presidential election, Teddy Roosevelt and the Progressive Party's rhetorical use and abuse of the Lincoln image was in full swing. However, this appeal to Lincoln was by no means limited to Roosevelt. Roosevelt's Democratic opponent also claimed the Lincoln inheritance. The 1912 election is sometimes characterized as a contest between Roosevelt's emphatically progressive New Nationalism and Woodrow Wilson's more moderate New Freedom. During the campaign, Wilson defended federalism, championed the idea of limited government, and heavily criticized Roosevelt's plans to endow independent regulatory agencies with vast discretionary power. Yet, despite their seeming disagreements, the similarities between Wilson and Roosevelt were arguably more significant than their differences. Both candidates adhered to the basic tenets of the progressive movement, and accordingly, in the name of history and progress, both publicly rejected the natural rights principles and constitutionalism of the American Founders.[1] Seeking to undermine public attachment to these principles, both claimed that the progressive movement was the rightful heir of Abraham Lincoln.

While Wilson perhaps appealed to the Lincoln legacy less frequently than Roosevelt did, his attempt to appropriate Lincoln in the rhetoric of American progressivism was no less significant. As part of the progressive movement, Wilson rejected the political theory of the American Founding. Informed by Hegel's philosophy of history, he denied the idea of a transhistorical, unchanging human nature, the idea that all men are equally endowed with natural and inalienable rights, and that the purpose of government is to secure these rights. The institutional measures designed to control the effects of the permanent problem of majority faction, particularly the concept of separation of powers, are deemed obsolete in light of historical progress. According to Wilson, such measures are not necessary in modern political life. Today we are capable of perfecting human nature. We can overcome the problem of self-interest and create a "genuine" democracy wherein the unified will of the people can be discerned and shaped by popular rhetorical leaders and then implemented by administrative experts in a rational, bureaucratic state.[2]

Wilson sought to incorporate Lincoln into this vision, but this led him, like Teddy Roosevelt, to offer a problematic interpretation of Lincoln. Wilson provided a reading of Lincoln that was at best fundamentally mistaken and, at worst, fundamentally misleading. Progressivism was hostile to the political theory that informed the American Founders and Abraham Lincoln. However, despite progressivism's theoretical foundations, the needs of popular political rhetoric seem to have forced the progressive movement to appeal to common reference points, commonly held convictions, and popular objects of veneration such as Lincoln.

Wilson attempted to appropriate Lincoln in the rhetoric of progressivism by focusing on three interrelated themes. First, as we might expect, was the theme of equality. In this Wilson was no different from other progressives in appealing to Lincoln's dedication to the idea that government ought to afford all men an equal chance in the race of life. Wilson attempted to connect the Lincoln image with his own plans to address the social and economic problems of modern industrial America through an equalization of the "conditions of opportunity for self-development."[3]

Second, Wilson attempted to incorporate Lincoln into the rhetoric of progress. He frequently appealed to the life of Lincoln as the embodiment of the American national spirit and as a metaphor for the long, incremental, evolutionary growth of our national destiny. In Wilson's political rhetoric, Lincoln did not serve as an example of the constant dedication to transhistorical natural rights principles but, rather, became the personification of the doctrine of progress and the historical overcoming of these principles.

Third, as part of his effort to transform American political institutions, Wilson wanted to open the nation up to progressive development through a restructuring and a reinterpretation of American constitutional government.

According to Wilson, the Founders' system of separation of powers must be abandoned and replaced with a more efficient, more flexible system capable of meeting the new and increasingly complex necessities of the modern age. This, Wilson believed, would require a new role for the American presidency, in which an active executive, as the embodiment of the will of the people, would provide the necessary leadership and rhetorical talent to lead the nation toward modern democracy. Wilson's chief model of this popularized rhetorical leader was, of course, Abraham Lincoln.

We will examine each of these themes in turn. However, before we examine his appeal to the Lincoln image, we should briefly consider Wilson's critique of the American regime. His rhetorical use of Lincoln was in the service of a profound attempt to change American political thought and institutions. Wilson once famously declared that the example of Abraham Lincoln vindicates America's faith in democracy.[4] To appreciate this statement fully one must try to understand just what Wilson thinks American democracy *is* or *should* be.

Wilson's Critique of the American Founding

As an academic and a politician Wilson contributed greatly to the influence of progressive thought upon American political development. Wilson's quarrel with what he referred to as the mechanistic spirit of "checks and balances" beneath the Founders' Constitution is familiar to most students of American government. Wilson endeavored to supplant the Constitution's separation of powers with a more "efficient" Constitution capable of meeting the demands of the current age. During his 1912 campaign for president Wilson proclaimed that "We are in the presence of a new organization of society. . . . We have changed our economic conditions, absolutely, from top to bottom; and, with our economic society, the organization of our life." Given that our society had changed so drastically, Wilson claimed, the "old political formulas do not fit the present problems; they read now like documents taken out of a forgotten age." A "new nation," Wilson argued, "seems to have been created which the old formulas do not fit or afford a vital interpretation of."[5] Wilson suggested that, since the Civil War, a new and increasingly complex industrial economy had rendered the political theory of the American Founding obsolete. New conditions required a government that was ready and able to confront new problems.

According to Wilson, every generation tends to think in terms of the dominant thought of its age. Wilson held that the American Founders had labored under the "Whig theory of political dynamics," a mechanistic theory of government modeled after Newtonian physics, the dominant theory of their age. According to Newtonian physics, Wilson explained, the various parts of the solar system are held in place by the attraction of gravity, "governed by the nice poise and balance of forces which give the whole system of the universe its symmetry and perfect adjustment." He argued that the English Whigs had attempted to frame a similar constitution, seeking to check and balance the throne institutionally. The English Whigs were practical statesmen, not theoretical men, in his view, and it took a theoretically minded Frenchman (Montesquieu) to explain to them just what they had done. They had balanced the departments of government by a series of "checks and counterpoises, which Newton might readily have recognized as suggestive of the mechanism of the heavens." Wilson asserted that one need only glance at the *Federalist* to see that the American Founders had adopted this same mechanistic, Newtonian view of politics.[6]

For Wilson, this very spirit of checks and balances must be overcome in the modern age if American democracy was to open itself to progress. He reasoned:

> The trouble with the [Whig theory of political dynamics] is that government is not a machine, but a living thing. It falls, not under the theory of the universe, but under the theory of organic life. It is accountable to Darwin, not to Newton. It is modified by its environment, necessitated by its tasks, shaped to its functions by the sheer pressure of life. No living thing can have its organs offset against each other, as checks, and live. On the contrary, its life is dependent upon their quick co-operation, their ready response to the commands of instinct or intelligence, their amicable community of purpose. Government is not a body of blind forces; it is a body of men, with highly differentiated functions, no doubt, in our modern day, of specialization, with a common task and purpose. Their co-operation is indispensable, their warfare fatal. There can be no successful government without the intimate, instinctive coordination of the organs of life and action. This is not theory, but fact, and displays its force as fact, whatever theories may be thrown across its track. Living political constitutions must be Darwinian in structure and in practice. Society is a living organism and must obey the laws of life, not of mechanics; it must develop.[7]

Wilson argued, however, that the Founders' Constitution, as such, was not a "machine governed by mechanically automatic balances." In essence, by viewing their government through the lens of the Whig theory of political dynamics, the American Founders had mischaracterized their own system. The organic nature of the Constitution is evident, Wilson claimed, despite the spirit of checks and balances that has traditionally framed our reading of it. Despite their embrace of the Whig theory, the Founders were still practically minded statesmen "with an experienced eye for affairs and a quick practical sagacity in respect of the actual structure of government, and they have given us a thoroughly workable model." According to Wilson, the Founders actually bequeathed to future generations a government "capable of vital and normal organic growth," able to be "eminently adapted to express the changing temper and purposes of the American people from age to age."[8]

Wilson's project was thus aimed specifically at how we interpret the Constitution. When read according to the Whig theory of political dynamics, Wilson claimed, the Constitution unnecessarily limits government, restricting its ability to adapt to the necessities of the times. This tendency is exacerbated in the modern age, when a new economic system forces us to reevaluate the relationship between labor and capital and to reassess the role of positive government in protecting its citizens.[9] On the campaign trail in 1912 Wilson suggested, "All that the progressives ask or desire is permission—in an era where 'development,' 'evolution,' is the scientific word—to interpret the Constitution according to the Darwinian principle; all they ask is recognition of the fact that a nation is a living thing and not a machine."[10]

For Wilson, if the nation is to be open to progress, we must not blindly adhere to the political formulas of the past. "Progress, development,—those are modern words," Wilson argued. "The modern idea is to leave the past and press onward to something new." Progress for Wilson was not merely improvement in the human condition but the necessary result of a purposeful, rational history. Wilson's thought owed much to Hegel's philosophy of history and the concept of the rational, bureaucratic state. His political thought assumed that history is rational and necessarily progressive and that every epoch of history is an improvement upon the one that came before it. Progress comes as the spirit of one age comes to replace another through the dialectic of history.[11]

According to Wilson's historicism it is a mistake to suggest, as the Founders and Lincoln had suggested, that there are self-evident truths applicable to all men at all times, independent of history. It is a mistake to assume an unchanging human nature and thus a mistake to assume that there are permanent political problems emanating from that nature. In constructing a regime designed to control the effects of faction, the Founders mistakenly assumed faction to be a permanent political problem. Insofar as human nature can "develop" over the course of human history, then the political arrangements designed to control the effects of faction are rendered not only obsolete but counterproductive. Wilson's historical critique of the Founding penetrated to the first principles beneath institutional concerns, for in positing that the seeds of faction are in fact not sown in the nature of man, free government can do more than merely control the effects of faction. Contrary to the political theory of the *Federalist,* the very causes of faction can be overcome by history. Limited government and institutional measures to control the effects of faction are rendered increasingly unnecessary. As history progresses and human nature improves, the way is opened toward a true unity of wills, a truly national sentiment. At the end of history, the most controversial of political questions will have been agreed upon and the emphasis in government turns from politics to administration. In the modern democratic state, the primary questions will be questions of means and not of ends.[12]

The institutional arrangements that Wilson wished to supplant were framed according to the belief that the purpose of government is to secure natural and inalienable rights. With Teddy Roosevelt, Wilson understood that the notion of natural and inalienable rights serves as the foundation of limited government. The spirit of checks and balances of which Wilson was so critical arose in the effort to secure such rights, and for Wilson the notion of natural and inalienable rights was as much an obstacle to progress as the spirit of checks and balances.[13] Given that the notion of natural and inalienable rights depends upon the possibility that there are abstract truths applicable to all human beings at all times, Wilson's historicism denies the very possibility of such rights. He asserted that although we tend to think of the Declaration of Independence as a highly theoretical document, "except for its assertion that all men are equal, it is not." In his view the Declaration is "intensely practical, even upon the question of liberty." Although the document "names as among the 'inalienable rights' of man the right to life, liberty, and the pursuit of happiness[,] . . . it expressly leaves to each generation of men the determination of what they will do with their lives, what they will prefer as the form and object of their liberty, in what they will seek their happiness." In brief, he argued, "political liberty is the right of those who are governed to adjust government to their own needs and interests."[14]

Liberty is thus no longer understood with any reference to natural and inalienable rights but is, rather, the continually changing, conventional result of a deal between the government and the governed. In Wilson's words, liberty is nothing more than a balancing between the "power of the government and the privilege of the individual." As the result of conventional agreement, and devoid of any basis in nature, the meaning of liberty is not subject to any limitations or guidelines save the will of the parties at the time of that agreement.[15] Lincoln had once declared "All honor to Jefferson, to the man who, in the concrete pressure of a struggle for national independence by a single people, had the coolness, forecast, and capacity to introduce into a merely revolutionary document, an abstract truth, applicable to all men and all times." Wilson, however, seemed so intent on reading the idea of natural and inalienable rights out of the American political tradition that anyone who subscribed to the idea, even the author of the Declaration of Independence, was deemed thoroughly "un-American." Jefferson, Wilson claimed, was too infatuated with the abstract philosophical thinking of the French Revolution to be considered a true American. Wilson deemed Jefferson's thinking "un-American in being abstract, sentimental, and rationalistic, rather than practical." For Wilson, the American tradition ought not to be understood in terms of a dedication to doctrinaire abstract natural rights principles but must be discussed as an organic, intensely practical tradition in which government can evolve and adapt to ever-changing circumstances.[16]

Wilson even went so far as to suggest that, if one is to really understand the Declaration, one should simply ignore its first two paragraphs.[17] Thus, according to Wilson, if we are truly to understand the Declaration we must read it in a strictly historical context, in isolation from the document's own fundamental statements on equality and natural rights. That is, one must read it differently from the way Lincoln did, who held that the principles of the Declaration applied to all men at all times, and who apparently voiced the same opinion of the document as was held by the men who had written and signed the document itself. As Lincoln's arguments on slavery repeatedly indicated, natural and inalienable rights place transhistorical limits upon what men might consent to, and these rights should continually guide our understanding of liberty and self-government. While Lincoln drew these notions from the political theory of the Declaration, Wilson sought to reinterpret the Declaration through a progressive lens, rejecting the theoretical core of the document, denaturing the rights professed therein, and rendering them merely positive or prescriptive rights.[18] For Wilson, in order for government to meet the challenges of modern society, the political thought of the American Founding must be transcended; and Wilson's use and abuse of Lincoln became central to this endeavor.

Wilson's effort to reshape the American constitutional order is well-traveled ground among students of American political development. Rarely, however, do we encounter much by way of a detailed examination of his use of the Lincoln image in this effort. A few commentators such as historians Merrill D. Peterson and Anthony Gaughan and sociologist Barry Schwartz do discuss Wilson's appeal to the Lincoln image. They do not really evaluate the plausibility of his treatment of Lincoln, however, nor do they focus more generally on the compatibility of progressivism and Lincoln's political thought.[19] Such considerations are more likely to come from the fields of American political thought and American political development. Yet, even here, few have concentrated specifically upon Wilson's use of Lincoln.

A notable exception is Pestritto's commentary on Wilson's political thought. While his analysis does not necessitate a detailed look at Wilson's use of Lincoln, Pestritto briefly calls our attention to what he refers to as Wilson's "misreading" of Lincoln. In a larger treatment of Wilson's historicism, Pestritto notes that Wilson once suggested he admired Lincoln as a statesman because Lincoln "did not have any theories at all." Pestritto claims that this apparent "misreading" is the result of Wilson's larger attempt to read the doctrine of natural and inalienable rights out of the American political tradition. While Croly had attempted to avoid the question of Lincoln's natural rights thinking by asserting that Lincoln was a model of progressivism "whatever his theories were," and Teddy Roosevelt implicitly did the same, Wilson would go so far as to attribute no theories to Lincoln at all.[20] Wilson's Lincoln did not hold that the Declaration contained an abstract truth applicable to all men at all times but, rather, was robbed of any abstract theoretical thinking altogether. It is this apparent "misreading" or misinterpretation of Lincoln that we shall examine here, and we shall find that Wilson recast Lincoln in the progressive mold, fit to serve him in an attempt to transform American political thought and institutions.

Wilson's Lincoln and the "Equalization of Conditions"

Wilson's misreading of Lincoln is particularly evident in his appeal to Lincoln as a symbol of equal opportunity. Wilson claimed that the progress of national development requires an "equalization of conditions" in response to the profound economic and political strains placed upon American society by the technological innovation and laissez-faire capitalism of the new industrial age. The increased exploitation of industrial workers and the pursuit of monopolistic economic power by special interests had rendered individuals incapable of providing for their own well-being. The rugged self-reliant individualism of the frontier age had given way to the vicious pursuit of wealth and power by big business, which had managed to co-opt the federal government and render it subservient to big business interests. Wilson's New Freedom was an effort to address these problems by strengthening the people's control over their government and, in turn, by strengthening the government's ability to deal with new economic conditions. To this end, the New Freedom included proposals for the nomination of congressmen and state officers through direct primaries, for the direct election of senators, for tariff reform, antitrust legislation, reform of the central banking system, and legislation for the improvement of working conditions.[21] Government, Wilson argued, must not continue to serve powerful special interests. The true purpose of government, he claimed, is to promote the equalization of the "conditions of opportunity for self-development." The very hope of society "lies in an infinite individual variety, in the freest possible play of individual forces." Government ought to work in the service of human individuality, understood in a particular way: the measure of the good regime is the extent to which it affords every individual "a fair chance to live and to serve himself."[22] Wilson did not necessarily seek to equalize incomes or material possessions among individuals but, rather, sought to equalize the preconditions for the individual's pursuit of self-development.[23]

In his effort to secure this equalization of conditions, Wilson often used the Lincoln example to persuade audiences that this pursuit was both desirable and illustrative of the American spirit. A key theme was Lincoln's claim that all men should have an equal chance to compete in the race of life. During the 1910 New Jersey gubernatorial campaign, Wilson argued that New Jersey Republicans had strayed away from the founding principles of their party, that they had "insensibly been led away from the ideals and standards of Lincoln," by allying themselves with special interests against the people.[24] Wilson asked:

> Do you suppose that Abraham Lincoln would have had anything to do with the Republican party either in this State or in this nation during the last two decades? Do you suppose that the great men who was [were] associated with Lincoln would recognize the party formed in order to effect the liberation of men from the bondage of ownership when the industrious effort of recent decades has been to establish another kind of industrial ownership? Don't let these men [the Republican Party] prate to us of the immortal example of

Lincoln until they show us that they are ready to follow it; then we will admit that they are of the lineage, otherwise we must proclaim that they are not.[25]

Seeking to associate the Republicans and big business with the slaveholders of Lincoln's day, Wilson continued this theme in the campaign rhetoric of the New Freedom in 1912. In an address to Chicago Democrats on Lincoln's birthday, he argued not only that the Democrats were the rightful heirs of Lincoln but that the Lincoln example was particularly relevant to the current situation in American society, a "critical turning point in history," when the nation must "make a choice whether it would divide or remain united upon a fundamental question of social structure." Lincoln had boldly declared, Wilson reminded his audience, that the nation could not continue to live half slave and half free. This statement, he claimed, "ought to be made now—that *as our economic affairs are now organized they cannot go on.*" The Lincoln example, according to Wilson, "illustrates the fundamental faith of democracy." The "richness of democracy," he suggested, "is in this—that it never has to predict who is going to save it. It never relies upon those of established influence. The gates of opportunity are wide open and he may enter who is fit." Playing on Lincoln's Gettysburg Address, Wilson claimed that Lincoln's example reminds us of the "birth of Freedom in the modern world," the "conception that every man stood naked and individual in his responsibility before his God and Maker and that the only test was the test of native worth and native principle."[26]

In Wilson's rhetoric, Lincoln became a symbol of individual opportunity, a symbol Wilson placed in stark opposition to modern-day Republicans, whom he routinely compared to slaveholders. In a 1912 campaign speech in Springfield, Illinois, he stated that, "when gentlemen proposing to legalize monopoly profess to speak in the name of Lincoln, it is as if those who professed and intended to perpetuate human slavery should have dared to speak in the name of the Great Emancipator. We are going to repudiate all this slavery just as emphatically as we repudiated the other."[27]

Wilson adopted Lincoln as a symbol of emancipation in order to argue for greater democratization in the service of a new equality of economic liberty. He suggested that the Democratic Party offered a return to the sympathetic leadership of Lincoln, a leadership in tune with the hearts and minds of the common man. In his 1912 campaign address "Lessons from Lincoln," Wilson proclaimed that the current economic and political situation in America required "nothing less than a new declaration of independence," to "proclaim against the economic forces which have been governing it." For Wilson, we cannot seek guidance from that "old" Declaration of Independence, apart from its description of the means by which men redefine the ends of government. The very notion of equality must be understood anew in light of modern circumstances. But we can look to Lincoln. Today, Wilson asserted, Lincoln "would have lined himself up with the men who are for a new order of things in the United States."[28]

Despite this effort to invoke Lincoln in the name of equality, Wilson's claim to act upon Lincolnian principles should be regarded with skepticism. Lincoln's pursuit of equality sought to secure equality of opportunity in light of transhistorical standards rooted in the Laws of Nature and Nature's God. As such, not only was this pursuit guided by the practical necessities of historical and political circumstance, but it was fundamentally guided by natural standards of right. Insofar as our pursuit of equality in civil society consists in an effort to secure inalienable rights grounded in nature, there are natural limits placed upon the objects and the means of that pursuit. Our natural equality not only suggests that the legitimate powers of government are derived from the consent of the governed, it also implies that there are limits as to what things the governed might rightfully consent to. Lincoln's pursuit of equality assumed the goodness of majority rule in principle but also held, with the American Founders, that the rule of the majority is defensible only insofar as it is reasonable, insofar as it rules without destroying the rights of the minority and without repudiating the natural rights basis of its own legitimacy. The primary problem of popular government is to construct the regime so as to foster a healthy rule of the majority that does not degenerate into rule by factious majorities. This understanding of free government structured and guided Lincoln's pursuit of equality.

Wilson, on the other hand, rejected the natural standards that guided Lincoln's equality and, as such, necessarily denied in principle that there are any limitations upon our pursuit of equality extrinsic to the will of the people and their government in a given historical or political circumstance.[29] In principle Wilson's equalization of conditions admits of no objective limit as to what we might consent to in the pursuit of equality or, for that matter, in our pursuit of any perceived good. While framed in the language of equality of opportunity, Wilson's equalization of conditions, in principle, moves toward the pursuit of equal results or, at the very least, does nothing to prevent this movement. Lincoln had presupposed that the pursuit of equality must be tempered by the requirement of consent, and consent is itself limited by the Laws of Nature and Nature's God. Wilson's equalization of conditions is limited only by our own will or, in the best case, by our faith in our own wisdom and beneficence. That Wilson wishes to address issues of national importance through economic and political reform is not in and of itself incompatible with Lincoln's political thought. However, the reasons, the *arguments* Wilson advances in support of such reforms, ultimately distinguish him from the American political tradition as it stood before the progressive movement.[30]

Beneath Wilson's attempt to incorporate Lincoln into his rhetoric of equalization of conditions, however, there is a more fundamental yet interrelated attempt to connect Lincoln and his political thought with the doctrine of progress. In his Gettysburg Address, Lincoln had spoken of a "new birth of freedom." Lincoln's new birth of freedom consisted in a rededication to the natural rights principles of the Declaration. Wilson's New Freedom consists in something very different, a profound and far-reaching restructuring of the American regime that required a self-conscious and deliberate break with the principles Lincoln sought to restore.[31] If he was to connect the Lincoln image to his call for the equalization of conditions, Wilson needed to divorce Lincoln from the natural rights tradition and appropriate him into the rhetoric of progress.

Wilson's Lincoln and the Idea of "Progress"

In February 1909, on Lincoln's birthday, Wilson delivered a speech in Chicago suitable to the occasion. This speech—entitled "Abraham Lincoln: A Man of the People"—is worth examining in detail. As one of the more extended treatments of Lincoln in Wilson's political rhetoric, it contains several of the elements that define his appeal to the Lincoln image. Wilson's stated purpose here was to "recall the character and achievements" of Lincoln and to "attempt to expound . . . the meaning of his life, [and] the significance of his singular and unique career." Wilson sought to place Lincoln in the proper historical context for, according to Wilson, neither political ideas nor those who hold such ideas can be understood in isolation from the historical circumstances that give rise to them. The nineteenth century, Wilson claimed, was a unique era for America:

> It is a very long century that separates us from the year of his [Lincoln's] birth. . . . [T]hat far year 1809 stands very near its opening, when men were only beginning to understand what was in store for them. It was a significant century, not only in the field of politics but in the field of thought. . . . Modern science came into the world to revolutionize our thinking and our material

enterprises just about the time that Mr. Lincoln was uttering those remarkable debates with Mr. Douglas. The struggle which determined the life of the Union came just at the time when a new issue was joined in the field of thought, and men began to reconstruct their conceptions of the universe and of their relation to nature, and even of their relation to God.[32]

By placing Lincoln in historical context, Wilson served not only an analytical need but also an important rhetorical need. He incorporated the symbol of Lincoln into the rhetoric of progressivism and called attention to the idea of progressive, evolutionary growth and development by placing the coming of Lincoln alongside the coming of Darwin (the two men were born on the same day in the same year). According to Wilson, while the scientific world was responding to the publication of *On the Origin of Species,* Lincoln was partaking in the beginnings of a profound change in American government. Both Darwin and Lincoln were, Wilson suggested, signs of historical progress in the nineteenth century.

This theme of organic growth, of evolutionary development, comes to dominate Wilson's praise of Lincoln as a man of the people. Wilson offered Lincoln as the personification of the doctrine of progress. Wilson's Lincoln is the result of an incremental development, almost imperceptible to anyone except those fortunate enough to be standing at the end of the process. Wilson emphasized Lincoln's slow, "almost sluggish" personal and political development as a metaphor for the slow development of our political thought and institutions. Lincoln slowly went from one success to another (although his short-sighted contemporaries perceived these successes as failures) until a great crisis arose that matched Lincoln's singular talents. Every little step in Lincoln's life, like every stage in American political history, was a necessary stage of development.[33] Wilson had made a similar statement in his 1894 essay "A Calendar of Great Americans." Here he claimed that Lincoln arose to political greatness through a long, slow process of development. Like the idea of liberty, Wilson suggested, Lincoln was "always a-making." Lincoln was the "supreme American," in which all the elements of American life were slowly harmonized. "To the Eastern politicians," Wilson claimed, "Lincoln seemed like an accident; but to history he must seem like a providence." According to Wilson, Lincoln embodied the whole of the American spirit, a spirit that is "progressive, optimistically progressive, and ambitious of objects of national scope and advantage." Wilson argued that no single man, "unless it be Lincoln, has ever proved big or various enough to embody this active and full-hearted spirit in all its qualities."[34]

In "Abraham Lincoln: A Man of the People," Wilson noted the most admirable of Lincoln's characteristics. He offered Lincoln's honesty, his wit, and his disinterestedness as necessary qualities of leadership, but he also singled out Lincoln's "studiousness," and in doing so, he made an interesting remark:

> [W]hat commends Mr. Lincoln's studiousness to me is that the result of it was he did not have any theories at all. Life is a very complex thing. No theory that I have ever heard propounded will match its varied pattern; and the men who are dangerous are the men who are not content with understanding, but go on to propound theories, things which will make a new pattern for society and a new model for the universe. Those are the men who are not to be trusted. Because, although you steer by the North Star, when you have lost the bearings of your compass, you nevertheless must steer in a pathway on the sea,—you are not bound for the North Star. The man who insists upon his theory insists that there is a way to the North Star, and I know, and everyone knows, that there is not—at least none yet discovered. Lincoln was one of those delightful students who did not seek to tie you up in the meshes of any theory.[35]

Wilson's professed Burkeanism is clear in this instance, and his criticism of doctrinairism is reminiscent of Burke's criticism of the French philosophes, but is it correct to suggest that Lincoln's study resulted in his holding no theories at all? Lincoln's prudence resided in the application of theoretical principles in light of practical circumstances.[36] As we have seen, Lincoln clearly understood that in politics there is often a disjunction between theory and practice. Indeed, this insight into the imperfect nature of political practice is foundational to the idea of prudential statesmanship. But it is wrong to suggest that Lincoln did not engage in abstract thinking. After all, was it not Lincoln who time and again took his moral and political bearings from the natural rights principles of the Declaration, which, in his opinion, contained an "abstract truth, applicable to all men and all times"? This is what Pestritto calls Wilson's "misreading" of Lincoln. Wilson's purpose in this speech is to divorce Lincoln from abstract, natural rights thinking and to employ him as an example of progress.[37]

On the campaign trail in 1912, Wilson would eventually characterize Lincoln as a somewhat self-conscious agent of progress. In October 1912, Wilson claimed that when Lincoln faced Douglas and the slave interest he was in effect saying, "You are looking at the situation as another generation has looked at it; you are looking at rights, at human rights, as another generation has looked at them. This generation looks at them [human rights] with clarified vision."[38] Here Wilson presented his Lincoln as self-consciously breaking with the American political tradition in order to usher in a new understanding of rights. This statement might seem odd, given that Wilson's Lincoln was a man with "no theories at all." In whatever respect Wilson's Lincoln believed in "human rights," it is clear that they were rights not grounded in nature or abstract theory. Again, we encounter a recasting of Lincoln to fit the progressive project. And we should not overlook the obvious. I am aware of nothing in Lincoln's speeches and writings to suggest that he looked at human rights in a "new" way, or with "clarified vision." In fact, Lincoln clearly and consistently suggested the very opposite opinion. If one were to sum up Lincoln's position using Wilson's language, one would have to suggest that, contra Wilson, Douglas and the slave interest were, in fact, *not* "looking at the situation as another generation had looked at it," and *not* "looking at human rights as another generation had looked at them." In his speech on the *Dred Scott* decision, throughout the Lincoln–Douglas debates, and elsewhere, Lincoln always maintained that the South's attempt to exclude the Negro from the Declaration of Independence, to deny that all men equally possessed natural and inalienable rights, was a deliberate break with the opinion of the Founding generation. Wilson mischaracterized the dispute between Lincoln and Douglas. Lincoln claimed to look at rights as another generation—the Founding generation—had looked at them and accused Douglas and Taney of departing from that tradition.

However, one might nevertheless object that, even if we cannot unqualifiedly equate Lincoln with progressivism, there did seem to be a "progressive" tone to much of Lincoln's political rhetoric. Was Wilson not justified in suggesting that Lincoln embraced a certain notion of "progress"? After all, Lincoln did sometimes speak of the principles of progress. Indeed, his characterization of the Declaration of Independence seemed to hinge upon the idea that it contemplated the "progressive improvement in the condition of all men everywhere." And Lincoln held that, in the pursuit of the standard maxim of equality promised in the Declaration, the American republic had seen a "steady progress toward the practical equality of all men." Yet it seems difficult to argue that by "progress" Lincoln meant anything approaching the doctrine of progress as espoused by Wilson and the progressives who invoked Lincoln's name.[39] We encounter the use of the same word, but with different meanings.

Lincoln's Understanding of "Progress"

In American political rhetoric, although we frequently encounter the term *progress*, as Ceaser has argued, the usage of the term sometimes obscures the fact that what we think of as "progress" usually contains not one but, rather, two ideas.[40] One idea that we have already noted in Wilson's thought is the "law" or "doctrine" of progress associated with the philosophy of history. This notion of "progress" contends that history is a rational, willful agent and that there is a definite "progressive" movement to history that can be discerned by human beings. According to this line of thinking, there can be no principles true, everywhere and always, independent of historical circumstance. The second idea, the idea shared by the American Founders and Abraham Lincoln, is "progress" understood simply as improvement or advancement. According to this notion of "progress," we can discern certain trends in history, and there is certainly room for human advancement through reflection and choice. But according to this view there is no definite movement to history itself, and "progress" is by no means guaranteed by history.[41] This understanding of "progress" is compatible with the idea that there are certain principles true everywhere and always, applicable to all human beings, independent of history or circumstance.

Given his embrace of the transhistorical principles of the Declaration, that Lincoln did not adhere to the notion of "progress" as espoused by Wilson should be clear enough. But there are certain instances in Lincoln's speeches and writings where the distance between the two men's thinking is made particularly clear. Take, for example, Lincoln's October 16, 1854, speech at Peoria on the Kansas-Nebraska Act, where he suggested that the act was a rejection of the founding attitude toward slavery, an attitude that was hostile to the principle of slavery, and that tolerated the institution only by necessity. "Little by little, but steadily as man's march to the grave," Lincoln suggested, "we have been giving up the OLD for the NEW faith. . . . The spirit of seventy-six and the spirit of Nebraska, are utter antagonisms; and the former is being displaced by the latter." But Lincoln claimed that this movement, this new spirit of Nebraska, could and must be arrested. He argued that the existence of slavery, with its probable expansion into the West, is viewed by the "liberal party throughout the world" as the last "retrograde institution in America," an institution that "is *undermining the principles of progress,* and fatally violating the noblest political system the world ever saw."[42] The spirit of the age, the spirit of Nebraska, was not a spirit of progress but a spirit of regression. For Lincoln, progress consisted in a return to the old, to the spirit of 1776, to the principles of the Declaration. Simply put, if history was moving at all, it was moving in the wrong direction. The spirit of Nebraska suggested to Lincoln that the eventual death of slavery throughout the world was by no means a given.

Lincoln denied the idea of progress as Wilson understood it. Another example occurs in his response to Justice Taney and the *Dred Scott* decision. Taney had argued that, since the authors of the Declaration of Independence had tolerated slavery, they could not have included the Negro in the Declaration's "all men are created equal." However, Taney also asserted that the public attitude toward the Negro and the institution of slavery had improved since the time of the Founding. Lincoln's arguments against the idea that the Founders excluded the Negro from the Declaration's "all men are created equal" clause are generally familiar.[43]

For our purposes here, we should note Taney's assumption about the progressive improvement in the public status of the Negro in American society. Lincoln denied this particular assumption of "progress," and as Pestritto observes, it was an assumption not limited to Justice Taney. Woodrow Wilson made the same assumption. In his history *Division and Reunion, 1829–1909,* Wilson viewed the American Civil War through a Hegelian lens. Here, slavery and the war itself were unfortunate—but necessary—steps in a great dialectic that ultimately strengthened and further centralized the national government. From this point of view, slavery and the war helped to foster progress toward the modern democratic state. Wilson characterized the Jacksonian era and the years leading up to the war as an era of progressive improvement in American attitudes toward the Negro. The institution of slavery, he claimed, had come under increasing scrutiny during this period. Wilson interpreted these things as a sign of the increasingly democratic spirit of the age.[44]

As Pestritto observes, Wilson's assumption of progress during the Jacksonian era is subject to the same criticisms Lincoln levied at Justice Taney. Wilson reasoned, like Taney, that the public attitude toward the Negro and slavery had grown more enlightened since the Founding. Lincoln held precisely the opposite view, suggesting that the regress in public attitudes toward slavery and the Negro was the result of an increasing disbelief in the natural equality.[45] Unlike Wilson, Lincoln did not assume "progress" but, rather, held that the fate of American liberty was not at all certain. For Lincoln, the existence of that liberty was dependent upon the belief in natural equality as the theoretical basis for self-government.

To argue, as Wilson did, that the antebellum period was a time of "progress" in attitudes toward slavery might seem rather odd. This period witnessed the rise of new and increasingly extreme arguments to defend not the unfortunate *necessity* of tolerating slavery where it existed but the very *principle* of slavery itself. During this time we find the emergence of arguments suggesting that slavery, to use John C. Calhoun's language, was a "positive good" for both master and slave. Calhoun would publicly argue in 1838 that the demand for abolition had "produced one happy effect" in that it forced the South to "look into the nature and character" of domestic slavery and to "correct many false impressions that even we had entertained in relation to it." Many in the South, Calhoun explained, had once believed that slavery was "a moral and political evil," but "that folly and delusion are gone; we see [slavery] now in its true light, and regard it as the most safe and stable basis for free institutions in the world."[46] The antebellum period also saw the rise of racial science, which would come to influence the vice president of the Confederacy, Alexander Stephens.[47] Wilson's characterization of this era as a time of progress in attitudes toward slavery only makes sense when viewed, as Wilson viewed it, in light of the notion of a progressive history. What Lincoln had regarded as a fundamental threat to the perpetuation of self-government Wilson can brush aside as merely a necessary step in the dialectical process of national development. Unlike Wilson, however, Lincoln understood progress to consist in a firm, continued adherence to the natural rights principles of the Declaration, principles that Wilson's notion of progress decidedly rejects. Indeed, Wilson's measure of progress is the degree to which a nation is able and willing to reexamine, and ultimately reject, the first principles that define Lincoln's notion of progress.[48]

However, one point of contact between Lincoln and the unqualified faith in human progress might lie in Lincoln's lifelong embrace of technological innovation and internal improvements.[49] But we should be cautious in equating Lincoln's hopes for human improvement and Wilson's progressivism. One of the most revealing statements of Lincoln's opinions on technology and human "progress" occurred in his 1858–1859 "Lectures on Discoveries and Inventions."[50] Lincoln's concern here was to examine the relationship between technological innovation and free government, and the "Lectures" are best understood when read in conjunction with Lincoln's statements on free labor.[51] Eugene Miller offers an excellent, rare, analysis of these neglected lectures and their relation to Lincoln's free labor doctrine. He persuasively demonstrates that the key issue in the lectures concerns the possibility of a democratic statesmanship capable of "reaping the benefits of modern technology while avoiding its dangers." While Lincoln surely believed that technological innovation helped foster free government, he also understood that the desire to master nature through modern technology could lead to enslavement rather than to liberation. Lincoln observed that advances in technology had been used, were being used, and would most probably continue to be used to perpetuate and extend the institution of slavery.[52]

For our purposes, it is useful to single out a particular overriding theme in Lincoln's "Second Lecture," in which he discussed a persona he referred to as "Young America." Lincoln's characterization of Young America helps us to clarify the distance between his understanding of "progress" and that of Wilson and the progressive movement. "We have all heard," Lincoln claimed "of Young America. He is the most *current* youth of the age. Some think him conceited, and arrogant; but has he not reason to entertain a rather extensive opinion of himself? Is he not the inventor and owner of the *present*, and sole hope of the *future*?" According to Lincoln, Young America satisfied his wildest desires with goods and luxuries carried to him from all corners of the globe, made available to him through modern, steam-powered transportation and novel telegraph communication. By right of possessing it, Young America owned most of the world, and what he did not possess he owned by right of desiring it and the intention of possessing it. Lincoln characterized Young America as having an overwhelming desire for more, in particular, a desire for land. "As Plato had for the immortality of the soul," Lincoln suggested, "Young America has a 'pleasing hope—a fond desire—a longing after' territory."[53]

Young America had a "great passion—a perfect rage—for the '*new*.'" In his burning desire for new territory he claimed to be "a great friend of humanity," who desired this territory not out of selfish motives but, rather, as a means to spread freedom to the rest of the world. According to Lincoln, Young America "is very anxious to fight for the liberation of enslaved nations and colonies, provided, always, they *have* land, and have *not* any liking for his interference." As for those without land and those who actually desired Young America's help, they could wait a few hundred years longer. Lincoln argued that Young America was also rich, particularly rich in knowledge. "He knows all that can possibly be known" and "is the unquestioned inventor of '*Manifest Destiny.*'" Coupled with his perfect rage for the new, Young America had a horror for all things old, particularly for that unfortunate, behind-the-times curmudgeon "Old Fogy."[54]

In speaking of the brash persona of Young America, Lincoln called to mind the Young America movement, an upstart faction within the Democratic Party that sought to oust the party rank and file (whom they described as the party's "old fogy wire-pullers"), gain control of the party, and secure Douglas's presidential nomination in 1852.[55] Douglas and the Young America movement embraced the idea of Manifest Destiny and believed that, through political, intellectual, and technological progress, American borders were destined to press ever outward, spreading freedom in their wake. There is, of course, a certain irony in Lincoln's praise of Young America. He did not offer an unqualified or uncritical embrace of "progress," technological or otherwise.[56] Rather, Lincoln criticized the notion of Manifest Destiny for its unflinching embrace of all things new against all things old and venerable. True progress, Lincoln argued, can be had through observation and reflection. But Manifest Destiny, not unlike the progressive movement, evoked a faith in a progressive history.[57] Lincoln recognized that the success or failure of American institutions is not a matter of fate or destiny. In particular, he saw that the progress of technological innovation could be used, not to spread freedom but to perpetuate and spread the institution of slavery in new and innovative ways.[58] Arguments aimed at justifying the "progress" of American expansion into the West and beyond became increasingly intertwined with arguments justifying the intrinsic rightness of human slavery. As we have seen, Lincoln understood such arguments to be a fundamental threat to free government.

Lincoln's qualified embrace of technological progress was comparable to his position on the progress of political ideas and institutions. In his famed "Speech at Cooper Institute," Lincoln offered one of his more extended arguments against Taney and Douglas's position that Congress had no right to forbid slavery from the western territories. Douglas claimed that the Founders had understood the slavery question as well as, if not better than, the current generation did. Lincoln agreed. In an effort to exploit this statement Lincoln attempted to prove that the Founders, in fact, held that Congress could legislate with respect to slavery in the territories, the best example of which being the exclusion of slavery in the Northwest Ordinance. But, it is important to note, Lincoln warned against his being misunderstood. While the Founders offered guidance on the slavery problem, Lincoln argued, we are not "bound to follow implicitly in whatever our fathers did. To do so, would be to discard all the lights of current experience—to reject all *progress*—all improvement." If we would "supplant the opinions and policies of our fathers in any case," Lincoln claimed, we should do so only "upon evidence so conclusive, and argument so clear, that even their great authority, fairly considered and weighed, cannot stand."[59]

One might think this language sounds similar to the evolutionary, organic, "living constitution" rhetoric of Wilson and the progressives. But Lincoln's idea of "progress" here referred to the possibility of improving upon the Founders' policies through reflection and choice. We might use our reason to determine the best means by which we might pursue the legitimate ends of American government in securing natural and inalienable rights. The Founders' opinions and policies must be carefully considered and weighed against our own. There is no presumption that the progressive march of history had necessarily rendered those opinions and policies obsolete. Unlike Wilson and the progressives, Lincoln's "improvement" or "progress" here refers not to overcoming or transcending the Founders' opinions and policies but to reflecting upon them in an effort to fulfill their principles.

Wilson's Lincoln and Presidential Leadership

In "Abraham Lincoln: A Man of the People," Wilson did more than merely offer Lincoln as a metaphor for the doctrine of progress, however. He singled out Lincoln as an example upon which to build progressive leadership for the twentieth century. Wilson urged that we must have "the leadership of sane, genial men of universal use like Lincoln, to save us from mistakes and give us the necessary leadership in such days of struggle and difficulty." Wilson suggested that we cannot rest content merely to remember the actions of men like Lincoln. Rather, we must produce "timely remedies, suitable for the existing moment." We must create leaders "in a kind of our own."[60] Like Teddy Roosevelt, Wilson held that Lincoln belonged to the bygone age of the western pioneer democrat. Contrary to his earlier assertion that Lincoln was the product of a long, slow developmental process, Wilson argued Lincoln's development "can not be said to have been a slow process." The age of the western pioneer was a time in which states were made as fast as men, where maturity was demanded of men quickly, where men could be "picked out in the crude" and "refined out in a single generation into pure metal." The problem facing the current generation, Wilson urged, was how to re-create such leaders of men in the modern industrial age. But, Wilson argued, if we are to re-create men such as Lincoln for our own time, we must first understand just what it is we must re-create. If Lincoln is best understood as a "man of the people," just what does this mean?[61]

A "man of the people," Wilson explained, has his roots in the experience of the people but does not allow his roots to hold him forever at the level of the common man. While the man of the people draws his inspiration from the experiences of the people, he becomes a leader of men by rising "above the level of the rest of mankind." Such a man has an "outlook" above the people's heads and sees "horizons which they [the people] are too submerged to see." The man of the people "has lifted himself to a new place of outlook and of insight." He is the leader of the people, "not because he speaks from their ranks, but because he speaks for them and for their interests." According to Wilson, "It was in this sense that Lincoln was a 'man of the people.'" And, for Wilson, the emergence of this kind of popular leader is a key component in opening the nation to the march of progress. Consider the following:

> A great nation is not led by a man who simply repeats the talk of the street-corners or the opinions of the newspapers. A nation is led by a man who hears more than those things; or who, rather, hearing those things, understands them better, unites them, puts them into a common meaning; speaks, not the rumors of the street, but a new principle for a new age; a man in whose ears the voices of the nation do not sound like the accidental and discordant notes that come from the voice of a mob, but concurrent and concordant like the united voices of a chorus, whose many meanings, spoken by melodious tongues, unite in his understanding in a single meaning and reveal to him a single vision, so that he can speak what no man else knows, the common meaning of the common voice. Such is the man who leads a great, free, democratic nation.[62]

Of course, contrary to Wilson, we have already seen that Lincoln did not claim to profess a "new principle for a new age" but, rather, urged a continual rededication to the principles of the Declaration and the American Founding. But, as Pestritto notes, Wilson's commentary on Lincoln as a man of the people is useful for what it suggests about Wilson's own understanding of presidential leadership.[63]

Wilson argued that the economic and political crises of the early twentieth century called for men such as Lincoln, "more audibly, more imperatively, than did the tasks of the time when civil war was brewing and the very existence of the Nation was in the scale of destiny." According to his thinking, "when a nation begins to be divided into rival and contestant interests by the score, the time is much more dangerous than when it is divided into only two perfectly distinguishable interests which you can discriminate and deal with." In Lincoln's time, Wilson asserted, there were two clearly identifiable interests—the Union and the Confederacy. But Wilson insisted that, in his own time, there were many rival interests. According to Wilson, this made the leadership of a "man of the people" even more necessary in the twentieth century.[64]

Wilson argued that American democracy required progressive visionary leadership if it was to overcome the stifling spirit of checks and balances and open itself to progress. There must be men of talent who would lead the people, guiding their political development toward the modern democratic state. For Wilson, a leader of men sees the direction in which history is moving. Although through intellect and talent he has risen to a level above the generality of men, the leader of men has a genuine sympathy and fellow-feeling with the common man. The leader of men has the rare ability to understand the common will of the people, even when there might seem to be no truly common opinion among them. In this sense, the leader of men was a kind of interpreter and rhetorician, able to discern what the people did not or what they only dimly comprehended as their own interest. According to Wilson, this art of interpretation was the foundation of popular leadership. The leader can interpret the people's will and can articulate that will back to the people in a comprehensive, understandable form. The leader, Wilson argued, "must read the common thought: he must test and calculate very circumspectly the preparation of the nation for the next move in the progress of politics."[65]

For Wilson, the possibility of leadership in government is severely impeded to the extent that the regime is infected with the spirit of checks and balances.[66] Early in his academic writings Wilson's proposed remedy was to reform the American Constitution to resemble the British Parliamentary system. By establishing cabinet government in the United States, Wilson hoped to establish a tighter relationship between the executive and legislative departments. Although Wilson understood Congress as the supreme department of the national government, he believed that there was no genuine leadership in the legislative department, particularly because of the manner in which Congress was organized. According to Wilson, complicated rules of behavior, a weak and decentralized party system, and above all, the standing committee system, all inhibited national leadership and true deliberation. Yet by 1908, in his *Constitutional Government in the United States,* Wilson turned his attention toward the presidency as the best source of energetic, progressive national leadership.[67]

Wilson argued that the president, being the only person nominated by an entire party, is especially suited to serve as a party leader. By virtue of being elected by the entire nation, the president is also the only public officer who can legitimately claim to represent the entire nation. The president is uniquely suited to serve as the "vital link of connection" between the party and the public. Wilson understood the president to be the sole national leader, the embodiment of the will of the people, and the only public officer who can truly claim a national mandate.[68] We recall that Wilson suggested the Constitution had always been more adaptable to change than the Whig theory of political dynamics would admit. He applied this general observation to the office of the national executive in particular, which he suggests "has been one thing at one time, another at another, varying with the man who occupied the office and with the circumstances that surrounded him."[69]

The American Founders, Wilson claimed, had looked upon the president much the way the English Whigs had looked upon the king, as merely the legal executive, endowed with merely "negative" authority. The veto power, for example, was but a negative power against the legislative. According to this view, the executive had no positive or guiding authority in creating national policy. But over time, Wilson suggested, the American presidency had begun to transcend this merely negative or reactive authority. As the appointed representative of the voice of the people and as party leader, Wilson's president becomes the chief legislator of the nation, actively pursuing national policy goals through an increasingly close relationship with Congress. The structure of the Constitution, Wilson claimed, had surely limited this increasingly active role, but it had not prevented it. The executive was an organic institution, adaptable to the necessities of the time. Wilson's focus upon the individuals filling the office of the president calls our attention not toward the constitutionally defined office itself, but solely toward the leadership of those holding the office.[70]

According to the Founders' understanding of presidential authority, although executive power is ultimately derived from the sovereignty of the people, that authority is defined and structured by the people's Constitution. While the Founders had clearly sought to create an independent, energetic executive, that energy was provided by the Constitution itself. To guard against the dangers of majority faction and demagoguery, the Founders sought to create an executive independent from Congress, and insulated from the temporary whims of public opinion. However, in a development that Wilson helped to effectuate, the necessary independence and energy of the executive came to be understood differently. The independence of the executive has increasingly come to be seen as a special sort of independence that derives not from the Constitution but by virtue of a mandate conferred directly by the people themselves. At the heart of the modern presidency (what Ceaser has referred to as the "plebiscitary" presidency) is the notion that the president, rather than Congress or the political party, is the embodiment of the will of the people. Underlying this view is the belief that the will of the people is most authoritatively expressed not in the Constitution but in the results of current public opinion, expressed by way of presidential elections results, and (increasingly today) public opinion polls. Insofar as the president's authority is derived directly and independently from the people, the definition of the rights and duties of executive authority is potentially determined by public opinion, rather than the people's Constitution.[71]

Wilson's ultimate remedy to the spirit of checks and balances was the plebiscitary presidency, a deliberate attempt to energize the presidency from outside the Constitution in the name of the people.[72] Wilson believed Lincoln was a useful model upon which to build the plebiscitary presidency. Some of Lincoln's critics also see the roots of the modern plebiscitary presidency in Lincoln. Kendall and Carey claim that Lincoln was a precursor to modern presidents such as Wilson and the two Roosevelts, basing his claim to authority on plebiscitary power.[73] Gottfried Dietze calls our attention to the fact that progressive and modern liberals such as Teddy Roosevelt, Wilson, and Franklin Roosevelt frequently looked to Lincoln's arguments on emergency powers in order to justify broadened executive power in the domestic realm. Dietze argues that Lincoln's administration fostered the aggrandizement of the presidency and opened the way for the development of an omnipotent national executive thought to embody the will of the people.[74] Such observations might suggest that Wilson succeeded in claiming Lincoln as a model for the plebiscitary presidency. Some of Lincoln's greatest supporters—and some of his staunchest critics—would probably think that Wilson was justified in claiming Lincoln as a model for the plebiscitary presidency. Herman Belz observes that many believe Lincoln to be the "prototype of twentieth-century presidential government, ruling through rhetorical leadership of public opinion rather than an adherence to the text and forms of the Constitution."[75]

Some might see something approaching the plebiscitary presidency in Lincoln's July 4, 1861, message to Congress in special session. The constitutionality of Lincoln's actions in response to Ft. Sumter (his appropriation of funds from the U.S. Treasury, his declaration of the naval blockade, his expansion of the army and navy, and his suspension of the writ of habeas corpus) is still hotly debated. In his message to Congress in special session, Lincoln argued that these actions were taken on "what appeared to be a *popular demand,* and a *public necessity.*" Lincoln seemed to imply that, in times of crisis and emergency, the legitimacy of the executive's actions are determined, if only temporarily, both by necessity *and* by "popular demand." Lincoln's suggestion resembles Locke's argument for executive prerogative in the fourteenth chapter of his *Second Treatise.*[76]

According to Locke, in all well-framed governments, the common good of the commonwealth requires that some powers be left to the discretion of whoever holds the executive power. The legislature cannot make quick decisions when necessary and cannot frame laws for every situation that may confront the health and safety of the commonwealth. It thus falls upon the executor of the laws, Locke claimed, to wield prerogative power, that is, the "Power to act according to discretion, for the public good, without the prescription of the Law, and sometimes even against it." Locke understood the potential that prerogative power could be abused, and he argued that the ultimate check upon its misuse resides in the people's right of resistance. For Locke prerogative power can exist outside positive law and, as such, must be subject to limits embodied in the "Law antecedent and paramount to all positive Laws of men"—that is, the natural right to appeal to the sword. To put it simply, for Locke the ultimate judge of the legitimacy and extent of executive authority is the judgment of the people.[77]

Some have argued that, by appealing to a *popular demand* in defense of his actions, Lincoln came very close to positing one of the central tenets of the plebiscitary presidency. Suggesting the people shall be the judge of executive authority might entail the idea that executive authority is structured and legitimated by current and potentially momentary public opinion, at least in times of crisis or emergency.[78] To argue that current public opinion determines the scope of executive power contradicts constitutional government, according to the political theory of the American Founding. Although all power is ultimately derived from the people, the most authoritative expression of the will of people regarding the powers of government is embodied in the Constitution, not in the opinion of the day. While the people themselves decide who shall hold the office of president, the powers of the office are defined by the Constitution as the fundamental law. Claiming Lockean prerogative, an American president could appeal outside the Constitution and directly to the people as the source and arbiter of executive power.[79] As noted in our discussion of Teddy Roosevelt's stewardship theory, Lincoln's claims to prerogative power were made in reference to emergency or crisis situations that threatened the very existence of the regime. Lincoln made such arguments in defense of temporary policies meant to preserve the Constitution. Such measures were not meant to extend beyond the crisis at hand; they were not intended to apply to the normal workings of the executive, under normal circumstances.[80] However, after Teddy Roosevelt, Wilson, and especially FDR, the language of crisis has become routine in the rhetoric of the plebiscitary presidency, with many perceived problems labeled "crises" upon which to declare war. The argument for emergency powers has been extended to address everyday politics. It is well understood that even if a case can be made for a breadth of discretionary, emergency powers in the executive, experience suggests that the exercise of such power might become more commonplace than was originally envisioned.[81] Divorced from constitutional restraints, discretionary power would appear to become the rule rather than the exception in the plebiscitary presidency, with the people passing judgment on the use of executive authority.

But Lincoln was nevertheless a poor model for Wilson and the progressives' vision of the plebiscitary presidency. Although Lincoln immediately defended his actions at the beginning of the war by arguing that they were taken on "what appeared to be a *popular demand,* and a *public necessity,*" this was an anomaly in Lincoln's statements on executive authority as Benjamin Kleinerman has ably demonstrated.[82] Lincoln consistently and meticulously defended his actions on constitutional grounds, particularly appealing to the president's unique constitutional duty to take care that the laws be faithfully executed (Article II, Section 3) and to the presidential oath of office to preserve, protect, and defend the U.S. Constitution (Article II, Section 1, Clause 8). As Kleinerman argues, the necessity of preserving the Union, not popular demand, became the central defining feature of Lincoln's suggestions on discretionary executive authority.[83]

We should also note that, insofar as Wilson's vision for the presidency requires rhetorical leaders of men to move the people beyond the principles of the Founding, Lincoln would again prove a poor model. The Lincoln of 1861 never strayed far from the Lincoln of 1838. That is to say, his famed analysis of the Caesarian danger in his 1838 Lyceum Address and his call for constant dedication to the Constitution and the laws never disappeared from his understanding of popular government. Throughout his career, Lincoln's political rhetoric was always aimed at turning the people back toward the Constitution and the principles of the Founding, not at overcoming the principles of the Founding in light of history and progress.

Nevertheless, in his own rhetorical effort to lead public opinion in the direction of history, Wilson would continue to offer Lincoln as the best example of the interpreter-leader of men. In a 1912 address at Williams Grove, Pennsylvania, Wilson again presented Lincoln as the supreme interpreter and shaper of public opinion. Like Herbert Croly and Teddy Roosevelt, Wilson offered a detached and disinterested Lincoln who was able to rise above the particularism and individualism of the average American in order to pursue the national interest. At Williams Grove, Wilson suggested the following:

> I thank God that we have lived to see a time when men are beginning to reason upon the facts and not upon party tradition. I believe in party tradition, but I believe in it only as founded upon eternal principles of justice. I have heard a great deal said about the fathers of the Republic not only, but a great deal said about the fathers of the Republican party. I have heard men speak very familiarly in these later days of the great Lincoln and assume that they are acting in his spirit, when all the world knows how open the heart of Lincoln was to the pulsations of every other heart that beat among his fellow men. Lincoln's glory was not merely that he was a man of the people but that by study, learning the lessons of the people's life, he, in the fullness of time, lifted himself above the general mass.... [Lincoln] looked away from groups of politicians [and] said "You have forgotten the traditions of the Republic. You listen to your own voices. You do not hear the unspoken commands, the inaudible whispers, of the public conscience. I do not hear you; I hear only the mandate of the people."[84]

Wilson's remarks here are interesting. According to Wilson, one ought to follow party tradition only insofar as that tradition is founded upon "eternal principles of justice," but such principles would surely seem to be denied by Wilson's historicism. More significant, however, are Wilson's use of the phrase "mandate of the people" and his association of Lincoln with this phrase, which are perhaps deliberate. The "mandate of the people," Wilson suggested, resides in the "unspoken commands" and "inaudible whispers" of the "public conscience." For Wilson, the "mandate of the people" cannot be found in the Constitution, for in listening to this mandate the leader of men seeks to transcend the Constitution. As we have seen, at the heart of the plebiscitary presidency is the idea that the will of the people is most authoritatively expressed not in the Constitution but in contemporary public opinion. This opinion is often said to be expressed in presidential election results. Supposedly acting as the most authoritative representatives of the people, plebiscitary presidents have often claimed national mandates for their chosen policy agendas. The association of Lincoln with the idea of the presidential "mandate" is not limited to Wilson at Williams Grove. Some of Lincoln's most vocal critics have made this very same connection.

Lincoln and the Presidential Mandate

We have seen that some of Lincoln's conservative critics see his dedication to equality as dangerous, and they have connected that dedication to the twentieth-century plebiscitary presidency. Willmoore Kendall, for example, sees a danger in an executive office that is aimed at "transforming the American political system into a *plebiscitary* political system, capable of carrying through *popular mandates*." Central to this transformation, Kendall suggests, is the glorification of the presidency and the attempt to make presidential elections the "central ritual of American politics—so that . . . a newly elected president with a majority will be able to plead, against a recalcitrant Congress, that *his* mandate must prevail."[85] Today, Kendall claims, "the Caesarism we all need to fear is the contemporary liberal movement, dedicated like Lincoln to egalitarian reforms sanctioned by mandates emanating from national majorities—a movement which is Lincoln's legitimate offspring." Kendall and Carey suggest that "this belief in a mandate is so dominant" that it would be virtually impossible to "cite all those who have at one time or another publicly professed it." Yet "in one fashion or another," they rightly observe, "every major presidential candidate in recent years has subscribed to it."[86] Kendall and Carey's concerns about Lincoln, equality, and the plebiscitary presidency point to fundamental questions about the American presidency and the nature and scope of executive power. Despite the fact that Kendall in the 1960s associated the plebiscitary presidency with the American political left, experience has shown that the modern presidency has been embraced by American intellectuals and politicians across the political spectrum. The manner in which the Lincoln presidency fits into this transformation has long been a source of intense debate among historians and political scientists. Some critics of the modern presidency school contend that there is not, in fact, a stark division between the "traditional" vision of the presidency and the "modern" presidency.[87] To draw a rigid distinction between the Founders' presidency and the presidency as it functions today—with Wilson as the crucial dividing line—

might underestimate incremental changes that contributed to the rise of the plebiscitary presidency over time. This is particularly true when one considers the idea of the presidential "mandate."[88]

Richard J. Ellis and Stephen Kirk offer a thoughtful reevaluation of the modern presidency literature, tracing the underdeveloped roots of the notion of the presidential mandate back to Thomas Jefferson's characterization of the election of 1800 as a declaration of the "public sentiment," which "burst open the doors of honor and confidence to those whose opinions they more approved." While Jefferson had asserted that the "will of the nation, manifested by their various elections, calls for an administration of government according with the opinions of those elected," he did not aggressively pursue this position to expand presidential authority in any sustained or systematic way.[89] The crucial step in the idea of the presidential mandate, Ellis and Kirk suggest, came with Andrew Jackson, who characterized the 1832 presidential election as a popular referendum on the question of the National Bank. Jackson claimed that the people had retained him, in part, on the basis of his position on the bank. The people, he argued, approved his intent to act upon the principles of his veto message.[90]

The Whig opposition to the Jacksonian presidency is well documented, and it suffices here to note that, in opposition to Jackson's theory of the mandate and executive authority, the Whigs maintained that presidential elections were nothing more than a means of selecting a chief national officer to execute the laws and defend the Constitution of the United States.[91] Ellis and Kirk remind us that among the most articulate defenders of the Whig view was a young Abraham Lincoln. In an 1848 speech to the U.S. House of Representatives, young Lincoln defended Zachary Taylor's Whig view of executive power as being defined and structured by the Constitution, condemning the Jacksonian notion of the presidential mandate. Young Lincoln argued that it was impossible to infer the public's policy preferences from election results. During an election campaign, there are simply too many questions considered and too many positions taken. The whole of these positions is "strung together" in one candidate, and in voting for a candidate the public "must take all or reject all." The people, Lincoln claimed, cannot "take what they like, and leave the rest." According to Lincoln, we cannot single out any particular policy as central to a candidate being elected. Therefore, we cannot argue that a particular candidate's election to office is an indication of the public will on any particular issue. Lincoln argued that the Democrats' claim to the contrary was "a most pernicious deception."[92]

By condemning the idea of the presidential mandate, young Lincoln condemned one of the guiding assumptions of the plebiscitary presidency. However, Ellis and Kirk suggest, ironically, despite Congressman Lincoln's best efforts to force "the Jacksonian genie back into the bottle," it would be President Lincoln who would eventually "shatter the bottle" altogether, solidifying the idea of the presidential mandate in American politics. Ellis and Kirk claim that, during the 1864 presidential election campaign and shortly thereafter, Lincoln appeared to adopt the idea of the presidential mandate.[93]

Throughout the campaign, Lincoln and the Republicans had framed the presidential election as a national referendum on the slavery issue. A vote for Lincoln was a vote for Union, a vote for the war, and by extension, a vote for an amendment abolishing slavery as a necessary means to preserving the Union after the war.[94] While Lincoln himself never explicitly used the term *mandate* to refer to his reelection, Ellis and Kirk contend that he did exploit the idea of the mandate in his December 6, 1864, State of the Union Address.[95] In this sense, Lincoln seemed to contribute to a core tenet of the modern plebiscitary presidency that Woodrow Wilson sought to institutionalize.

In his 1864 State of the Union, Lincoln continued to push for an amendment to the U.S. Constitution abolishing slavery throughout the Union. Nearly six months prior to the address, a proposed amendment to this end had passed the Senate, but it did not get through the House. In the State of the Union, Lincoln argued that Congress should reconsider and pass the proposed amendment. His argument here is worth considering. Although "the abstract question is not changed," Lincoln claimed, "an intervening election shows, almost certainly, that the next Congress will pass the measure if this [Congress] does not. Hence there is only a question of *time* as to when the proposed amendment will go to the States for their action. And as it is to go, at all events, may we not agree that the sooner the better?" Lincoln emphatically suggested that the recent election imposed no duty upon members of Congress to change their views or their votes. Nevertheless, given that the Republicans had just gained an overwhelming majority in the House, the amendment was sure to pass in the next Congress. The argument here is one of practical politics. Lincoln suggested that, as long as the amendment is going to pass, Congress should get on board and begin to prepare for Reconstruction. Yet Lincoln did not stop there. He then argued that the recent election had pointed the direction in which public sentiment was tending, characterizing the election as the "voice of the people now, for the first time, heard upon the question" of slavery and its abolition. Thus, President Lincoln, contrary to the Whig congressman

Lincoln in 1848, suggested that we can discern the public sentiment on a specific policy through election results. "The most reliable indication of public purpose in this country," Lincoln argued, "is derived through our popular elections."[96]

Observers such as Ellis and Kirk are right to suggest that the idea of the presidential mandate might have pre-Wilsonian roots, and clearly the rise of the plebiscitary presidency depends in part upon the belief that popular mandates can be discerned in the results of national elections. Lincoln did frame the 1864 election as a referendum on slavery, and he did suggest that public opinion on a given proposal or group of proposals can be discerned in election results. This does appear to contradict the Lincoln of 1848. However, we cannot make enough of the fact that Lincoln suggested the recent election imposed no duty upon members of Congress to change their views or votes on the proposed amendment. The election, according to Lincoln's argument, merely indicated the people's agreement with their elected representatives as to the desirability of preserving the Union, and the best means of doing so. Lincoln said nothing to suggest that he believed the election itself had imposed a moral or political duty upon the other departments of government to acquiesce in the president's agenda. Insofar as there was a duty placed upon Congress to pass the amendment, according to Lincoln, this duty was to save the Union, with the election merely indicating the people's dedication to this same end.

The Lincoln offered up by the American political left is often not all that dissimilar from the Lincoln we find on the right. The fact that Woodrow Wilson and Kendall and Carey both chose to connect Lincoln with the presidential mandate is a case in point. Ellis and Kirk's argument suggests there might be something to this connection. But aside from the idea that an election might indicate current public opinion on a given issue, nothing in Lincoln's actions during the war suggests he should be regarded as a precursor to the extra-constitutional "leadership" of the plebiscitary presidency, despite Wilson's claims to the contrary.

Conclusion

Wilson's effort to incorporate Lincoln into the rhetoric of progressivism and the plebiscitary presidency is closely related to the idea of equality as a political goal for American government. Wilson's attempt to transform the American presidency is based in part upon his effort to introduce an equalization of conditions for self-development into American society. However, Lincoln's understanding of equality, and its pursuit, ultimately distinguishes him from the progressives and their heirs. The progressive pursuit of equality rests upon fundamental assumptions about human nature and the purpose of government that are very different from those held by Lincoln.

Lincoln's pursuit of equality was informed fundamentally by the natural right principles of the American Founding, principles that impose limits upon the means and objects of government by consent of the governed. The progressives sought to transcend these first principles and to overcome the institutional arrangements founded upon them. For Wilson this process would be spearheaded by the president, acting as the leader of men. The consequences of this progressive rejection of natural rights and limited government constitutionalism are significant. Once the ends of government are divorced from standards of right, independent of particular circumstances, the pursuit of equality is unlimited in principle and potentially points far beyond Lincoln's equality of opportunity. The progressive appropriation of the Lincoln image obscures the details of Lincoln's equality and helps to create a Lincoln steadfastly dedicated to equality, albeit an equality without any reference whatsoever to the idea of natural and inalienable rights. In this respect Wilson and the progressives denature Lincoln as thoroughly as they denature equality and the Declaration of Independence. As a consequence, both the ends and means of American democracy change significantly.

This attempt to appropriate Lincoln into an expanded and denatured pursuit of equality would not stop with Woodrow Wilson and the progressives. In bringing much of Wilson's vision for American politics into the middle of the twentieth century, Franklin D. Roosevelt would bring Wilson's Lincoln with him. In his speeches and writings, FDR would adopt the progressives' Lincoln and transform him into a proto-New Dealer and a model for a new understanding of American statesmanship.

FOUR

Franklin Roosevelt's Lincoln

LINCOLN'S POLITICAL THOUGHT and the basic tenets of American progressivism are incompatible. We have seen, however, that the progressives nevertheless sought to incorporate Lincoln into their political rhetoric. In the progressives we find a historicized Lincoln who has been divorced from natural right, and divorced from the principles of the Declaration of Independence as Lincoln himself seems to have understood them. We also find in the progressives' image of him a Lincoln who is relatively unconcerned with constitutional formalities and structures, a Lincoln more suited to the progressive effort to overcome institutions such as the separation of powers in the name of history or progress. Consequently, with the progressives, we are presented with a Lincoln who is wholly dedicated to the pursuit of equality, but this equality has no basis in natural and inalienable rights, no connection with limited government, and seemingly little appreciation for constitutionalism. Equality remains a goal in the progressives' Lincoln, but this goal is severed from any objective justification for the reasons it is a choice-worthy goal, other than that it is good to associate equality with the historical notion of "progress," unlimited by natural standards or constitutional forms. The effort to render Lincoln a precursor to modern egalitarianism is made much easier once the Lincoln image is thoroughly divorced from Lincoln's own political thought.

The explicit rejection of the natural standards that guided Lincoln's equality denies in principle that there are any limitations upon our pursuit of equality extrinsic to the will of the people and their government in any given historical or political circumstance. While some might suggest the progressives were not in practice radical egalitarians, their arguments, in principle, admit no objective limits as to what we might consent to in pursuit of greater equality.[1] The progressive pursuit of equality was intertwined with an effort to reconstruct American political institutions in order to get around constitutional formalities (such as representation, separation of powers, and the amendment process) that might stand in the way of "genuine" democracy. In particular, we have seen the rise of the idea that the modern plebiscitary presidency has both the right and the duty to pursue expanded notions of equality in the name of national "mandates." All of these transformations have roots in progressive political thought.

Filmmaker Ken Burns asserts that, in following the Lincoln example, America is still "constantly trying to enlarge the definition and deepen the meaning of 'all men are created equal.'"[2] Historian Barbara Fields suggests that Lincoln and the Civil War "established a standard that will not mean anything" until we have "finished the work" we started. If some citizens "live in houses and others live on the street," Fields asserts, then "the Civil War is still going on. It is still to be fought, and regrettably, it can still be lost."[3] As Hayward has suggested, and given our understanding of Lincoln's equality, it seems hard to associate such language with Lincoln.[4] To suggest that the *influence* of the Declaration's "all men are created equal" might be "spread" and "deepened" is not to suggest that its *meaning* might be "enlarged" or "deepened." In this, Lincoln was clear. The authors of the Declaration "defined with tolerable distinctness, in what respects they did consider all men created equal—equal in 'certain inalienable rights, among which are life, liberty, and the pursuit of happiness.'"[5]

The *influence* of the truth of natural equality might be spread and deepened, but its *meaning* remains the same. Moreover, to suggest, with Fields, that as long as some "live in houses and others live on the street, the Civil War is still going on" seems a generally un-Lincolnian sentiment. Could we really suggest Lincoln would contend that, insofar as there are some people living in poverty, the Civil War is still being fought? Aside from its rather free use of the term *civil war*, this statement seems to convey a utopianism uncharacteristic of Lincoln's political thought.[6]

Nevertheless, this language should sound familiar to us. When Fields asserts that the Civil War is still being fought as long as "some live in houses and others live on the street," we might reasonably think not of Lincoln but of Franklin Roosevelt. Fields's remarks are reminiscent of Roosevelt's famous statement that America cannot be content if "some fraction of our people—whether it be one-third or one-fifth or one-tenth—is ill-fed, ill clothed, ill-housed, and insecure."[7] And Burns's phrase "enlarging the definition and deepening the meaning of 'all men are created equal'" also sounds more like Roosevelt than Lincoln.[8] We shall find that Roosevelt himself summed up Lincoln's statesmanship in similar terms and provided another step in the incorporation of the Lincoln image into the modern rhetoric of equality. Using Lincoln in the rhetoric of the New Deal, Roosevelt helped to further a movement from formal equality of opportunity to an open-ended modern egalitarianism. On a course cleared by the progressives, FDR rhetorically connected the Lincoln image to a new, expanded pursuit of equality, a "redefinition of rights" divorced from the natural rights principles and constitutionalism that had informed Lincoln's statesmanship.

Roosevelt's Lincoln in the Rhetoric of the New Deal

In his handling of the Great Depression and the Second World War, Franklin Roosevelt proved a master of political rhetoric. Like Lincoln, he was seemingly able to give the right speech at the right time and to offer a struggling American people the necessary hope to endure potentially overwhelming crises. Defending his New Deal policies and his foreign policy during the Second World War, FDR frequently claimed that he continued the Lincolnian tradition. According to Roosevelt, both he and Lincoln believed that the purpose of American government is to help the governed meet new challenges as they arise. Simply put, if the general government is to secure the safety and happiness of the American people, it must be given the necessary means to fix perceived problems. With respect to the New Deal, FDR's use of Lincoln peaked between 1938 and 1939, although it had begun several years earlier. Ultimately, Roosevelt came to appropriate him into the New Deal rhetoric as a "liberal" politician to be included alongside Thomas Jefferson, Andrew Jackson, Woodrow Wilson, and Teddy Roosevelt.[9]

Despite the progressives' efforts to appropriate Lincoln, the Republicans still clung firmly to their own claim to Lincoln's legacy into the 1930s. It is well understood that Franklin Roosevelt self-consciously sought to remedy this, incorporating the Lincoln image into his own political rhetoric. Mario Cuomo and Lincoln scholar Harold Holzer have written on the various attempts to claim Lincoln and suggest that the "Democrat who worked most assiduously of all to seize the Lincoln legacy was Franklin Delano Roosevelt."

David Donald notes that, with FDR, we see "another serious effort" to "raid the Republican closet and steal the stovepipe hat." According to Donald, Roosevelt assumed "the mantle of the Great Emancipator" and took his "pick of garments" from the "clothes closet of American history." Roosevelt, Donald claims, "understood what was meant by a 'usable past.'" Likewise, Michael Lind argues that the progressives, who came to call themselves liberals in FDR's Democratic Party, "rewrote history" and attempted to "enlist Lincoln as a political ancestor." According to Lind, what the "New Deal liberal historians and intellectuals did was breathtaking in its audacity." By seizing the Lincoln image the "New Deal intellectuals succeeded in crafting a new version of the American past."[10]

As early as April 1929, as governor of New York, FDR had already begun to challenge the Republicans' claim to the Lincoln legacy. Writing to Jefferson biographer Claude Bowers, Roosevelt claimed that "I think it is time for us Democrats to claim Lincoln as one of our own. . . . The Republican Party has certainly repudiated, first and last, everything he stood for."[11] By the early 1930s, in the dispute over what could and should be done about the Great Depression, Herbert Hoover and FDR engaged in a quarrel over just who in fact the true heirs of Lincoln really were. For example, in a radio address on February 12, 1931, President Hoover claimed that he could find no precedent, not even in Lincoln's handling of the Civil War, for a greater centralization of government as a means to combat the economic crisis of the Depression.[12] By 1932 Roosevelt had retaliated by going on the offensive on the campaign trail, frequently invoking Lincoln in support of his policy proposals and questioning the Republicans' claim to Lincoln's inheritance. By 1934, as president, Roosevelt would be invoking Lincoln as a defense against Hoover and critics of the New Deal. According to FDR, the current economic crisis was akin to the crisis of the Civil War, and the national government had both the right and the duty to take increased and novel steps in addressing this crisis.[13]

The appeal to Lincoln had become a staple in Roosevelt's political rhetoric. For example, in January 1936, Roosevelt wrote a tribute to Lincoln, to be read on his birthday to the Lincoln Association of Cleveland, Ohio:

> Abraham Lincoln was not a son of the North or the South. Born in Kentucky and nurtured in the very heart of our land, the scope of his intellect and of his sympathies was co-extensive with the length and breadth of our domain. Nor could Abraham Lincoln have come from any class that did not know, through daily struggle, the grim realities of life. Self-sustained,

self-educated, and grounded in common sense through contact with his fellow man, he developed that homely philosophy with which we have come to associate his name and with which he was to solve the problems of a distraught nation.

From such an origin and from such a school, there emerged a character destined to *transfuse with new meaning the concepts of our constitutional fathers* and to assure a Government having for its broad purpose the promotion of the life, liberty, and happiness of all the people.[14]

Here Roosevelt offered more than a praise of Lincoln's humble virtues, common sense, and sympathy with the common man. He offered a window into his own understanding of democratic statesmanship by praising Lincoln as destined to transfuse the concepts of the Founders with new meaning.[15] Roosevelt's Lincoln redefined the Founders' principles in light of changing historical circumstances, ushering in new, deeper concepts of equality, liberty, and happiness. Such a redefinition, it seems, was necessary (and will always be necessary) in order to "solve the problems of a distraught nation." Roosevelt sought to identify his own idea of statesmanship with Lincoln's, and he used the Lincoln example rhetorically as a justification for a new understanding of our fundamental political principles.

In fall 1936, Roosevelt closed his presidential campaign at Wilmington, Delaware. He told his audience that he thought it inappropriate to give a "political speech" on such an occasion. Rather, Roosevelt said, he could "better describe the kind of liberty which our Administration has sought and continues to seek by reading to you the simple words of a great President who believed in the kind of liberty that we believe in—the great President who preserved the American Union." Roosevelt went on to read excerpts from Lincoln's April 1864 address to a sanitary fair in Baltimore. Roosevelt claimed that, although these words were nearly three-quarters of a century old, they nevertheless still applied in 1936:

> The world has never had a good definition of the word liberty, and the American people, just now, are much in want of one. We all declare for liberty; but in using the same word we do not all mean the same thing. With some the word liberty may mean for each man to do as he pleases with himself, and the product of his labor; while with others the same word may mean for some men to do as they please with other men, and the product of other men's labor. Here are two, not only different, but incompatible things,

called by the same name, liberty. And it follows that each of the things is, by the respective parties, called by two different and incompatible names—liberty and tyranny.[16]

Then, Roosevelt said, Lincoln offered one of his "homely examples":

> The shepherd drives the wolf from the sheep's throat, for which the sheep thanks the shepherd as his liberator, while the wolf denounces him for the same act as the destroyer of liberty. . . . Plainly, the sheep and the wolf are not agreed upon a definition of the word liberty; and precisely the same difference prevails today among us human creatures . . . and all professing to love liberty. Hence we behold the processes by which thousands are daily passing from under the yoke of bondage, hailed by some as the advance of liberty, and bewailed by others as the destruction of all liberty.[17]

Lincoln at Baltimore had claimed that, by abolishing slavery, the people of Maryland had been doing something to define liberty, and the wolf's dictionary had been repudiated. Roosevelt concluded by suggesting that, in 1936, the people had "again been doing something to define liberty. And the wolf's dictionary" had again been repudiated.[18] Roosevelt deemphasized the context surrounding Lincoln's remarks, but the point was still clear: the New Deal understanding of liberty was akin to Lincoln's understanding of liberty—for each man to do as he pleases with himself and the product of his labor. Powerful industries and corporations, on the other hand, held to the slaveholders' understanding of liberty—to do as they please with other men and the product of other men's labor. According to FDR, echoing the rhetoric of progressives such as Teddy Roosevelt and Woodrow Wilson, those who fought for social and industrial justice through the policies of the New Deal were the rightful heirs of Abraham Lincoln. Those who fought for the interests of modern industry and big business were modern-day slaveholders with no claim to Lincoln's legacy. As Ronald Rietveld observes, Roosevelt repeated this same speech the next two times he closed his campaign in Wilmington, in 1940 and 1944.[19]

Like the progressives before him, Roosevelt held that the excesses of an unrestrained, free-market, industrial economy made it impossible for many Americans to provide for themselves without the aid of national government. The Founders' understanding of the purpose of government in securing inalienable rights was deemed insufficient to secure our safety and happiness. For Roosevelt, history demonstrated the need for government to aid in securing equality of opportunity by establishing and promoting new, primarily economic, "rights." Roosevelt's new conception of rights was intricately tied to a new understanding of American liberalism, borrowed in part from the political writings of John Dewey in the late 1920s and early 1930s. The progressives struggled with what they regarded as the overly individualistic liberal tradition of the American Founding. Dewey, however, sought to transform progressivism into a new type of liberalism, in which the state becomes the guarantor of individual well-being and security. For Dewey, the true purpose of government was to foster the "liberation of individuals for free self-initiated expression."[20]

In the introduction to the 1938 volume of his *Public Papers and Addresses*, as a response to his political opponents Roosevelt argued that there had always been two parties during times of crisis in American history—the "liberal" and the "conservative," with the liberal party being the more "progressive" and the conservative the more "reactionary." According to Roosevelt, the duty of the liberal party (that is, the duty of men such as Thomas Jefferson, Andrew Jackson, Abraham Lincoln, Woodrow Wilson, and Teddy Roosevelt) is to find new remedies to meet new problems as they arise. This would help to ensure that "the average person has the right to his own economic and political life, liberty, and pursuit of happiness." FDR claimed that this was the New Deal theory of government. He contended that this same theory of government was expressed by Lincoln when he said (in his Fragments on Government) that "the legitimate object of government is to do for a community of people whatever they need to have done, but cannot do at all, or cannot do so well for themselves, in their separate and individual capacities."[21]

Roosevelt's use of the term *liberal* shows Dewey's influence, but what is perhaps most significant here is not merely the use of this term to describe a variant of progressivism. Rather, Roosevelt had connected this new liberalism to the idea of equal "rights." Dewey, while urging for a new American liberalism, did not so much connect this liberalism to a new idea of rights but, rather, suggested that the success of liberalism depended upon the reform of local communities as forums for educated public inquiry.[22] In New Deal liberalism, however, we find an apparent union of the individualistic, "Jeffersonian" rights language of the old, formal liberalism and the newer rhetoric of progressivism. The old liberal tradition was not presented explicitly as an enemy as much as it was incorporated into a new liberal tradition. To understand liberalism anew, it must be divorced from merely "procedural" concerns about the scope and structure of government. Roosevelt's task was to associate liberalism primarily with the aspirations of government.

Viewed in this light, Roosevelt suggested, we could look back into our political history to see that, in essence, the liberal pursuit had always been fundamentally the same. In January 1938, at a Jackson Day Dinner address, Roosevelt argued that in "these recent years the average American seldom thinks of Jefferson and Jackson as Democrats or of Lincoln and Theodore Roosevelt as Republicans." Rather, Americans tend to remember these presidents for their "attitude toward the fundamental problems that confronted" them. Such men stood out, Roosevelt argued, for "the constructive battles they waged, not merely battles against things temporarily evil but battles for things permanently good—battles for the basic morals of democracy, which rest on respect for the right of self-government and faith in majority rule." According to Roosevelt, although they understood majorities can make mistakes, these presidents believed passionately that the "rule of a small minority" makes worse mistakes. In the long run, the instincts of the common man "work out the best and safest balance for the common good." This, Roosevelt claimed, "is what I mean by the battle to restore and maintain the moral integrity of democracy."[23] For Roosevelt, what united these presidents (including Roosevelt himself) was their passionate belief in majority rule and their willingness to engage in battle to preserve self-government.

In his July 3, 1938, address at Gettysburg, a speech occurring on the seventy-fifth anniversary of the battle of Gettysburg, Roosevelt again invoked Lincoln in defense of the New Deal. Here he claimed that, in the Gettysburg Address, Lincoln had restated the purposes for which the nation was founded. The great task we must always face is to preserve under the changing conditions of each generation a "people's government for the people's good." Roosevelt suggested that "Sometimes the threat to popular government comes from political interests, sometimes from economic interests, sometimes we have to beat off all of them together. But the challenge is always the same." Roosevelt thus argued that, like Lincoln, he must again seek to preserve the people's government under changing circumstances, this time emphasizing the particular economic threat to the people's good. Again, Roosevelt argued that the liberal pursuit had always been the same. According to Roosevelt, in 1938 his audience faced a crisis "as fundamental as Lincoln's, fought not with glint of steel, but with appeals to reason and justice on a thousand fronts—seeking to save for our common country opportunity and security for citizens in a free society." Lincoln had led the people through a war and, ultimately, toward peace and unity. So too must Roosevelt engage in battle and lead the nation toward a new peace and unity in 1938.[24]

This appeal to unity was a common theme in his appeal to Lincoln. That same year in Denton, Maryland, Roosevelt would suggest that, as for Lincoln, a great part of his duty as president had been to do what he could to bring the people back together again after a divisive struggle. But at Gettysburg, Roosevelt had provided some insight into just what it meant to achieve this unity, and why we should want to achieve it. Roosevelt's new unity was not an end in itself but, rather, a precondition by which we might pursue new and increased ends in the name of democracy. Roosevelt claimed that Lincoln understood "a democracy can keep alive only if the settlement of old difficulties clears the ground and transfers energies to face new responsibilities. Never can it have as much ability and purpose as it needs in that striving; the end of the battle does not end the infinity of those needs."[25] To follow Lincoln's example is not only to recognize the need for unity but to understand that democracy must continually strive to face new responsibilities.

According to Roosevelt, what united Lincoln with other "liberal" presidents was his supposed understanding that government must continually seek out and solve problems that confront the governed in securing their needs. This, Roosevelt reasoned, was genuine democracy. In his January 1939 Jackson Day Dinner Address, Roosevelt claimed that twenty years had to pass before Andrew Jackson's principle of *true* democracy could be reborn in the next real *democrat*—Abraham Lincoln.[26] This statement sparked another heated exchange with Hoover and the Republicans. In his February 12, 1939, speech at the Lincoln Day Dinner, Hoover argued, "Those who adhere to the traditional liberalism upon which the Republic was founded and which Lincoln sustained are crowding away from the pseudo-liberalism of the New Deal. . . . Whatever this New Deal system is, it is certain that it did not come from Abraham Lincoln." Soon after, in an article that appeared in *New Republic* on March 8, 1939, Max Lerner suggested that there is a "new and revived Lincoln image in the making" as "almost providentially made for our present crisis." Lerner specifically attributed the source of this revival to Franklin Roosevelt.[27]

By January 1940, FDR was taking his appeal to Lincoln in a different direction, suggesting that Lincoln's statesmanship transcended partisan concerns. In his January 8, Jackson Day Dinner Address, Roosevelt claimed, "I do not know which party Lincoln would belong to if he were alive in 1940—

and I am not even concerned to speculate on it. . . . I am more interested in the fact that he did the big job which then had to be done—to preserve the Union and make possible, at a later time, the united country that we all live in today." According to Roosevelt, Lincoln's "sympathies and his motives of championship of humanity" had made him "the legitimate property of all parties—of every man and woman and child in every part of our land."[28] By the 1940 presidential campaign, Roosevelt was turning increasingly to the Lincoln example not so much to defend the New Deal but to help address the challenges of a potential world war. In June 1940 Roosevelt met with leaders of the American Youth Congress, who criticized the president for having abandoned the domestic concerns of the New Deal in the face of foreign threats to our safety. Responding to one student, Roosevelt asked if the student had read Sandburg's *Lincoln*. When the student admitted that he had not, Roosevelt responded, "the impression was that Lincoln was a pretty sad man, because he could not do all he wanted to do at one time, and I think you will find examples where Lincoln had to compromise a little to gain something." Lincoln, FDR suggested, "had to compromise to make a few gains. Lincoln was one of those unfortunate people called a 'politician' but he was a politician who was practical enough to get a great many things for his country. He was a sad man because he couldn't get it all at once. And nobody can."[29] As Rietveld notes, such statements seemed fitting for a reluctant third-term presidential candidate.[30]

In comparing his own situation to that of Lincoln, Roosevelt emphasized Lincoln's purpose to serve the greater good but also his practicality and willingness to compromise when necessity dictated doing so.[31] Clearly, one must sometimes be willing to accept what is less than perfect in light of practical circumstances. And one can, of course, draw reasonable parallels here between Lincoln and Roosevelt. Both steered their country through times of national crisis. Neither was able to do all he wanted at one time, yet both were practical enough to do a great many things for their country. However, we should not lose sight of the fact that FDR associated Lincoln with a notion of progressive leadership similar to that which we encountered in the thinking of Teddy Roosevelt and Woodrow Wilson. Teddy Roosevelt built upon Croly's appeal to Lincoln and sought to associate his Lincoln with a redefinition of our most fundamental rights in light of historical circumstances, a progressive attempt to make "the rights of man . . . real and living." Wilson's Lincoln self-consciously looked upon rights with clarified vision, uttering a "new principle for a new age." In suggesting that Lincoln gave "new meaning" to the concepts of American Founders, FDR readopted but also redirected the Lincoln image as a model of progressive leadership, which he claimed requires the redefinition of rights "in terms of a growing and changing social order."[32]

Despite Roosevelt's attempt to incorporate Lincoln into the New Deal rhetoric, the New Deal order represented a self-conscious break with the liberalism of Lincoln and the American Founders. When Roosevelt described Lincoln as a character destined to give new meaning to the concepts of the Founding, he did not identify these concepts, but we are fairly safe in assuming they included the notion of equality. Given that Lincoln's views on equality were voiced in light of the problem of slavery and the South's denial of the natural equality of all men, does FDR acquiesce in Taney's argument that blacks were excluded from the Declaration's "all men are created equal"? Does he suggest that the Founders did not include the Negro in the Declaration and that the Founders' Constitution was a proslavery document? If so, this is the same view that was roundly rejected by Lincoln, who repeatedly suggested it was his duty to *resist* the transfusion of "new meaning" into the idea of equality. He specifically resisted the attempt—made on the part of Calhoun, Douglas, Taney, and the Southern slave interest—to "redefine" the concepts of the Founders by reading the natural equality of all human beings out of the American political tradition. Lincoln always claimed he was reiterating rather than improving upon the Founders' understanding of equality.[33] Nevertheless, Roosevelt used his Lincoln as a precursor to a new understanding of equality, and a new kind of liberalism.

Dewey, Lincoln, and FDR's Pragmatic Liberalism

The direct influence of Dewey's efforts to redefine liberalism on Roosevelt and his speechwriter Adolf Berle is particularly illustrated in one of the "founding documents" of the New Deal, Roosevelt's Commonwealth Club address of 1932.[34] In constructing this now famous campaign address, Berle and Roosevelt closely followed Dewey's critique of classical liberalism. Dewey understood his new liberalism to be a deliberate response to the classical, formal liberalism of eighteenth- and nineteenth-century America. The traditional emphasis upon economic individualism, natural and inalienable rights, limited government, and separation of powers was deemed insufficient to secure individual liberty after the closing of the frontier and the rise of the modern industrial economy. Like Croly, Teddy

Roosevelt, and Wilson before him, Dewey sought to craft a more flexible notion of individualism that was adaptable to the demands of the day and compatible with the strong, centralized, administrative state deemed necessary to temper the excesses of the new economy.[35]

Having had a major influence on the progressives, political pragmatism then came to the New Deal through the influence of Dewey in the early 1930s. The idea that the New Deal contained some element of pragmatism is commonly encountered in the relevant literature. Yet the extent to which the New Deal is pragmatic, and in just what sense it is pragmatic, is not always agreed upon. The commitment to planning as a method of solving social and economic problems was common among those whom Sidney Milkis labels as the "more zealous New Dealers." They emphasized "benign administration" as the remedy for what they regarded as the inherent weaknesses of the U.S. Constitution. "As such," Milkis explains, "the efforts to strengthen the state during the New Deal period were not truly an adaptation of constitutional principles and mechanisms, but a repudiation of them." FDR's genius, Milkis contends, consisted in the fact that he fundamentally transformed the American regime without actually appearing to do so, yet this transformation is hard to discern because of the "pragmatism so central to FDR's statesmanship."[36]

Arthur Schlesinger, Jr., one of the foremost historians of Roosevelt and the New Deal, claims that Roosevelt was the "eternal pragmatist," and he characterizes the New Deal as little more than experimental "trial-and-error pragmatism." Elaborating on the New Deal's experimental character, Schlesinger argues that the repeated charges—that the New Deal had no core doctrine, that it was improvised and opportunistic, and that it was guided only by circumstance—were all true. But, Schlesinger contends, these characteristics represented its very strength, for "the advantage enjoyed by the pragmatists over the ideologists was their exceptional sensitivity to social and human reality."[37]

However, as Milkis suggests, New Deal pragmatism was more than mere indirection or purposeless drift. Rather, it was guided by a "rather well thought out plan to reshape the working of American democracy."[38] On this note, Robert Eden usefully characterizes New Deal thought as a variant of "pragmatic liberalism," as opposed to formal or classical liberalism. Pragmatic liberalism, Eden explains, is a "strain of modern or postmodern politics that does not stand upon liberal forms and constitutional formalities; that is in principle always willing (if not eager) to strike down the formalities upheld by classical liberalism, in favor of results, consequences, and programs that promise to *actualize* liberalism in its fundamental purposes."[39] Eden helps us to understand the difference between pragmatic and formal liberalism by noting pragmatic liberalism's animus against modern natural right. The old, formal liberalism rested upon the Lockean proposal (here we might say the Lincolnian proposal) "that reasonable men might turn to nature to discern the essential purposes of civil society and of government." Pragmatic liberalism, on the other hand, repudiates this proposal as metaphysics, "in favor of an essentially historical mode of critical thinking; there are no self-evident truths; the Declaration of Independence has no epistemic significance."[40]

Pragmatic liberalism's rejection of modern natural right thinking and indifference to constitutional forms are necessarily related. The old liberalism's reliance upon "merely" procedural concerns (like separation of powers, the rule of law, and limited government) is predicated on the belief that one can comprehend man's nature. The old liberalism assumes that human nature is necessarily imperfect and that political power is prone to be abused by those who wield it, be it the one, the few, or the many. Thus, power must be distributed and structured in such a manner that it remains constitutionally balanced and limited. As we observed in our discussion of the progressives, particularly in our brief look at Wilson's critique of the Founders' Constitution, insofar as this view of nature is rejected then the concern with constitutional forms based upon these assumptions is deemed obsolete, and even counterproductive.

Eden contends that, although there is indeed a connection between Dewey's pragmatism and the New Deal, this connection has often been overstated. Conventional wisdom suggests that New Deal pragmatism was simply derivative of Dewey; Eden's thesis is that the pragmatic liberalism of the New Deal actually moved beyond Dewey. Rather than overtly rejecting the principles of the Declaration of Independence in an effort to transcend those principles, the New Deal's pragmatic liberalism sought to create the appearance that it was firmly rooted in the traditional liberalism of the American regime, thus ushering in a "pragmatist teaching" conveyed in a "Lockean guise."[41] This merits our consideration. Roosevelt would rhetorically appeal to the formal liberal tradition that the New Deal was attempting to supplant, and this appeal is closely connected to his use of the Lincoln image.[42]

Dewey developed what would become his classic *Individualism Old and New* in a series of articles that appeared in the *New Republic* from 1929 to 1930. The initial article in the series, entitled "The House Divided against

Itself," would become the first chapter.[43] America in 1929, Dewey argued, was a house divided against itself—in that the political tradition is "itself double." On the one hand, Americans were dedicated to "the ideal of equality of opportunity and of freedom for all without regard to birth or status, as a condition for the effective realization of that equality." According to Dewey, this was the "genuinely spiritual element of our tradition." Yet, on the other hand, Dewey reasoned, "our institutions embody another and older tradition" of industry and business for profit, which had grown increasingly powerful with the coming of the machine age. Our "law and politics and the incidents of human association" depend upon this combination of machine and money. The result, Dewey argued, "is the pecuniary culture characteristic of our civilization. The spiritual factor of our tradition, equal opportunity and free association and intercommunication, is obscured and crowded out."[44]

Eden rightly wonders why Dewey chose to call to mind Lincoln's "House Divided" speech in an article dedicated to overcoming the formal liberalism of eighteenth- and nineteenth-century America. After all, Eden suggests, Dewey could have reasonably seen Lincoln as the "epitome of formal liberalism in action." Eden reminds us of the context surrounding the House Divided speech: Lincoln challenged Douglas for a seat in the Senate, accepting the formalities of the American party system. Lincoln defended the Declaration of Independence and the Constitution against what he believed to be a Southern slave conspiracy dedicated to overcoming what Eden describes as the "founding principles of the liberal regime, to its political economy, to all the formal rights of property and person that were required both in logic and by experience to actualize those principles."[45] Dewey, however, held that such formalities, and the fundamental principles upon which they were based, were anachronistic and must be overcome in the modern world.

To understand Dewey's version of the "House Divided," Eden suggests, one must appreciate that Dewey portrayed himself as Lincoln's successor, as a savior of liberalism. Yet, while Lincoln was able to rely upon the old individualism and liberal constitutional forms to save liberalism in the face of the slavery crisis, Dewey argued that contemporary liberals no longer had that option. Formal liberalism must be replaced by pragmatic liberalism. For Dewey, one need only look to the hardships of the average American in the modern industrial economy to see that the old liberalism could not stand up to the new pressures being placed upon it. Indeed, the principles of the old liberalism—natural and inalienable rights (especially individual property rights), limited government, separation of powers, and constitutional formalism—were used to justify what Dewey regarded as the extreme individualism of modern America.[46]

According to Dewey, the current confusion and frustration of the American individual was the result of an undue faith in the abilities of the old liberalism to meet modern demands. Eden suggests that Dewey probably chose the title "The House Divided" as a deliberate provocation, as an open invitation to see the differences between his new individualism and the old liberalism by calling the Lincoln example to mind right up front. Lincoln, therefore, was being used as an "emblem of popular trust misplaced." If the "soul of the old individualist was a house divided," Eden contends, then "Lincolnian statesmanship perpetuated that division or prevented its resolution." If equality of opportunity and individual freedom were to be actualized, then the Lincoln example must be transcended.[47] To follow the Lincoln example, connected as it was to the old liberalism of the frontier economy, would only frustrate matters in the modern industrial economy, causing more harm than good. According to Eden, Dewey's project demanded that Lincoln's political principles be consciously abandoned, "while creatively reinterpreting Lincoln as an unwitting precursor of pragmatism."[48]

FDR's rhetorical use of Abraham Lincoln illustrates just such a reinterpretation, and if much of the scholarly literature on Lincoln's statesmanship is any indication, that reinterpretation appears to have been rather successful. Although an exhaustive discussion of references to Lincoln's "pragmatism" is beyond the scope of this study, relevant histories and commentaries on Lincoln's statesmanship are riddled with references to Lincoln as the quintessential pragmatic decision maker. Some scholars note a remarkable similarity between Lincoln and FDR, in that both men shared a specifically "pragmatic" method or style of presidential leadership. Here we encounter a problem in that in everyday usage, the terms *pragmatism* and *pragmatic* are often taken to mean, in a simple sense, flexible or "not doctrinaire."[49] Indeed, many studies of Lincoln's statesmanship take care to suggest that his supposed pragmatism consisted in a flexible and realistic "method" or "leadership strategy," in service of higher, "principled" ends.[50] But, Eden suggests, the commonplace usage of the term *pragmatism* must be qualified in discussing the New Deal. In American politics, pragmatism was introduced as more than a mere disposition to improvise. Rather, pragmatism represented a deliberate break with the notion that there are truths applicable to all men at all times. Whatever the common usage of the term *pragmatism* has become, pragmatism as it came to light in the progressives, Dewey, and the New Deal began with the rejection of the guiding principles of Lincolnian statesmanship. Above all, pragmatism began by rejecting the premise that there are self-evident truths rooted in nature.[51]

The New Deal helped to institutionalize the rhetoric of pragmatism in American political discourse. Prior to the twentieth century, presidential speechmaking consisted largely in attempts to articulate the principles of republican government. Even in late nineteenth-century speeches, the general aim was to show how a new direction of policy was consistent with the American political tradition. The aim was not merely to discuss why a given proposal constitutes "good policy" but, rather, to show how that policy squared with the Constitution and the principles of republican government.[52] The New Deal played no small role in helping to transform this discourse concerning the principles of republicanism and constitutionalism into the rhetoric of political pragmatism, wherein it would seem that the purpose of government is simply to solve perceived problems, and a constitution is often understood as nothing more than a grant of power for government to do so. But we must understand that, in actuality, FDR's rhetoric was not *simply* one of results-oriented problem solving. Roosevelt seemed to understand that, whatever we might concede to popular government's love of novelty, the success of the New Deal required more than mere professions of innovation and experimentalism. Rather, it required Roosevelt the rhetorician to frame innovation in familiar terms and recognizable themes. It often required (at least it still required in the 1930s and early 1940s) that the beginnings of a new tradition be couched in the language of the old tradition.[53]

The progressives understood this as well, and particularly in Woodrow Wilson we can observe something very important. For all of the progressive rhetoric about transcending the old liberalism associated with Croly's "Jeffersonian" horn of the American political tradition, Wilson knew that, as objects of popular veneration, the Declaration and the Constitution could not merely be thrust aside, at least not publicly. Rather, they must be reinterpreted in terms of progress and history, effectively denatured and historicized so as to seem congruent with the progressive vision. Wilson sought to establish the idea that, in reality, whether they knew it or not, every generation of citizens possessed both the right and the duty to redefine fundamental principles and political institutions in light of progressive history. Franklin Roosevelt would closely follow Wilson's progressive rendering of the Declaration and the Constitution. However, FDR appeared to go further than some progressives in his attempt publicly to square pragmatic liberalism with the first principles of American republicanism. Although prominent progressives such as Croly and Teddy Roosevelt insisted that the rights to life, liberty, and the pursuit of happiness must be redefined (or understood anew in light of historical and economic circumstances), Franklin Roosevelt placed a greater emphasis upon the language of individual rights than his predecessors did. Nowhere was this more apparent than in Roosevelt's 1932 Commonwealth Club address. This address served as a declaration of his intention to redefine rights in light of historical and economic circumstances. Such a redefinition illustrates the type of statesmanship Roosevelt attributed to Lincoln, that is, a statesmanship that would transfuse the principles of American republicanism with new meaning. Roosevelt's use of the Lincoln image and his own attempt to redefine rights are thus intimately connected.

The Commonwealth Club Address and the Redefinition of Rights

Roosevelt's Commonwealth Club address of 1932 is arguably one of the most important examples of political rhetoric in American history. With this address Roosevelt sought to change the popular understanding of the purposes and scope of government. The address clearly helped to usher in significant and lasting changes in American political development. Here Roosevelt claimed that the necessities of modern America, particularly the profound economic crises of the Great Depression, had placed new demands upon government. New circumstances required nothing less than a rewriting of the American "social contract," and government must take on a more active, more "positive" role in securing the social and economic well-being of the people.[54] As we have seen, this notion of statesmanship is not limited to the Commonwealth Club address. In his 1938 address at Gettysburg, for example, FDR claimed that Lincoln too had restated the purposes of the nation's Founding in order to preserve the "people's government for the people's good" in the face of changing circumstances.[55] We thus turn to the Commonwealth Club address not only to understand Roosevelt's justification of the New Deal but also to gauge how the Lincoln image fits into this justification. The address provides an example of the type of statesmanship that Roosevelt attributes to Lincoln, the "transfusion" of "new meaning" into "the concepts of our constitutional fathers." It also illustrates how far Roosevelt departed from Lincoln's principles, despite his repeated claims that the New Deal followed in a Lincolnian tradition.

Roosevelt's arguments will not seem entirely new to us. Above all, we might be reminded of Wilson's New Freedom. Wilson too had suggested that modern necessities demanded nothing less than a reinterpretation of the Declaration of Independence and the Constitution. Wilson too claimed to follow Lincoln in looking at rights with a new, clarified vision. Moreover, it is generally accepted that the New Deal institutionalized many of the measures proposed in the New Freedom, in particular, the consolidation of the modern presidency and the modern bureaucratic state. However, we need not rely on political scientists and historians to make this connection between the New Freedom and the New Deal. Roosevelt himself points us in this direction. During his acceptance speech at the 1932 Democratic national convention, Roosevelt announced his resolve "to resume the country's interrupted march along the path of real progress, of real justice, of real equality for all of our citizens, great and small. Our indomitable leader in the interrupted march is no longer with us," Roosevelt claimed, "but there still survives today his spirit. Many of his captains, thank God, are still with us, to give us wise counsel. Let us feel that in everything we do there still lives with us, if not the body, the great indomitable unquenchable, progressive soul of our Commander-in-Chief, Woodrow Wilson."[56] By Roosevelt's own admission, the New Deal is a rededication to the principles of the New Freedom—principles of "real progress," "real justice," and "real equality."[57]

In the Commonwealth Club address Roosevelt claimed to take his bearings from a fundamental and persistent question:

> The issue of Government has always been whether individual men and women will have to serve some system of Government or economics, or whether a system of Government and economics exists to serve individual men and women. This question has persistently dominated the discussion of Government for many generations. On questions relating to these things men have differed, and for time immemorial it is probable that honest men will continue to differ.
>
> The final word belongs to no man; yet we can still believe in change and in progress. Democracy, as a dear old friend of mine in Indiana, Meredith Nicholson, has called it, is a quest, a never-ending seeking for better things, and in seeking for these things and the striving for them, there are many roads to follow. But, if we map the course of these roads, we find that there are only two general directions.[58]

One should readily observe that, insofar as one holds with Lincoln and the Founders that all human beings are equally endowed with natural and inalienable rights and that the purpose of government is to secure these rights, then Roosevelt's persistent question was most eloquently answered by the Declaration of Independence—and reaffirmed by Lincoln. That is, government and economic systems would exist to "serve" individual men and women. Yet, even here, Roosevelt frames the question in such a way as to preclude the idea of securing natural and inalienable rights altogether. As Eden has argued, by identifying the purpose of government as *service* to the individual, Roosevelt suggested it cannot be sufficient for government to *secure* individual rights. Rather, government must be focused upon the *results* of the exercise of rights.[59]

Roosevelt suggested, we should also note, that the final answer to his persistent question "belongs to no man." As Charles Kelser argues, given his invocation of "change" and "progress," Roosevelt implied that the answer to this question is ultimately not attainable by human reason. The answer cannot be discerned by reference to the Laws of Nature and Nature's God. Rather, the answer is revealed by "change" and "progress"; in other words, the answer will have to be determined by progressive history. Roosevelt seems to have indirectly questioned the naturalness of the rights proclaimed in the Declaration of Independence. If government is not grounded in nature and the purpose of government is not to secure natural and inalienable rights, then how ought we to understand American democracy? We are to understand it as Roosevelt's friend Meredith Nicholson understands it, as "a quest, a never-ending seeking for better things." Following the progressives, and building upon the rhetoric of Wilson's New Freedom, Roosevelt sought to place American democracy upon new ground by identifying it with change and the doctrine of progress.[60]

We should again recall Roosevelt's characterization of Lincolnian statesmanship in his 1938 address at Gettysburg, which was phrased in terms quite similar to his remarks here in the Commonwealth Club address. Roosevelt argued that Lincoln's efforts to unify the nation were necessary in order to allow American democracy to fulfill its purpose, to continue once again its never-ending quest to face new responsibilities.[61] Roosevelt's description of the purpose of American democracy here in the Commonwealth Club address is identical to the vision of American democracy he would attribute to Lincoln six years later. As Kesler rightly observes, even if this formulation served the noble end of emphasizing America's ability to climb out of the Great Depression, it did so at a great cost by "unmooring America from its fundamental principles—from any permanent standard." In Roosevelt's vision of American democracy there was simply no place for the belief, shared by Lincoln and the American Founders, that the Declaration professed an abstract truth rooted in nature, applicable to all men at all times. Absent this standard, which Lincoln referred to as the sheet anchor of American republicanism, how are we to distinguish the "better things" we are seeking in our never-ending quest from the worse things? To what ends are our efforts directed and what means are we willing, or rightfully justified, to employ toward those ends?[62]

In the Commonwealth Club address Roosevelt suggested that there are many roads to follow in our never-ending seeking after better things. Political history had revealed, however, that we have generally followed one of two courses. Either we have accorded power to strong centralized government in pursuit of our desired ends, or we have sought to balance and limit the power of government in that pursuit. The initial growth of the nation-state, Roosevelt argued, was animated by a struggle to impose peace upon ruling barons and to develop a strong centralized government to protect the individual. But, in time, when the development of nations in Europe had been completed, the talented and ambitious creators of national governments came to overstep their mark and abuse their power. There came to be a feeling that government was conducted for the benefit of the few at the detriment of the many. The people thus sought to limit and balance government by establishing town councils, trade guilds, national parliaments, constitution, popular participation and control, thus placing limitations upon arbitrary power.[63] These two directions—strengthening and centralizing national government, on the one hand, and limiting and balancing national government on the other—were the defining features of Roosevelt's description of political history.

According to Roosevelt, the American colonies were born in this struggle. In a variation on Croly's Hamilton–Jefferson dichotomy, Roosevelt characterized the years after the American Revolution as a push and pull between these two horns of the political tradition. Roosevelt argued that the Jeffersonian side of that tension won out in the election of 1800, and "individualism was made the great watchword of American life. The happiest of economic conditions made that day long and splendid." Echoing the progressives, Roosevelt held that the field of individual opportunity was wide open in the age of the pioneer democrat. Government during this period had been called upon merely to produce the conditions by which individuals could live happily and securely. With the industrialization of

America there came great progress and a new dream for American life, the dream of an economic machine able to raise the standard of living for all Americans. But, Roosevelt explained, for the dream to be made real, we required the talents of ruthless and ambitious men—the "financial titans"—in order to finance and engineer these developments.[64]

Roosevelt argued that the advantages offered by the financial titans initially outweighed any concern about their "ruthless, often wasteful, and frequently corrupt" methods. There was "equal opportunity for all and the business of government was not to interfere but to assist in the development of industry." This, Roosevelt claimed, was done at the insistence of the businessmen themselves, through tariffs and subsidies. But, with the turn of the century, we reached our last frontier. According to FDR, clear-sighted men such as Teddy Roosevelt and Woodrow Wilson began to see that equality of opportunity was in grave danger. They saw that "the growing corporation, like the feudal baron of old, might threaten the economic freedom of individuals to earn a living." Roosevelt claimed that this potential danger had come to pass. A "glance at the situation today only too clearly indicates that equality of opportunity as we have known it no longer exists. Our industrial plant is built; the problem just now is whether under existing conditions it is not overbuilt." Roosevelt argued that, after the closing of the frontier, more than half of our people did not live on farms and could not derive a living by cultivating their own property.[65]

Clearly, Roosevelt proclaimed, we are in need of a "re-appraisal of values." The mere builder of industrial plants, the mere creator of railroads, and the mere organizer of corporations was probably as much a danger as a help. The day of the financial titan "to whom we granted anything if only he would build, or develop, is over." Roosevelt defined the new task at hand: "Our task now is not discovery or exploitation of natural resources, or necessarily producing more goods." Rather, our task had become the "soberer, less dramatic business of administering resources and plants already in hand." According to Roosevelt, with the New Deal, "The day of enlightened administration" had come.[66]

Just as the people had once accorded power to central governments in exchange for security, the people accorded power to the financial titans in exchange for prosperity. The people were once forced to limit and balance their system of government. They were now forced to do the same with regard to their economic system by centralizing and strengthening their political system. The new task of government in its relation to business, Roosevelt claimed, was "to assist in the development of an economic declaration of rights, an economic constitutional order."⁶⁷ The declaration of such rights, according to Roosevelt, was nothing more than a redefinition of the terms of the Declaration of Independence. To argue his case, Roosevelt characterized the Declaration as follows:

> The Declaration of Independence discusses the problem of Government in terms of a contract. Government is a relation of give and take, a contract, perforce, if we would follow the thinking out of which it grew. Under such a contract rulers were accorded power, and the people consented to that power on consideration that they be accorded certain rights. The task of statesmanship has always been the re-definition of these rights in terms of a growing and changing social order. New conditions impose new requirements upon Government and those who conduct Government.⁶⁸

The terms of the contract, Roosevelt asserted, are as old as the Republic, and as new as the new economic order. Note that Roosevelt followed Wilson's reading of the Declaration, with the terms of the social contract (which would seem to include not only the means but also, it is important to note, the ends of government) capable of being continually renegotiated. Our most fundamental rights—rights once claimed to be natural and inalienable—become rights "accorded" to us as the result of a deal struck between the people and their rulers.⁶⁹

Roosevelt's Wilsonian take on the Declaration illustrates the difficulty entailed in reading natural and inalienable rights out of the American political tradition. The formulation of the social contract as we find it in the Declaration suggests that governments are instituted among men to secure their natural (that is, preexisting, pre-political) and inalienable (that is, non-negotiable) rights. Indeed, the natural and equal possession of these rights is the theoretical basis of the people's right to give or withhold their consent in the first place. Roosevelt's reading of the Declaration obscured this fundamental premise and thus departed significantly from Lincoln's understanding of the first principles of American government.

There appear to be no natural and inalienable rights, properly understood, in FDR's version of the Declaration. The ends of government are open to perpetual redefinition, and any principled limits to the means we might consent to in pursuit of those ends no longer have any objective basis. Theoretically, then, the ends and means of government are merely subject to a collective determination of what the circumstances may demand, made by the people and their government. But, practically speaking, the Wilsonian plan for the administrative state found its home in the New Deal. The means of government were increasingly fashioned by administrative agencies, while the political side of the equation turned increasingly toward opinion leadership in the executive. Insofar as our most fundamental rights must be redefined, it helps if we have a proper leader, Wilson's rhetorically gifted "man of the people," to see into the future, discern the movement of history, and point us in the direction we must tend. Indeed, Roosevelt asserted that the very "task of statesmanship" consists in the redefinition of rights "in terms of a growing and changing social order." In order to keep pace with the growing and changing social order as of 1932, Roosevelt reasoned that the rights of the Declaration (the old terms of the social contract) must be redefined. Just as Lincoln had transfused the concepts of the Founding with new meaning, so too Roosevelt had to redefine those principles to allow for equality of opportunity in the modern industrial economy.

According to Roosevelt, as of 1932, the new terms of the contract could be summarized as follows. First, while every man has a right to life under the old terms of the contract, this right must be redefined or deepened. "Every man has a right to life," Roosevelt claimed, "and this means that he also has a right to make a comfortable living." While a man may decline to exercise that right, "it may not be denied him." The right to a comfortable living presupposes plenty, that there is enough for everyone to secure such comfort. We have "no actual famine or dearth," Roosevelt argued, and "our industrial and agricultural mechanism can produce enough and to spare. Our Government formal and informal, political and economic, owes to everyone an avenue to possess himself a portion of that plenty sufficient for his needs, through his own work."[70]

Second, Roosevelt suggested, according to the old terms of the contract, every man has a right to property, "which means a right to be assured, to the fullest extent attainable, in the safety of his savings. By no other means," Roosevelt argued, "can men carry the burdens of those parts of life which, in the nature of things, afford no chance of labor; childhood, sickness, old age." Third, Roosevelt claimed that the "final term of the high contract was for liberty and the pursuit of happiness." Again, Roosevelt emphasized the redefinition of these terms, suggesting that we have "learned a great deal of" liberty and the pursuit of happiness "in the past century." According to Roosevelt, these rights "mean nothing" unless both are ordered so that "one man's meat is not another man's poison." We know, Roosevelt argued, "that the old 'rights of personal competency,' the right to read, to think, to speak, to choose and live a mode of life, must be respected at all hazards. We know that liberty to do anything which deprives others of those elemental rights is outside the protection of any compact." However, if the task of statesmanship is the redefinition of the terms of the social contract in light of a changing and growing social order, we should rightly ask here on what basis are these rights of personal competency somehow inviolable? One can surely imagine new conditions that might require government to restrict "free speech," for example. Would not a defense of these rights, if they are to be defended, ultimately need recourse to the natural and inalienable rights of man? Similar to the progressives before him, Roosevelt was forced to avoid such notions in his redefinition of the Declaration of Independence. Here in the Commonwealth Club address, he robs himself of any principled defense of the goods he says we hold dear, like the rights of personal competency.[71]

Here I follow a particular illustration of Kesler's more general argument that, in turning away from the idea of nature and toward a faith in "change" and "progress," Roosevelt adopted a fundamentally historicist understanding of the principles of American republicanism.[72] If the Commonwealth Club address is rightly considered one of the founding documents of the New Deal, we should seriously question Roosevelt's repeated claims that the New Deal follows in the Lincolnian tradition. Roosevelt routinely sought to incorporate the Lincoln image into the New Deal rhetoric. But this forced him to obscure the fact that his own understanding of statesmanship as the redefinition of rights in light of history and circumstance was fundamentally at odds with the natural right principles of Lincolnian statesmanship. The Commonwealth Club address makes this clear.

But here we must note a wrinkle. On the basis of their rejection of natural right thinking some progressives sought to break openly with the "Jeffersonian" element of the American political tradition. FDR, however, readopted the rhetoric of that Jeffersonian element. As Milkis observes, by invoking the language of life, liberty, property, and the pursuit of happiness, Roosevelt framed progressive principles not as a repudiation or rejection of natural rights but, rather, as an expansion and fulfillment of those rights.[73] This, in part, is what Eden means in suggesting that, through the Commonwealth Club address, Roosevelt and Berle offered pragmatism in a "Lockean guise."[74] But Eden also leads us to consider perhaps a fundamental problem with classical Lockean liberalism. Eden prompts us to consider carefully Roosevelt's account of Western political history for it points us in a different direction, away from Kesler's argument on Roosevelt's apparent historicism.

Kesler is surely correct that Roosevelt's profession of faith in change and progress and his Wilsonian spin on the Declaration seem to convey a historicist rejection of the principles of the Declaration as Lincoln and the Founders understood them. But when one looks at Roosevelt's history (which takes up a great portion of the Commonwealth Club address), we find that on the surface it might not seem to be fundamentally historicist. As Eden suggests Roosevelt, if anything, seems to give a cyclical account of Western political history. The speech describes a continual ebb and flow between the granting and centralizing of political power to serve the people and the limiting and balancing of that power if and when it comes to be abused.

Of particular importance to Roosevelt's history in the Commonwealth Club address is Thomas Jefferson. Teddy Roosevelt had criticized the individualism of the "Jeffersonian" (here we might say "Lockean") horn of Croly's Jefferson–Hamilton dichotomy. Despite his reputation as part of the Jeffersonian wing of American progressivism, Woodrow Wilson had asserted that Jefferson, by virtue of his abstract, philosophical reading of the Declaration, was more French than American. But, contrary to the view that the New Deal was a fulfillment of a specifically Hamiltonian nationalism and executive power, FDR invoked the Jeffersonian tradition in the Commonwealth Club address, albeit in a very specific manner.[75] Roosevelt's Jefferson "did not deceive himself with outward forms. Government to him was a means to an end, not an end in itself; it might be either a refuge and a help or a threat and a danger, depending on the circumstances."[76] In short, Roosevelt's Jefferson served not as the epitome of classical, formal liberalism but, rather, as an example of pragmatic liberalism in action. As Eden explains, Roosevelt's political history and his appeal to Jefferson exploited the idea of Lockean prerogative power, the very notion of prerogative publicly employed by Jefferson in the purchase of Louisiana.[77] In fact, in the Commonwealth Club address, this willingness to sacrifice constitutional formalism for desired results becomes the central animating feature of Roosevelt's account of American political history. According to Roosevelt, in reality, the American people had always been dedicated to pragmatic, as opposed to formal, liberalism.

What Eden reveals is that Roosevelt and Berle formulated a political history based upon what one might regard as the extreme end of Lockean principles, in which the people accord unlimited prerogative power to princes (in this case the American executive) to deal with the demands of the times. The people had once accorded vast amounts of power to central governments in exchange for security. The financial titans were also once accorded seemingly unlimited power in exchange for material prosperity. In 1932 circumstances required that government, in particular the executive, once again be accorded this power to check an unlimited economic power that has become destructive of the common good.

Eden suggests that (unlike Dewey) Roosevelt and Berle attempted to transform the American polity not by soaring over and above it but, rather, by reaching down to its basic needs for security and survival, undermining formal liberalism in favor of pragmatic liberalism.[78] In effect, Eden claims, Roosevelt exposed the Machiavellian underbelly of Lockean political theory. Self-preservation or security at all costs became the order of the day. Rule by executive prerogative was made routine. The people hold the plebiscitary power not only to reject or accept the executive's actions after the fact but also to prescribe or proactively approve an executive's actions beforehand by electing a candidate to office on the basis of his proposals for the future.[79] This, of course, is the epitome of the idea of the presidential mandate. According to Eden, by falling back on familiar Lockean formulations, Roosevelt's Jefferson became a "ventriloquist's dummy" for proclaiming the new individualism of John Dewey. For Roosevelt, a new anti-formal and pragmatic liberalism was needed to protect individualism in the modern age. Similar to Machiavelli, Roosevelt appeared to take his bearing from the extreme case, treating the extreme case as the routine, institutionalizing government by prerogative as the norm.[80]

For Locke, prerogative power pointed to an unremitting but necessary tension within liberal constitutionalism. In Roosevelt's Commonwealth Club address, prerogative power became the defining feature of liberal government. As Eden suggests, Roosevelt attempted to convince the American people that they had never truly been a constitutional people. Even if they held up constitutional forms in word, their deeds showed them to have always been pragmatic liberals.[81] Again, we should question Roosevelt's wider claim to the Lincoln legacy. Roosevelt sought to incorporate the Lincoln example into the New Deal rhetoric, yet Lincoln had sought to reinforce Americans' dedication to their Constitution through public statements such as his Lyceum Address, in which he reminded his audience that the ills of democracy must be combated through a reverence for the Constitution and the laws.[82] Even Lincoln's arguments justifying his actions during the Civil War were generally framed in constitutional terms. In the Commonwealth Club address, Roosevelt did not remind his audience of the need for a reverence for the Constitution and the laws. Rather, like the progressives, he held that the solution to the ills of democracy necessarily lies outside the formal structures of the Constitution. This confidence in stepping outside the Constitution follows from the progressive rejection of the view of human nature and limited government shared by Lincoln and the Founders. We see this most clearly in FDR's re-adoption of the historicized, Wilsonian reading of the Declaration, a decidedly non-Lincolnian reading.

Eden suggests that Roosevelt purposefully conveyed the fundamentally historicist teaching of John Dewey in a Lockean guise. Yet he also alerts us to the fact that Roosevelt's historical sketch of the granting and retracting of unlimited political power does not seem to be fundamentally historicist. But this seemingly non-historicist sketch did nothing to destroy the historicism animating the Commonwealth Club address and the New Deal. The Commonwealth Club address was thus an odd mixture. In it Roosevelt spoke both of universal principles and a seemingly historicist faith in change and the doctrine of progress. He spoke of the Declaration of Independence and securing the individual rights to life, liberty, and the pursuit of happiness, while simultaneously appearing to question the Declaration's profession of the naturalness of those rights.

Kesler is correct to note that Roosevelt's Wilsonian interpretation of the Declaration, his praise of change and progress, and his apparent rejection of nature as the ground of our political principles, all suggest a progressive historicism. After all, Roosevelt himself framed the New Deal as a rededication to Wilson's New Freedom, as a continuation of the nation's briefly interrupted march toward "real progress."[83] Roosevelt would close his Commonwealth Club address with a statement of "Faith in America, faith in our tradition of personal responsibility, faith in our institutions," and "faith in ourselves." But we recall that the beginning of the address suggested that our faith ought to lie in change and progress.[84] It appears that, for Roosevelt, our faith in America, faith in our traditions and institutions, indeed our faith in ourselves, all depended upon a faith in the doctrine of progress. Our faith must depend upon the notion that history and circumstance have revealed to us—or perhaps more accurately, that they have revealed to leaders of men—that our most fundamental rights are both capable of and in desperate need of continual redefinition. Rights can and must be given new meaning. Roosevelt's profession of "faith in ourselves" hinged upon a faith that leaders of men are sufficiently wise to redefine our most fundamental rights and to alter our political institutions in light of historical progress, and that the people are sufficiently wise in their plebiscitary capacity to serve directly as the ultimate judge of those actions.

One cannot understand this redefinition of rights unless one considers it in light of Roosevelt's oft-repeated assertion that necessitous men are not free men. If men are to become truly free, then they must live beyond necessity. Government must take on new responsibilities in providing for the necessities of its citizens. Unhampered by the burden of securing the basic necessities of life, individual men and women might then turn their attention toward exercising those old rights of personal competency—to read, to think, to speak, and perhaps above all else "to choose and live a mode of life." The New Deal rhetoric, while indeed appealing to the idea of necessity and self-preservation, nevertheless points beyond necessity toward something that looks rather like the open-ended politics of individual self-development characteristic of Wilson and Dewey.[85] Roosevelt's "economic declaration of rights" emphasized what looked to be the Lockean language of individual rights. But Roosevelt helped to introduce a decidedly new conception of rights into American political thought and practice. Roosevelt's concept of economic rights prompts us to question not only his claim to Lincoln but also the effort on the part of many observers to connect Roosevelt's pursuit of equality with that of Lincoln.

The "Second" Bill of Rights and "Equality in the Pursuit of Happiness"

While Roosevelt mentioned his economic declaration of rights in the Commonwealth Club address, these proposed rights are commonly associated with his 1944 State of the Union Address. Here Roosevelt sketched his most detailed listing of these new economic rights.[86] Roosevelt famously proclaimed that, after the war, the one supreme objective for the future in the United States and for "all the United Nations, can be summed up in one word: Security." To achieve and maintain peace in the world, Roosevelt claimed, there must be security here at home, "not only physical security which provides safety from attacks by aggressors" but also "economic security, social security," and "moral security." "Freedom from fear," Roosevelt urged, "is eternally linked with freedom from want." It had become our duty to establish "an American standard of living higher than ever before known. We cannot be content," Roosevelt suggested, "no matter how high that general standard of living may be, if some fraction of our people—whether it be one-third or one-fifth or one-tenth—is ill-fed, ill-clothed, ill-housed, and insecure."[87]

Roosevelt argued that our republic "had its beginning, and grew to its present strength, under the protection of certain inalienable political rights—among them the right of free speech, free press, free worship, trial by jury, [and] freedom from unreasonable searches and seizures. They were our rights to life and liberty." However, Roosevelt continued, as our nation grew "in size and stature—as our industrial economy expanded—these political rights proved inadequate to assure us equality in the pursuit of happiness." We have come to realize that true individual freedom cannot exist without economic security and independence. "'Necessitous men,'" Roosevelt suggests, "'are not free men.' People who are hungry and out of a job are the stuff of which dictatorships are made."[88] We should consider his argument here, for it appears to be a more detailed example of how he meant to redefine the terms of the social contract.

First, Roosevelt claimed that our republic had its beginning—and grew to its present strength—under the protection of certain "inalienable political rights." The rights Roosevelt listed here are among the rights listed in the first ten amendments to the Constitution, established in civil society as means of securing what are properly regarded as inalienable rights, that is, the natural rights of the Declaration. In this way Roosevelt fostered an ambiguity between the natural and inalienable rights of the Declaration and the conventional rights meant to secure them. Rightly understood, civil and political rights established in civil society, while perhaps understood as inferences from our natural and inalienable rights, are neither natural nor inalienable but are subject to determination by the people and their representatives.

We might wonder why FDR chose to use the term *inalienable* to refer to these rights. However debatable his identification of political rights as inalienable might be (as was the case with the rights of personal competency), it is difficult to discern the ground upon which Roosevelt could suggest that *any* right is inalienable. This again illustrates how misleading his effort really was to incorporate Lincoln into the New Deal rhetoric. We recall that he had claimed in 1936 that the New Deal understanding of liberty was identical to Lincoln's idea of liberty as expressed in his 1864 Baltimore Address to a Sanitary Fair.[89]

Lincoln suggested that liberty might best be understood as each man's doing as he pleases with himself and with the product of his labor. But, for Lincoln, this idea of liberty was rooted in nature. According to the Declaration, the right to liberty is a natural and inalienable right. Given Roosevelt's Wilsonian reading of the Declaration, the New Deal theory of liberty cannot admit of any notion of liberty (or any other right) as a natural and inalienable right. The New Deal idea of liberty moves in principle beyond Lincoln's understanding of equal liberty. Lincoln's view of liberty was premised on the Lockean idea that each man ought to eat the bread he earns by the sweat of his own brow. Our natural and inalienable rights place limits upon what we might rightfully consent to, and limits upon what government may do in the name of the people. Lincoln's idea of equal liberty and his understanding of limited government thus are necessarily connected. But no such limits are present in Roosevelt's New Deal theory of liberty because the ends and the means of government are up for perpetual redefinition in light of historical progress. By denaturing the idea of liberty, Roosevelt sacrificed any objective defense of individual liberty and any objective defense of limited government.

Second, Roosevelt suggested that over time these political rights "proved inadequate to assure us equality in the pursuit of happiness." In his view we have come to realize that true individual freedom cannot exist without economic security and independence. Since necessitous men are not free men, then to be truly free it seems we must somehow overcome necessity.[90] In the Commonwealth Club address, he suggested that the terms of the social contract must be redefined so as to promote equality of opportunity in light of a changing and growing social order. Here, he offered a slightly different formulation, however. Our political rights, he claims, have proved inadequate to assure us equality in the pursuit of happiness—equality *in* the pursuit of happiness. To borrow Roosevelt's language, according to the "old terms" of the social contract, securing equal opportunity was understood as Lincoln understood it, that is, as securing one's right to pursue happiness under the rule of law but not necessarily securing equal results among individuals in that pursuit. In this sense, Roosevelt was correct to suggest that our political rights were inadequate to assure us equality in the pursuit of happiness. Indeed, our political rights cannot provide—and were never envisioned as capable of providing—equality *in* the pursuit of happiness. Rather, they were seen as a necessary means in securing the *right* of individuals *to* pursue happiness, exercising necessarily diverse and unequal talents in pursuit of their interests, and achieving diverse and unequal rewards in that pursuit. By emphasizing equality *in* the pursuit of happiness, Roosevelt implied that the true measure of equal opportunity lies not in the equality of the *right* to pursue happiness but, rather, in the *results* of the exercise of that right.

FDR claimed that, over time, certain "economic truths have become accepted as self-evident. We have accepted, so to speak, a second Bill of Rights under which a new basis of security and prosperity can be established for all—regardless of station, race, or creed." Among these new rights are:

> The right to a useful and remunerative job in the industries or shops or farms or mines of the Nation; The right to earn enough to provide adequate food and clothing and recreation; The right of every farmer to raise and sell his products at a return which will give him and his family a decent living; The right of every businessman, large and small, to trade in an atmosphere of freedom from unfair competition and domination by monopolies at home or abroad; The right of every family to a decent home; The right to adequate medical care and the opportunity to achieve and enjoy good health; The right to adequate protection from the economic fears of old age, sickness, accident, and unemployment; The right to a good education. All of these rights spell security. And after this war is won we must be prepared to move forward, in the implementation of these rights, to new goals of human happiness and well-being.[91]

Roosevelt understood that these economic rights were something new in American political discourse. There seems to be no conception of Roosevelt's "economic rights" in the political thought of the American Founding or in the thought of Abraham Lincoln. As Roosevelt had declared in the Commonwealth Club address, according to the earlier tradition of liberalism, government had been asked merely to produce the conditions by which one might pursue happiness. This was the guiding premise of Lincoln's pursuit of equality, in which individuals are afforded equal liberty to pursue happiness under the rule of law. In principle, Roosevelt's view of statesmanship consisted in redefining the right to pursue happiness into a right to happiness itself, at least happiness understood as material well-being or security.[92] Roosevelt's economic bill of rights clearly does not demand an equality of results in any *unqualified* sense. What it does do, however, is call for equality in particular or specific results in that pursuit (gainful employment, decent wages, and so on), elevating them to the status of "rights," or more accurately stated, entitlements.[93]

We should ask, however, just how Roosevelt envisioned this economic "bill of rights" in political practice. As Milkis reminds us, given the New Deal aversion to constitutional forms, it is not surprising that many New Dealers balked at this new emphasis upon what looked like formal rights. This ran against the New Deal faith in pragmatism and administrative discretion. Were these "economic rights" to be added to the Constitution as formal amendments? Like the progressives, the New Dealers tended to see the amendment process as unnecessarily cumbersome and inefficient. If government was to get down to the serious business of solving problems, institutional mechanisms like the amendment process must be eschewed in favor of new, more "efficient" means of getting results. By all accounts, Roosevelt neither expected nor desired that these economic rights be engrafted onto the Constitution as formal amendments. As Milkis suggests, a commitment to "economic" rights as formal legal rights might bind the new economic constitutional order in a "legal straightjacket." While Roosevelt was committed to new "economic" rights, these rights were best understood as "programmatic rights," secured through the pragmatic administration of the economy and a government freed from the "demands of formal constitutionalism."[94]

However, even if these rights were never intended to be added to the Constitution, Roosevelt's elevation of these rights certainly resonated with the American people. Milkis rightly suggests that, after the Roosevelt era, nearly every major public policy was characterized as a "right," asserted to confer constitutional status automatically to programs such as Social Security, Medicare, and food stamps. Whatever opinion one might harbor as to the desirability or necessity of such policies, with the New Deal came a new, more expansive understanding of rights. According to Milkis, the attempt to secure these rights required a "relentless government identification of problems and the search for methods by which these problems might be solved." This never-ending seeking after problems to solve in the name of securing perpetually redefined rights is the very essence of the New Deal's pragmatic liberalism.[95]

Cass Sunstein has argued that Roosevelt's second bill of rights is best understood as a statement of national aspiration, a set of national commitments, in effect, to which the nation ought to be forever dedicated.[96] Roosevelt's second bill of rights, as political rhetoric, illustrates an attempt to dedicate the nation to a set of propositions—that necessitous men are not free men, that individual freedom is impossible without economic security and independence, that the actualization of equality *in* the pursuit of happiness demands that we recognize certain "economic rights." In effect, through such highly visible rhetorical pieces as the Commonwealth Club address and the 1944 State of the Union, Roosevelt attempted to dedicate the nation to a new understanding of equality, in which the general government can no longer rest content merely to secure the conditions whereby individuals might pursue happiness. Rather, government must actively seek to secure at least a minimal or baseline equality of condition. And the engine of this change resided not in traditional constitutional forms and procedures but, rather, in a growing administrative bureaucracy and an increasingly powerful rhetorical presidency.

Franklin Roosevelt's Lincoln 129

We have seen that Roosevelt repeatedly asserted that the New Deal was both a continuation of Lincoln's understanding of liberal statesmanship and an attempt to fulfill Lincoln's understanding of liberty and equality. It is not difficult to understand why the Lincoln example might seem so attractive in this respect. Lincoln too had famously claimed that the nation was dedicated to equality as a national commitment, as the standard maxim toward which American government ought to strive. We can understand why historians might see an apparent similarity between Lincoln's words on equality and the rhetoric of FDR. We can understand why observers Kendall and Carey might be tempted to draw parallels between Lincoln and the New Deal, suggesting that Lincoln played a leading part in turning the American political tradition toward a presumed national commitment to equality, "which involves, *inter alia*, a restructuring of American society so as to produce a condition of equality" at the expense of all other legitimate political and constitutional goods. Our heroes today, Kendall and Carey claim, are those who would advance that presumed commitment, "the Warrens, Blacks, Douglases, along with the Wilsons, Roosevelts I and II, and Lincolns."[97]

The willingness of commentators to draw parallels between the New Deal pursuit of equality and Lincoln's equality would seem to be bolstered by the fact that Roosevelt himself tried to incorporate the Lincoln example into his New Deal rhetoric. But the New Deal redefinition of rights does more to distinguish FDR's pursuit of equality from Lincoln's than it does to connect the two in any simple fashion. Roosevelt's pragmatic liberalism, in a sense, "feels" like the old formal liberalism it attempts to supplant. That is, the New Deal rhetoric was surely framed in such a manner as to resemble the Lockean-Jeffersonian tradition of natural rights informing Lincoln's pursuit of equality. But the New Deal theory of rights is generally, and I think correctly, accepted as something new, something that moves beyond the old rights language of formal liberalism. What Berle and Roosevelt managed to do, particularly in the Commonwealth Club address, was to popularize a new notion of rights in American political discourse, a notion of rights that was consistent with New Deal liberalism and intricately bound to the pursuit of equality.

We should, however, refuse to concede any simple connection between Lincoln's pursuit of equality and Roosevelt's call for "equality in the pursuit of happiness." We must reiterate that Lincoln sought, insofar as it was possible and prudent, to secure equality of opportunity in light of transhistorical standards rooted in the Laws of Nature and Nature's

God. Not only was this pursuit guided by the practical necessities of historical and political circumstance, it was fundamentally guided by natural standards of right. Our natural equality not only suggests that the legitimate powers of government are derived from the consent of the governed but also implies that there are limits as to what things the governed might rightfully consent. According to Lincoln's principles, majority rule is defensible only insofar as it is reasonable, insofar as it rules without destroying the rights of the minority and without repudiating the natural rights basis of its own legitimacy.

In essence, Roosevelt's call for "equality in the pursuit of happiness" closely followed Wilson's equalization of the "conditions of opportunity for self-development." And Roosevelt, like Wilson, appeared to reject the natural standards that guided Lincoln's pursuit of equality. Thus, Roosevelt denied in principle that there are any limitations upon our pursuit of equality, or upon any other perceived end, extrinsic to our will under a given set of circumstances. It is arguable that the pursuit of equality has the potential to become unhinged from moderation when the distinction between rights and the results of the exercise of rights becomes obscured. We must recognize that one's rights and one's interests are not necessarily the same thing, and according to the political theory of the Declaration, American government exists to secure individual rights, not necessarily individual interests. The American Founders understood that the paramount task of republican government is to secure the permanent and aggregate interests of the community as well as the private, individual rights of citizens. The task is not one of securing individual interests; rather, it is one of securing one's individual right to pursue one's interests in a manner consistent with the common good.[98] This understanding follows from a view of human nature, shared by the Founders and Abraham Lincoln, in which the causes of faction are sown into the very nature of man, and hence the danger of faction cannot be transcended by history or rendered obsolete by social planning.

Here we should again note the relationship between pragmatic liberalism's rejection of modern natural right and its indifference to constitutional formalism. The old, formal liberalism's reliance upon constitutionalism and its dependence upon separation of powers, the rule of law, and limited government are based upon the notion that human nature is everywhere and always imperfect. Insofar as this view of human nature is rejected, then the concern with limited government and constitutionalism forms based upon this assumption is deemed obsolete. The pursuit of equality is therefore released from any principled constraints and severed from any need to balance equality against the necessity of constitutionalism. This problem is exacerbated once equality is associated with an understanding of rights entirely divorced from nature. The task of securing rights becomes conflated with securing the results of the exercise of our rights. This tendency is illustrated in Roosevelt's economic rights, which have come to be understood not as positive or civil rights but as "human rights." Paradoxically, Roosevelt's economic declaration of rights seems to contribute to a doctrinaire rhetoric of rights arising from a pragmatic tradition aimed at destroying the supposed doctrinairism and inflexibility of formal liberalism. Whatever the pragmatic and seemingly tentative character of Roosevelt's new declaration of rights, in political practice these rights have come to be applied to all human beings as such. These rights are counted among the legitimate and chief ends of government and consist in entitlements to be secured, often in exclusion of all other political and constitutional considerations.

One might wish to suggest, however, that we see something of this in Lincoln. After all, in his Fragments on Government, Lincoln suggested that the "legitimate object of government is to do for a community of people whatever they need to have done, but cannot do at all, or cannot do so well for themselves, in their separate and individual capacities." Roosevelt was fond of employing this passage in support of the New Deal. One might claim there is surely a similarity between Roosevelt and Lincoln in that each would claim government is duty bound to "do for a community" what cannot be done, or not done so well, by individuals acting alone. Let us address this suggestion by way of conclusion.[99]

Conclusion

Although Roosevelt sought to connect the New Deal pursuit of equality to the Lincoln example, we should reemphasize that Lincoln's Fragments on Government were merely fragments. Indeed, although they seem intended as pieces of a lecture, there is no documentary evidence that such a lecture was ever given or even that one including these fragments was ever intended to be given. Thus, we must admit the possibility that for some reason the fragments apparently never saw the light of day. One might nevertheless suggest that there is an apparent similarity between Roosevelt and Lincoln here, in that each would claim that good government must "do for a community" things that cannot be done, or done so well, by people in their separate and individual capacities.

Lincoln, no less than Roosevelt, understood that the common good requires government sometimes either to provide for those who cannot provide for themselves or to help them provide for themselves. Surely, Lincoln and Roosevelt would agree that things such as employment, decent wages, adequate shelter, and medical care are highly desirable goods. Indeed, some are vital in providing for the lives of citizens. People need things such as food, shelter, and medical care in order to survive, and government, according to the political theory of the Founding, is instituted among men first to secure the right to life. But, as Jaffa suggests, according to the political principles informing both Lincoln and the Founders, there is no a priori rule in such matters. To characterize such intermediate goods simply as fundamental rights runs the risk of conflating means with ends. The end of government in securing natural and inalienable rights is not subject to deliberation but, rather, is held to be an inference from the Laws of Nature and Nature's God, principles deemed true everywhere and always. Yet the manner in which such things are to be done—whether privately or publicly, whether by local governments, state governments, or the general government—are matters of deliberation and prudence. Simply stated, the determination of just what the people can or cannot do as well, or not so well, for themselves is open to debate. Since such concerns ultimately point in the direction of taxation, they are regarded as matters of legislative prudence. This is because such things are properly not so much regarded as the ends of government (that is, not as fundamental rights in and of themselves) but, rather, counted as among the means by which we seek to secure natural and inalienable rights to life, liberty, and the pursuit of happiness.[100] Lincoln did suggest in the "Fragments" that government must sometimes secure goods that citizens cannot provide in their separate and individual capacities. But, it is important to note, Lincoln did not characterize such public goods and services as a necessary imperative of equality, nor simply as a matter of right in and of themselves. To suggest that Lincoln somehow believed one's rights are being secured only insofar as certain results in the exercise of those rights are equalized is surely incorrect.[101]

Roosevelt's declaration of economic rights helped to usher in a new era of rights in American political discourse, in which the distinction between our fundamental rights and the results of our exercising those rights has become increasingly blurred. The manner in which we understand our rights fundamentally shapes our understanding of the nature and the purpose of government. Our understanding of the proper ends of government will necessarily shape our opinions about the proper means of government.[102]

Insofar as the pursuit of equality in American society is wrapped up with the notion of "equal rights," the manner in which we understand rights directly shapes our understanding of the meaning of equality and the manner in which that equality is to be pursued. Lincoln understood the equality of all men as, above all else, an equality of rights. In his view, to pursue equality was to secure, insofar as it was possible and prudent, the equal liberty of individuals to exercise their rights in pursuit of their interests under the rule of law. We have seen that some of Lincoln's conservative critics argue that he leaves the door open for the rise of an unfettered modern egalitarianism that is hostile to all inequalities and constitutional forms. I believe this understates the real differences between Lincoln's equality and modern egalitarian notions such as economic rights. However, even if we concede that by simply talking about equality Lincoln somehow contributed to the misuse of his speeches and writings by modern egalitarians, the door is opened wider—it may be taken off its hinges—once the pursuit of equality is severed from any basis in natural rights and limited government constitutionalism.

FIVE
Lyndon Johnson's Lincoln

AFTER THE NEW DEAL, the Lincoln image continued to be associated with what many referred to as "expanded" or "deeper" notions of equality. If the Lincoln image underwent a revitalization in Roosevelt's New Deal, then the rhetorical appeal to that image exploded from the late 1950s to mid-1960s during the American civil rights movement. In the summer of 1963, standing on the steps of the Lincoln Memorial in Washington, DC, Martin Luther King, Jr., reminded his audience that one hundred years ago Abraham Lincoln had signed the Emancipation Proclamation. Yet, one hundred years later, King suggested, "the Negro is still not free . . . the life of the Negro is still sadly crippled by the manacles of segregation and the chains of discrimination." King argued that the civil rights movement was an attempt to cash a "check," to fulfill a promise offered by the authors of the Declaration of Independence and the Constitution that "all men would be guaranteed the unalienable rights of life, liberty, and the pursuit of happiness." King went on to his famous proclamation: "I have a dream that one day this nation will rise up and live out the true meaning of its creed: 'We hold these truths to be self-evident—that all men are created equal.'"[1]

In 1964 and 1965 Lyndon Johnson too would adopt the Lincoln image as his own, incorporating Lincoln into the rhetoric of the Great Society and promising to make real the "promise of America"—that in due time weights should be lifted from the shoulders of all men, that all men should have an equal chance. According to Johnson, when Lincoln signed the Emancipation

Proclamation he freed the black man from the chains of slavery, but he could not free him from the burdens of bigotry and discrimination. Thus, Johnson suggested, emancipation remained merely a *proclamation* and not a *fact*. The self-professed aim of the Johnson administration was thus to *make* it a fact. Echoing the language of the Gettysburg Address, Johnson frequently claimed that if we could make emancipation a fact we could finally fulfill the "unfinished work" of Lincoln and the men who died at Gettysburg.[2]

I have argued that Lincoln's equality was an equality of opportunity for individuals to pursue their interests under the rule of law, while expecting an inequality of results or outcomes in that pursuit. For Lincoln, and the men who framed the Reconstruction Amendments, equal opportunity was understood as the security of individual rights of person and property and access to the legal system that enabled individuals to pursue their interests under the rule of law.[3] The federal civil rights and voting rights legislation of the middle 1960s were meant to help secure these ends by removing racial, ethnic, and religious discrimination against individual citizens, and to ensure that no citizen is denied the right of suffrage on account of race or color. Yet there was a growing sentiment that mere legal protections were insufficient to integrate black citizens into American society. Johnson himself would eventually suggest that the problem of racial injustice was more complex than anyone had previously understood, growing more critical by the moment. In the memoirs of his administration, Johnson claimed that even though the Civil and Voting Rights Acts began a process by which the barriers to freedom had begun to fall, "these legislative victories served to illuminate the full dimensions of the American dilemma . . . the time would come when we would realize that legislative guarantees were not enough."[4]

According to Johnson, for all the successes of the 1960s in securing the rights of black Americans, these citizens nevertheless remained "excluded from real equality." Both North and South were often unwilling to grant the "social acceptance and compassion that would make the formal rights meaningful."[5] Johnson argued that the interconnectedness of the problem of racial discrimination with problems of poverty, educational opportunity, housing, delinquency, and unemployment "could not be solved entirely by laws, crusades, or marches." The "effect on the black man of centuries of discrimination had become all too visible in the form of apathy, hatred, anger, and violence. The problems at this stage could not be solved by goodwill and compassion; they required large expenditures of public funds."[6] To secure real equality for blacks, and for all Americans, the federal government had to fund and implement programs to solve societal problems thought to frustrate the full and equal exercise of our rights.

As part of this effort, Johnson appealed to the Lincoln example in support of the Great Society, claiming to take up Lincoln's unfinished work in a new era of emancipation. However, in doing so, he departed fundamentally from Lincoln's equality of individual opportunity under the rule of law. In his 1965 Commencement Address at Howard University, Johnson boldly proclaimed the administration's intention to move beyond mere "legal equity" to "human ability," to achieve not just "equality as a right and a theory but equality as a fact and equality as a result."[7] Similar to Teddy's Roosevelt's claim to make rights both real and living, Johnson came to suggest that formal or procedural rights are worth nothing unless the results of our exercising those rights are equally enjoyed. Johnson ceased to strive to secure individual equality of opportunity as Lincoln understood it and, rather, argued unambiguously for an equality of results. This illustrates just how far he had departed from the Lincolnian tradition. Like the progressives and FDR, while rhetorically invoking Lincoln's legacy Johnson rejected Lincoln's principles.

Johnson's Lincoln and the War on Poverty

On the anniversary of Lincoln's birthday in February 1964, speaking on the steps of the Lincoln Memorial, Johnson set the tone for his use of the Lincoln image, referring here (as he would frequently refer) to the "promise" of America. "More than a century and a half ago," Johnson reminded his audience, "Abraham Lincoln was born. It is nearly a century now since his death. But it is his birth that we celebrate, and the new birth of freedom that he promised. This, he said, was the promise of our nation's birth—the 'promise that in due time the weights would be lifted from the shoulders of all men, and that all should have an equal chance.'" Again invoking the language of the Gettysburg Address, Johnson continued, "This is the unfinished work to which we, the living, must dedicate ourselves." According to Johnson, this work will have remained undone "so long as there is a child without a school, a school without a teacher, a man without a job, a family without a home; so long as there are sick Americans without medical care or aging Americans without hope; so long as there are any Americans, of any race or color, who are denied their full human rights; so long as there are any Americans, of any place or region, who are denied their human dignity." Lincoln's words, Johnson suggested, "have become the common covenant of our public life. Let us now get on with his work."[8]

Just one month later, Johnson would deliver his now famous 1964 Special Message to Congress proposing a nationwide war on poverty, the goal of which was arguably framed in Lincolnian terms—to create "an America in which every citizen shares all the opportunities of his society, in which every man has a chance to advance his welfare to the limit of his capacities." Johnson used a rhetoric that might bring to mind Lincoln's rhetoric of equal opportunity, to lift artificial weights from all shoulders, to afford to all an equal chance in the race of life. "We have come a long way toward this goal," Johnson admitted, but he insisted that we "still have a long way to go." Once again calling to mind Lincoln's words at Gettysburg, Johnson claimed that the "distance which remains is the measure of the great unfinished work of our society. To finish that work I have called for a national war on poverty. Our objective: total victory."[9]

In the fall of 1964, Johnson often recurred to the Lincoln example, rhetorically associating the abolition of slavery with the abolition of poverty. Speaking in Dayton, Ohio, Johnson suggested that a "great American President led this Union in a war against slavery 100 years ago. Lincoln abolished slavery in the United States. Today we are starting another war to abolish poverty in the United States among our people." In Chicago Johnson told his audience, "We have declared war on poverty, and we mean all-out war. Abraham Lincoln, a product of Illinois, abolished slavery 100 years ago. And now the Democratic Party adopts as its program the abolishment of poverty." Johnson would make nearly identical statements in Pittsburgh, Milwaukee, and New York. Speaking at his alma mater, Southwest Texas State College in San Marcos, Texas, Johnson reminded his audience, "It was a hundred years ago in 1864, that Abraham Lincoln abolished slavery in this country. A hundred years later, here in the hills of home, we are inaugurating a movement to abolish poverty in this county." Johnson would go on in this speech to urge "every student of this college, every faculty member, to pledge himself not to the Emancipation Proclamation that Lincoln signed a hundred years ago, or not to freeing the slaves, but, instead, to declaring a war and abolishing poverty in this land."[10]

However, to suggest with Johnson that Lincoln's work will remain unfinished—as long as "there is a child without a school, a school without a teacher, a man without a job, a family without a home," as long as "there are sick Americans without medical care or aging Americans without hope"—takes liberties with Lincoln's understanding of the standard maxim of equality. We certainly hear echoes of the rhetoric of the New Deal in the passages above, and such assertions are commonplace among historians, political scientists, and politicians. But it seems difficult to associate the arguably utopian language of ending poverty or abolishing homelessness with Lincoln's pursuit of equality.

Lincoln, of course, believed that the nation ought to encourage material prosperity. His support of free labor and technological innovation were intricately tied to his belief that the equality principle promotes a wider distribution of wealth and a higher standard of living for all Americans if they are allowed to enter into society as free and equal participants under the rule of law. But there is simply no evidence that suggests Lincoln understood the equality of the Declaration of Independence to mandate a national effort to abolish poverty in the United States. No matter how one feels about Johnson's policies, or the intended outcomes of those policies, his *arguments* depart sharply from Lincolnian political thought. One must always note that, as the ends to which government is dedicated become unlimited, the necessary means commensurate to those ends become, in principle, unlimited as well. Nothing could be further from Lincoln's understanding of American democracy. Although Johnson framed the war on poverty in Lincolnian terms, as an effort to lift artificial weights from all shoulders, Johnson here had more in common with Franklin Roosevelt than with Abraham Lincoln. While Lincoln rightly understood that government might have to take a role in helping to provide for those who cannot provide for themselves, his pursuit of equality of opportunity did not guarantee one a home, education, employment, and so on.[11] Once again (see previous chapters), it is simply not the case that Lincoln believed one's rights are secured only insofar as results in the exercise of those rights are equalized.

But the war on poverty is but one part of a much larger whole for Johnson. According to Johnson, the necessary interconnectedness of poverty, family breakdown, educational and employment opportunity, and medical care are all related to the issues of race and civil rights in America. His attempt to enlist Lincoln in support of the war on poverty is unpersuasive. But Johnson also employed the Lincoln example in the most obvious, and most plausible of places, in particular, as part of his push for the 1964 Civil Rights Act and the Voting Rights Act of 1965.

Johnson's Lincoln and the Civil Rights Act of 1964

Speaking to a group of civil rights leaders in April 1964, Johnson suggested that "A hundred years ago Lincoln freed the slaves of their chains, but he did not free the country of its bigotry. A hundred years ago Lincoln signed the Emancipation Proclamation, but until education is unaware of race, until employment is blind to color, emancipation will be a proclamation, but it will not be a fact." In this, and in several other speeches on civil rights, Johnson turned to Lincoln, relying upon an explicit distinction between emancipation in law or theory and emancipation in actuality or practice. In his view, the Civil Rights Act of 1964 was an attempt to help make emancipation a fact. He explained to his audience the intention of the new civil rights bill, claiming that "None of the provisions in this bill would create preferential treatment for one race or another. This would be a direct violation of the bill itself." Johnson suggested that all the bill would do "is to see that service and employment will not be refused to individuals because of their race or their religion or where their ancestors were born."[12] This contention appears across Johnson's rhetoric in 1964. In January, speaking to Plans for Progress volunteers, Johnson had urged business leaders pledged to address discrimination in employment to "pick up where Lincoln left off." Addressing Treasury Department officials in April, and the President's Commission on Equal Employment Opportunity in May, Johnson claimed that the administration's purpose was to follow Lincoln, to make emancipation a fact, by rendering education "unaware of race" and "employment blind to color." Both before and after the passage of the Civil Rights Act in July, repeatedly and reasonably appealing to the Lincoln example, Johnson claimed the bill was meant to assure that individual achievement in American society would be based upon individual talents and abilities and not upon the accidental qualities of ethnicity, religion, race, or color.[13] Intended to prohibit discrimination against individuals on the basis of arbitrary distinctions such as race, ethnicity, or religion, the Civil Rights Act, as written and passed by Congress, seems consistent with Lincoln's understanding of equality and its pursuit through established representative institutions.[14]

Johnson's victory in securing the passage of the Civil Rights Act, as well as an intervening landslide electoral victory for the Democratic Party in November, prompted him to claim a national mandate regarding his civil rights agenda. By his own admission, Johnson intended to take full advantage of this political momentum.[15] Almost immediately, his rhetoric opened up to point toward goals greater and more expansive than the mere removal of arbitrary legal barriers to equal opportunity for individuals. In December 1964, in his remarks at the National Urban League's Community Action Assembly, Johnson employed a familiar theme, claiming that "It is more than 100 years since Abraham Lincoln charged the living to dedicate themselves to the unfinished work of the dead at Gettysburg." He added immediately that even Lincoln, "with his deep sense of man's imperfections, could not know that a century later we would still be striving to abolish racial injustice."[16] Johnson thus suggested that our national goal was not merely to remove arbitrary, discriminatory barriers to individual opportunity, and not merely to establish laws or enforce existing laws to address the problem of racial injustice, but to abolish racial injustice entirely.

Despite his appeal to Lincoln, Johnson here seems much closer to the progressives, with their faith in the perfectibility of human nature through social planning, than he does to Lincoln.[17] To identify discrimination on the basis of race as illegal and to improve the legal means by which individuals might have recourse to address racial discrimination are not inconsistent with Lincoln's understanding of the standard maxim of equality. And Johnson claimed that the 1964 Civil Rights Act was rightly aimed at securing such goals. However, as we are beginning to see, Johnson's rhetoric in support of this legislation would begin to point beyond the principles of the legislation itself. Along the way, Johnson would also stray from the core principles of Lincoln's understanding of politics. One must wonder if the attempt to abolish injustice is asking much from human beings and asking much from the political. Lincoln, time and again, prudently recognized that in all events, under all circumstances, we shall have human beings both silly and wise, both good and bad. With his belief in an unchanging and complicated human nature and his profound understanding of the human condition, Lincoln understood that our natural love of justice and our natural selfishness stand in *eternal* antagonism.[18]

Johnson refers to Lincoln's "deep sense of man's imperfections," and it is this very sense of man's imperfections that suggests Lincoln would have doubted the prudence of the attempt to abolish injustice from political life. To believe that one could do so would be to expect more from the political than Lincoln thought human beings—at least, most human beings, most of the time—were willing or able to offer. Lincoln would probably have expected that, one hundred years later, Americans would still struggle with the problem of racial injustice. This is not to suggest that the attempts to ensure citizens are secure in their property and persons and to ensure that citizens are equal before the law are not noble and choice-worthy goals. And Lincoln surely anticipated the possibility of, and looked forward to, improvement in education and public opinion, laws, and institutions. But his repeated statements as to the necessarily complex and imperfect character of our shared human nature suggest a realistic acknowledgment that the problem of injustice, racial or otherwise, cannot be completely abolished from the American experience because man's imperfections cannot be expunged from the human soul.

Moreover, it is by no means clear here what Johnson's understanding of justice actually is. On the one hand, for Johnson, to abolish racial injustice seems to have something to do with passing and enforcing the 1964 Civil Rights Act. Racial justice would seem to require that individual citizens not be legally denied equal opportunity based on race, ethnicity, or religion. Again, this seems consistent with Lincoln's understanding of equal liberty. But Johnson's rhetoric pushes beyond the idea of equal protection of equal rights.[19] He appears to suggest that justice, racial or otherwise, might reside in the enjoyment of the many guarantees or equal results promised by the war on poverty. Johnson's notion of the nature of justice departs from Lincoln's notion of justice as equal opportunity rooted in natural and inalienable rights. Johnson's rhetoric again points beyond the legislation of the Civil Rights Act, and beyond Lincoln's political principles.

Johnson's Lincoln and the Voting Rights Act of 1965

After the passage of the Civil Rights Act and the 1964 election, Johnson used the opportunity to push forward by securing the passage of a new voting rights bill to address widespread discrimination in voter registration in the southern states. Speaking to the National Urban League's Community Action Assembly in December 1964, Johnson returned to familiar rhetoric when he claimed that "One of the Presidents that I admire most signed the Emancipation Proclamation 100 years ago. But emancipation was a proclamation and not a fact. It shall be my purpose and it is my duty to make it a fact." Once again, Johnson elaborated on what this would require, and now he states that, "Until every qualified person regardless of the house where he worships or the State where he resides or the way he spells his name or the color of his skin—until he has the right unquestioned and unrestrained to go in and cast his ballot in every precinct in this country, I am not going to be satisfied." Johnson then asserted, "The finest compliment that I can pay to the Negroes of America is to say that if their constitutional rights are protected as mine are protected, if they have the privilege of voting as I am privileged to vote, then all these other problems will take care of themselves."[20]

Johnson himself would later comment on the extreme importance of the Lincoln example to his own push for the voting rights bill. Johnson wrote in his memoirs that, on the way home from the Capitol after his 1965 Message to Congress on Voting Rights, he found himself passing by the Lincoln Memorial. "There had always been something haunting for me in that statue of Lincoln," Johnson claimed, "so life-like and so clear-cut a reminder of the persistent gap between our promises and our deeds. Somehow that night Lincoln's hopes for America seemed much closer." Four months later, Johnson returned to the Capitol to sign the Voting Rights Act of 1965. He claimed that, at this historic moment, he was reminded of Martin Luther King's suggestion at Montgomery, "We are on the move now.... Selma has become a shining moment in the conscience of man." In return, Johnson proclaimed, "So we will move step by step—often painfully, but I think with clear vision—along the path toward American freedom." These words, Johnson reminded us, were spoken in the Capitol rotunda, directly in front of a statue of Abraham Lincoln.[21]

Johnson's 1965 Special Message to Congress on Voting Rights was entitled "The American Promise," the very phrase he consistently associated with the Lincoln image. Explaining his understanding of that promise, he opened the address with the now famous words, "I speak here tonight for the dignity of man and the destiny of democracy." Our nation, Johnson claimed, was "the first nation in the history of the world to be founded with a purpose," a "promise to every citizen that he shall share in the dignity of man." Elaborating on this idea, Johnson invoked an arguably Lincolnian theme in explaining that human dignity rests in a man's "right to be treated as a man equal in opportunity to all others. It says that he shall share in freedom, he shall choose his leaders, educate his children and provide for his family according to his ability and his merits as a human being."[22] According to Johnson:

> Our fathers believed that if this noble view of the rights of man was to flourish, it must be rooted in democracy. The most basic right of all was the right to choose your own leaders.... Yet the harsh fact is that in many places in this country men and women are kept from voting simply because they are Negroes.... The Constitution says that no person shall be kept from voting because of his race or his color. We have all sworn an oath before God to support and to defend that Constitution. We must now act in obedience to that oath.... To those who seek to avoid action by their National Government in their own communities; who want to and who seek to maintain purely local control over elections, the answer is simple: Open your polling places to all

your people. Allow men and women to register and vote whatever the color of their skin. Extend the rights of citizenship to every citizen of this land. There is no constitutional issue here. The command of the Constitution is plain.[23]

The Fifteenth Amendment holds that no state shall deny any citizen of the United States the right to vote on the basis of race or color. Moreover, Congress had the express authority to enforce this amendment with appropriate legislation. Thus, Johnson argued, "there is no issue of States rights or national rights. There is only the struggle for human rights."[24] (It is not clear whether Johnson suggested that the right of suffrage is indeed a "human right," that is, a right that belongs to all human beings as such, or whether suffrage is a necessary *precondition* for individuals to pursue or secure their human rights).

Even if the proposed voting rights bill passed, Johnson argued, "the battle will not be over," for this legislation is part of a wider movement. It is part of the effort of black Americans to "secure for themselves the full blessings of American life." Just as he had done in his arguments for the war on poverty and the Civil Rights Act of 1964, Johnson again turned to Lincoln and reminded his audience that "a century has passed, more than a hundred years, since the Negro was freed. And he is not fully free tonight." According to Johnson, "A century has passed, more than a hundred years, since equality was promised. And yet the Negro is not equal." Echoing the language of Lincoln's 1862 letter to James C. Conkling, Johnson declared, "A century has passed since the day of promise. And the promise is unkept."[25]

Following Johnson's argument, if America is to make good on Lincoln's promise, citizens must not be denied the right to vote on the basis of race or color. Suffrage, Johnson claimed, is a right of citizenship, a civil right (perhaps even a human right, belonging to all humans as such). However, years of political practice and understanding suggest that suffrage was, in fact, not generally understood to be a right of U.S. citizenship as such (to say nothing of a human right) but, rather, a political right enjoyed by qualified citizens, a right traditionally defined by the state governments. Properly speaking, the Fifteenth Amendment did not "give" any citizen the right of suffrage but rather prohibited states from denying the right of suffrage based on race. However, throughout his voting rights address, Johnson repeatedly referred to suffrage as a right or a privilege of citizenship. This tends to obscure the fact that suffrage had traditionally been understood as a political right rather than a civil right proper, for a civil right belongs to all citizens, as such.[26]

Johnson blurred such distinctions when he was speaking about rights, one of the most interesting examples of which occurred when he claimed that, while the proposed voting legislation would be widely regarded as a "civil rights" bill, "most of the program" he recommended—the wider program of the Great Society—"is a civil rights program. Its object is to open the city of hope to all people of all races." All Americans, Johnson declared, must have the right to vote. But "to exercise" the privileges of citizenship "takes much more than just legal right. It requires a trained mind and a healthy body. It requires a decent home, and the chance to find a job, and the opportunity to escape from the clutches of poverty." Thus, Johnson placed emphasis not only upon the formal right of suffrage but also upon the effective exercise of that right. To ensure that the right of suffrage is equally exercised requires much more than preventing discrimination and disenfranchisement. According to Johnson, "people cannot contribute to the Nation if they are never taught to read or write, if their bodies are stunted from hunger, if their sickness goes untended, if their life is spent in hopeless poverty just drawing a welfare check. So we want to open the gates to opportunity. But we are also going to give all our people, black and white, the help that they need to walk through those gates."[27]

"Civil Rights" and the Great Society

Johnson's arguments in support of civil and voting rights pointed beyond the issues of discrimination and suffrage. By identifying the bulk of the Great Society as a "civil rights program," Johnson implied that citizens, as such, have (or should have) a right to all the goods promised by the Great Society. In his 1964 Commencement Address at the University of Michigan, Johnson offered one of his more detailed explanations of the ends of the Great Society, declaring that the Great Society demanded the complete abolition of poverty and racial injustice. Yet even these goals were said to be only the beginning. The abolition of poverty and racial injustice were merely the *foundations* upon which the Great Society was to be erected. According to Johnson, the Great Society sought to ensure that the "city of man secures not only the needs of the body and the demands of commerce but the desire for beauty and the hunger for community." It sought to ensure that "the demands of morality, and the needs of the spirit, can be realized in the life of the Nation." Johnson asked the Michigan graduates to join him in the battle "to give every citizen the full equality which God enjoins and the law requires, whatever his belief, or race, or the color of his skin, . . . [the battle to] give every citizen an escape from the crushing weight of poverty, . . . [the battle] to make it possible for all nations to live in enduring peace—as neighbors and not as mortal enemies." To build the Great Society was a battle "to build a richer life of mind and spirit."[28]

Thus, securing equality for all citizens, ending racial injustice, and abolishing poverty were the foundations upon which the larger aims of the Great Society are built. These aims moved well beyond mere equality before the law, well beyond equal opportunity to pursue happiness, toward the satisfaction of human wants, even our spiritual longings. The Great Society demanded nothing less than the satisfaction of the human soul. If we are to understand "most" of the Great Society to be a "civil rights" program, as Johnson asserted, then is not the implication here that all citizens as such have a "civil right" to the goods promised by the Great Society? This not only takes us beyond civil and political rights as they had traditionally been understood, it also moves us even beyond the economic rights espoused by Franklin Roosevelt.

There is an important sense in which Johnson's understanding of rights did have some basis in what came before, particularly in the idea that citizens have a right to be free from fear and free from want, but FDR's new understanding of rights was phrased largely in terms of material well-being or economic security. Johnson's rhetoric suggested a further development. All citizens now have a right to psychological or spiritual satisfaction, a right that is to be secured by the general government.[29] Clearly, we have come a long way from the idea of merely preventing discrimination in housing, education, employment, and voting. But this is the way Johnson's suggestions lead us. Johnson abandons Lincoln's understanding of equality while continuing to appeal to Lincoln's legacy. Enacted by the elected representatives of the people, legislation such as the civil and voting rights bills is compatible with Lincoln's equality. Lincoln did believe that, in due time, black citizenship and suffrage were legitimate rights to be achieved in the name of equality.[30] But in Johnson's rhetoric, the idea of equality of rights is expanded to encompass more than Lincoln's understanding of formal equality of individual citizens before the law. All citizens, according to Johnson, have a right to the entitlements of the Great Society, which include not only the right to material security but also the right to psychological or spiritual satisfaction. Johnson made arguments that pointed far beyond the notion of securing equal liberty by enforcing the Reconstruction Amendments, and in doing so, he abandoned the Lincolnian tradition he claimed to follow.

Johnson Relativizes the Lincoln Example

We recall that on February 12, 1964, Johnson had promised to finish Lincoln's work, to fulfill the "promise of America." In the course of the following year, Johnson consistently presented himself as following the Lincolnian example, but he also claimed to move beyond what Lincoln was either willing or able to achieve in the circumstances confronting him. Johnson vowed to make Lincoln's mere proclamation of emancipation a fact, to turn mere words into a tangible reality.[31] Speaking on February 12, 1965, Johnson again appealed to the Lincoln image, this time at a White House luncheon honoring Lincoln's birthday. These remarks are worth examining in detail, for this speech marks, I believe, something new in Johnson's appeal to Lincoln. However, his language and his argument will sound familiar. His suggestions will sound very much like those of the progressives.

Johnson here suggested to his audience that this nation's greatness can be measured by the qualities of the men it honors, and that it is a tribute to America that it continues to hold up Abraham Lincoln as an object of national reverence. History, nature, events, and character all combined to create Lincoln, a leader and an ideal worthy of our allegiance. Elaborating on that ideal, Johnson remarked:

> It is the work of historians to try and separate fact from myth, the real man from the legend. But nothing we learn can diminish Lincoln. For his importance to us is not in the facts of his life, but in what he has come to mean, and the way along which he commands us. Almost alone among the figures of history we honor him not so much for what he did, but for what he stood for; not so much for the acts he performed, but the spirit of that ideal America he embodies. Each generation of Americans stands charged before the court of history, to answer Lincoln's challenge to the American will and the American heart. The answer to that charge is our measure, not his.[32]

To follow Lincoln's example, Johnson explained, is to stand with Lincoln for Union, to enlarge the liberties of all the American people, and to stay true to the Declaration of Independence, that is, to lift the weights from the shoulders of all men, to afford all an equal chance.

These may well be Lincolnian goals, but we should notice just what Johnson claimed here. The importance of the Lincoln example, according to Johnson, is not found in the facts of Lincoln's life. We are said to honor Lincoln not so much for what he did, not so much for the actions he performed, but rather, for what he has *come to mean* to us over time. Perhaps Johnson was attempting to save the Lincoln image from potential debunkers, from those who would dispute the integrity of the Lincoln example on the grounds that Lincoln was not wholly committed to human equality or did not do enough to foster that equality.[33] Perhaps Johnson was responding to those who might claim Lincoln was nothing more than a self-serving politician who took advantage of the slavery crisis for political gain. Indeed, the work of revisionist historians such as Richard Hofstadter had come to the fore over the previous several years, focusing on Lincoln the ambitious politician and his "self-made myth." And only a few short years later Lerone Bennett would publish his influential *Ebony* article on Lincoln as a white supremacist, a piece that gave voice to an increasing dissatisfaction with the Lincoln "myth" among many in the emerging Black Power movement.[34]

Whatever the case, "nothing we learn can diminish Lincoln," according to Johnson, because Lincoln's words and deeds as Lincoln himself might have understood them do not really matter. Rather, Lincoln is worthy of our admiration because of what he has *come to mean* to us today. Today we stand before the "court of history" in trying to finish Lincoln's work, and we are charged to live up to the Lincoln example as it *appears to us in our time*.[35] The meaning of the Lincoln example is thus not defined by any merits or faults intrinsic to Lincoln, his words, or his deeds. For Johnson, the real meaning of the Lincoln example is thus provided by our changing interpretations of that example over time. Here we encounter something very similar to what we observed in the progressives' Lincoln.[36] A historicized or relativized Lincoln example is flexible enough to help deemphasize the fact that Johnson's general claim to act on Lincolnian principles seems difficult to square with the Great Society's expanded notion of equal rights and its utopian rhetoric of abolishing poverty, racism, and injustice. To maintain his appeal to the Lincoln example (an example he admits is of great rhetorical importance in American politics), Johnson downplays the content of Lincoln's equality in order to focus upon what the Lincoln example comes to mean over time.

The progressives and FDR historicized the Declaration of Independence, historicized the proposition that all men are created equal, and historicized the Lincoln example. In similar fashion, Johnson suggests the Lincoln example is best understood as it comes to be understood over time. Once Lincoln's importance is severed from the facts of his life and the specific content of his thought, then the Lincoln example is capable of meaning whatever we want it to mean. One must wonder, of course, how far this idea can be stretched before the Lincoln example is rendered essentially meaningless, before it is merely an empty vessel into which we might pour varied and contradictory interpretations of equality, however much they may or may not comport with Lincoln's words and deeds. We recall that Woodrow Wilson had endeavored to establish the notion of a "living constitution," flexible enough to meet the needs of the times. Here, Johnson seeks to establish a "living Lincoln," adaptable to the sentiments of the day and suited to serve the goal of equality however that goal might come to be defined. Promising to fulfill Lincoln's work, Johnson would nevertheless move beyond Lincoln's vision of equality of individual rights under the rule of law. Johnson would urge that the next great stage in the battle for civil rights, the next stage in our fulfillment of the promise of America, requires that we pursue more than mere equality of individual opportunity but, rather, an equality of group results.

The Howard Address and Equality of Results

On June 4, 1965, Johnson delivered a commencement address at Howard University entitled "To Fulfill These Rights."[37] The Howard address is generally recognized as one of the most important presidential speeches on the idea of equality in contemporary American political history. The address is representative of an important shift in the way we talk about equality as a goal for American society, a shift that continues to resonate in our political discourse today. It marks one of the first times an American president specifically and unambiguously argued modern times demand that American government should seek to secure not merely equality of opportunity among individuals but equality of results among groups. The Howard address helped to set the stage for what would come to be known as "affirmative action" policies from the late 1960s until the present day. Johnson repeatedly claimed that he sought to continue Lincoln's "unfinished work" by lifting artificial weights and fulfilling the promise of America. But in seeking to move beyond equality of opportunity to equality of results, Johnson moved beyond and in fact rejected Lincoln's idea of equality. The Howard address is worth examining in detail because it illustrates just how far Johnson has strayed from Lincoln's principles, despite his numerous attempts to seize the Lincoln mantle.

To understand fully the context of the Howard address, it is particularly important to note the release in March 1965 of Daniel Patrick Moynihan's controversial *Report on the Negro Family*. The Moynihan Report suggested that the legacy of slavery and years of racial discrimination and bigotry had trapped many black Americans in a cycle of despair, alienation, and seemingly inescapable poverty.[38] In the years between the *Brown* decision and the Civil Rights Act of 1964, the report claimed, "the demand of Negro Americans for full recognition of their civil rights was finally met." However, Moynihan warned that a "new crisis in race relations" was emerging. We were beginning to witness a "new period" in which "the expectations of the Negro Americans will go *beyond civil rights* . . . they will now expect that in the near future equal opportunities for them as a group will produce roughly *equal results,* as compared with other groups."[39] According to Moynihan, these expectations would not be realized any time soon, not even in the distant future, unless the federal government took account of the problem of racism and the legacy of slavery. The federal government had to make, in Moynihan's words, "a special effort" to address the problems of delinquency, unemployment, alienation, and ultimately, the "Negro family structure."[40]

Johnson began the Howard address (which Moynihan had a large part in drafting) by recognizing the advances made toward the security of civil rights for all Americans. Johnson singled out *Brown v. Board,* and the civil rights legislation of 1957, 1960, and 1964 as a series of victories and he looked forward to the passage of the voting rights bill in the near future.[41] Yet, while the Voting Rights Act of 1965 would be the latest in this series of victories, Johnson argued, it would not—it simply could not—be the last step. Quoting Winston Churchill, Johnson declared that the voting rights bill "is not the end. It is not even the beginning of the end. But it is, perhaps, the end of the beginning." This beginning was the removal of legal discrimination and the guarantee of formal protections for the property and persons of black Americans. This beginning, Johnson suggested, was freedom, and the "barriers to that freedom are tumbling down." This freedom is "the right to share, share fully and equally, in American society—to vote, to hold a job, to enter a public place, to go to school." Freedom "is the right to be treated in every part of our national life as a person equal in dignity and promise to all others." But, Johnson continued to suggest, this mere "freedom is not enough":

> You do not wipe away the scars of centuries by saying: Now you are free to go where you want, and do as you desire, and choose the leaders you please. You do not take a person who, for years, has been hobbled by chains and

liberate him, bring him up to the starting line of a race and then say, "you are free to compete with all the others," and still justly believe that you have been completely fair. Thus it is not enough just to open the gates of opportunity. All our citizens must have the ability to walk through those gates. This is the next and the more profound stage of the battle for civil rights. We seek not just freedom but opportunity. We seek not just legal equity but human ability, not just equality as a right and a theory but equality as a fact and equality as a result.

To this end, Johnson argued, "equal opportunity is essential, but not enough." That is to say, merely rendering it such that individuals might legally exercise their diverse abilities and talents in the pursuit of their interests is insufficient to secure our desired ends. Although "[m]en and women of all races are born with the same range of abilities," ability is "stretched or stunted by the family that you live with," the "neighborhood you live in," the "school you go to," and the "poverty or richness of your surroundings." Ability, Johnson argued, "is the product of a hundred unseen forces playing upon the little infant, the child, and finally the man."[42]

Now, there is much to consider here in these few words. We should note first that Johnson claimed this new understanding of equality represented "the next and the more profound stage of the battle for civil rights." While the Howard address closely followed the language of the Moynihan Report, we should recall that Moynihan had suggested there was an urgent necessity to go *beyond* civil rights in order to foster equality of results. That is, Moynihan had suggested a difference between civil rights on the one hand and results in pursuit of our interests on the other. In the Howard address, Johnson blurred this distinction. He characterized this new pursuit of equal results not as a step *beyond* civil rights but, rather, as the next stage in the battle *for* civil rights. This again suggests that, in Johnson's public rhetoric, the notion of civil rights included something more than formal equality of individual citizens before the law. Rather, civil rights included the material and spiritual goods of the Great Society.

Johnson publicly announced this new goal of equality by way of a variation on Lincoln's race of life metaphor. But for Lincoln, we recall, the race of life was meant to convey an individual-regarding equality of rights, an equal opportunity under the rule of law to pursue one's interests, while expecting an inequality of results among individuals in that pursuit. As Samuel Beer observes, Johnson's variation on the race of life metaphor, building on the thesis of the Moynihan Report, conveyed a new egalitarianism that departed sharply from Lincoln's understanding of equal opportunity as the protection of individual rights. Johnson promoted a modern egalitarianism centered upon the idea of equality of group results.[43]

With Johnson, the term *equal opportunity* thus took on a different meaning, shifting from the idea of ensuring that individuals must be treated equally by the procedures, or rules of the game, to the idea of equalizing the probabilities of achieving a given result in the race.[44] As David Zarefsky argues, the *initial conditions,* or the chance to enter the race, had defined the older notion of equal opportunity—the notion, we observe, shared by Lincoln and the American Founders. In Johnson's formulation, equality of opportunity is now defined by the *terminal conditions,* or the results of the race. What Johnson and Moynihan did was to suggest that, if opportunities were truly equal in American society, then one would expect the number of "winners" from a certain group or class of citizens in the race of life would be roughly proportional to that group's overall population in the wider society. A disproportionately low ratio of winners to entrants in the race thus becomes prima facie evidence that opportunity is not truly equal.[45]

Thus, a pursuit of equality that was once centered upon securing the procedural, formal rights of individuals to pursue their interests under the rule of law becomes one of securing group results, although these ends are often referred to as group rights. In this, Johnson partakes in a significant departure from American constitutional theory, for it had always been understood that rights belong not to groups but to individuals, and that the U.S. Constitution attempts to secure the rights of individuals.[46] What would come to be known as "affirmative action" policies addressing inequalities in education, politics, and employment would not significantly begin to take hold until the Nixon administration, largely through a series of bureaucratic and judicial reinterpretations of the 1964 Civil Rights Act. However, the rationale beneath Johnson's Howard address helped to pave the way for this new group-specific, results-oriented understanding of equality in American political discourse.[47] Now, irrespective of whether one agrees with the policy implications of Johnson's redefinition of equal opportunity, it is undeniable that the Howard address breaks fundamentally with the first principles of American democracy as these principles had traditionally been understood. Despite Johnson's broader effort to incorporate Lincoln into his political rhetoric, the principles beneath the Howard address demonstrate how far Johnson actually departed from the Lincolnian heritage he claimed for the Great Society.

Conclusion

Some claim that Lincoln set a precedent for various forms of modern egalitarianism when he claimed that we ought to strive toward the standard maxim of equality and ensure that all have an equal chance in the race of life. One can understand why observers might see at least a surface similarity between Lincoln's words on equality and the rhetoric of Lyndon Johnson. But, once again, Johnson's redefinition of rights was akin to Franklin Roosevelt's attempt to redefine the foundational premises of American democracy. While Johnson appealed to the Lincoln image in his political rhetoric, his redefinition of rights clearly illustrated his rejection of Lincoln's understanding of equality.

Again, Lincolnian political thought would suggest that the pursuit of equality has the potential to become separated from moderation when the distinction between rights and the results of the exercise of rights becomes obscured. Here, in principle, we find the same problem we encountered with FDR's economic rights. However, Johnson's notion of rights added to FDR's political and economic goods the psychological and spiritual goods of the Great Society. According to Johnson, the bulk of these goods ought to be considered "civil rights" belonging to all citizens. Johnson in his rhetoric employed Lincoln and his race of life metaphor to effect this change, which leads some to suggest that Johnson builds upon Lincolnian foundations. In his defense of free labor as morally and economically superior to chattel slavery, Lincoln did sometimes employ the metaphor of the race of life. This metaphor has come under attack from different ideological circles. The metaphor is sometimes found to be intellectually or philosophically unsatisfying, and some argue that in the end it begs more questions than it answers.[48]

When the race of life metaphor is pushed to its extreme, detached from Lincoln's first principles about the nature and purpose of popular government, then one can certainly understand the issue here. For some, one of the persistent problems with the race of life metaphor is that it seems difficult to determine where the "starting line" is, or just when the race begins for an individual. We might find it difficult to determine just what constitutes a "fair chance" in the race of life. Would ensuring a fair start in the race not require that we address past inequalities and injustices for groups, or even specific individuals, so as to create an equality of talent or ability at the starting line? If this were somehow possible, would this not require that government infringe on individual liberty for some in the name of results for others? Would it not require that government regulate traditionally private concerns on an unprecedented level? The race of life metaphor might seem to move in this direction but only when abstracted from the context in which Lincoln used it.

Lincoln held that a fair chance in the race of life meant that one's chances in the race are determined by one's abilities, rather than by artificial legal distinctions that would arbitrarily force one to run the race with imposed burdens or that would disqualify one from entering the race at all. For Lincoln, this was a formal equality before the law, which accepted an inequality of results among individuals because of their necessarily diverse and unequal attributes and abilities. Lincoln thus drew a clear distinction between equality of rights, on the one hand, and equality of abilities, on the other. For Lincoln, to ensure an equal start in the race of life was to ensure equality before the law to exercise *unequal* abilities. Lincoln's race of life metaphor was not meant to call for an *equalization* of abilities. Any reading of Lincoln's statements on equality makes this clear. Those who argue that an equal chance in the race might demand more than Lincoln's limited equality of rights can provide are correct, if an "equal chance" means that all citizens should have equal abilities in the race. Of course one might then ask if the race of life metaphor would make any sense at all, because the race would presumably always end in a tie. It can be argued that Lincoln's race metaphor is limited by certain assumptions and might not hold up when abstracted from those assumptions.

In this sense, Lincoln's race of life metaphor is limited, because it is ultimately based upon his first principles regarding the natural equality of all men, the limits of human nature, and the necessity of limited government. If our goal is the modern egalitarian and utopian ends of the Great Society (an end to all war, injustice, and poverty), then this requires not only an infinitely malleable and perfectible human nature but, perhaps, an unlikely union of absolute power and absolute wisdom in order to secure such goods. A government of unlimited ends requires a government of unlimited means, which is by definition unjust according to Lincoln's political thought. Taking his bearings from the premise that we are all equally endowed with natural and inalienable rights that cannot be consented away, Lincoln held that legitimate government is by definition limited government.[49] It thus remains difficult to identify Johnson's arguments with the Lincoln example. As a statesman Lincoln used his metaphor in the service of a limited constitutional government with the duty of preserving the natural and inalienable rights of its citizens. For Lincoln, to ensure an equality of abilities, results, or conditions among individuals or groups would require something more than limited constitutional government is reasonably capable of providing, and something more than it is rightfully entitled to provide.

SIX

Barack Obama's Lincoln

WITH THE BICENTENNIAL of Lincoln's birth in 2009, we have witnessed yet another explosion of interest in our sixteenth president, fueled not only by the bicentennial but by the political rhetoric of Barack Obama. In February 2007, just two days before Lincoln's birthday, Obama announced his candidacy for the U.S. presidency in Springfield, Illinois. Obama was standing in front of the old Illinois State Capitol—the site of Lincoln's famed House Divided speech—and the power and purposefulness of this symbolism was unmistakable. Obama's declared purpose was to answer the call to rise up, like previous generations of Americans, and to do what needed to be done, to fulfill what he sometimes identifies as the "promise" of America. Obama suggested that our unyielding faith, dating back to the founding of the nation, is that we will fulfill this promise in the face of impossible odds. This, Obama claimed, is what "Abraham Lincoln understood." Laying out the themes of his presidential campaign, Obama offered the numerous reforms necessary to live up to this charge, as he understands it: reshaping the economy to provide for greater equality of opportunity; establishing higher standards for education and better pay for teachers; affordable college tuition; increased funding for scientific research; broadband lines in both city and countryside; better benefits and retirement plans for the nation's workers; the abolition of poverty in the United States; universal health care; energy independence; the defeat of terrorism, an end to the Iraq war, and improved benefits for veterans; and a rebuilding of the

U.S. military. If we can begin this work, Obama suggested, we might begin to live up to the promise of America, to prove our fidelity to the American creed. According to Obama, the Founders and Abraham Lincoln understood that the unique and most commendable quality of American democracy is that it can be changed.[1]

Obama argued that these goals can be realized only through unity and conviction. Calling to mind Lincoln's famous words, Obama suggested that, divided, we are bound to fail. Americans must join together to fix contemporary problems. While Americans have historically been plagued by a growing cynicism about the possibilities of politics, Obama claimed that a different future is possible. We can know this, he explained, if we consider the life of a "tall, gangly, self-made Springfield lawyer." Lincoln tells us that there is "power in words," that there is "power in conviction," that "beneath all the differences of race and region, faith and station, we are one people," and that "there is power in hope." Employing the language of Lincoln's House Divided speech, Obama referred to Lincoln's part in helping to organize "strange, discordant, and even hostile forces" to form the Republican Party in the fight against slavery. In similar fashion, Obama and his supporters today must stand together, united, "gathered from the four winds" to see the fight through.[2]

Obama argued that he had run for the presidency in order to gather with his audience to "transform a nation," to "win the next battle for justice and opportunity." Invoking the language of the Gettysburg Address, Obama professed his desire to "take up the unfinished business of perfecting our union, and building a better America," to "finish the work that needs to be done, and usher in a new birth of freedom on this Earth."[3] Just shy of two years later, Obama chose "A New Birth of Freedom" as the theme for his presidential inauguration ceremonies. Upon being elected, Obama famously followed Lincoln's train route to Washington, ate the food Lincoln had eaten at his inaugural luncheon, and took the oath of office using the Bible Lincoln had used at his inauguration. For the two years leading up to Obama's inauguration, academics and journalists frequently made the ubiquitous Obama-Lincoln connection. The substance of that comparison ranged from the thoughtful and observant to the downright pedestrian and silly. Countless articles appeared in the press noting the similarities between Obama and Lincoln. Some focused on the substance of their ideas. Some considered their temperaments, rhetorical skill, "leadership," or "management style." Others noted that both are talented, self-made men from humble roots. Still others observed that both are tall, thin lawyers that began their improbable rises to the White House from the state of Illinois.[4]

It is important to note, however, that Obama himself is widely recognized for his own cultivation of the Obama-Lincoln comparison. In his attempt to incorporate the Lincoln image into his political rhetoric, Obama repeatedly identified himself with Lincoln and famously compared Lincoln's experiences leading up to the Civil War with his "own struggles."[5] Like many politicians before him, in speeches, writings, and interviews Obama frequently claimed that Lincoln serves as a constant source of guidance and inspiration. Coinciding with Obama's rising popularity was the publication of Doris Kearns Goodwin's masterful and widely recognized *Team of Rivals: The Political Genius of Abraham Lincoln.*[6] Obama enthusiastically praised the book, and observers quickly noted an apparent similarity between Lincoln's selection of his cabinet and Obama's potential picks for his own advisors, including rival Hillary Clinton. Goodwin's frequent praise of Obama's intelligence and temperament in the news media served to feed the growing Obama-Lincoln comparison.

There is also, of course, the historic importance of Obama's election. No matter how one might feel about Obama's politics, or about the comparisons to Lincoln in terms of ideas, policies, character, or rhetoric, one can easily understand the relevance of Lincoln's legacy to Obama's election to the presidency. One wonders how any person watching Obama's victory speech in Grant Park could have remained unmoved, just before the bicentennial anniversary of Lincoln's birth. Recalling Lincoln's efforts to realize the principle of equality by lifting the artificial weights of slavery, many academics, journalists, and Obama himself have regularly suggested that, if not for Lincoln's legacy, such a monumental election might not have been possible.

Yet none of this means that Obama's frequent appeals to the Lincoln legacy should go unquestioned, however popular, eloquent, or moving those appeals may be. The foregoing discussion suggests that Obama's claim to carry on Lincoln's task is nothing new. As we have observed, the effort to paint oneself as the modern Lincoln is certainly not novel. In fact, it is rather unremarkable. In many respects, Obama's Lincoln is merely a more recent variation on a preexisting theme, a stock progressive appeal to Lincoln repackaged for a new audience. Obama's Lincoln is clearly indebted to the Lincoln that was offered by progressives such as Herbert Croly, Teddy Roosevelt, and Woodrow Wilson, and characteristic also of the modern rhetoric of FDR and Lyndon Johnson. A brilliant rhetorician, Obama often draws upon similar—if not identical—themes as those who have come before him. As such, his effort to claim the Lincoln inheritance encounters difficulties similar to those found in those previous appeals to Lincoln. Obama's use of Lincoln deserves discussion, for it offers a fresh example of the progressive claim to the Lincoln inheritance. And this claim, once again, is expressly tied to Lincoln's notion that the standard maxim of equality is to serve as a goal toward which American democracy should strive.

Obama, Lincoln, and the Principles of the Declaration of Independence

Clearly, Obama and his speechwriters are fond of peppering his political speeches with Lincolnian phrases and rhetoric. Take, for example, Obama's 2008 victory speech, wherein he incorporated two of the most memorable phrases in American political history, both of which belong to Lincoln. Obama first congratulated and praised all of his supporters for proving that "more than two centuries later a government of the people, by the people, and for the people has not perished from the Earth." This, Obama declared, "is your victory."[7] This statement was received with thunderous cheers and applause from the massive audience of supporters gathered in Grant Park. But, despite the power of Lincoln's words, one wonders exactly what Obama suggested here. Would a Republican victory have spelled the end of American democracy?[8] Obama seems to suggest that this is the case, presenting his victory as a vindication of Lincoln's understanding of free government. The implied message is simple: a Democratic victory is a fulfillment of Lincoln's vision of American democracy. A Republican victory is a threat to Lincoln's vision of American democracy.

Later in his address, in a professed effort to foster bipartisanship and unity after a divisive election, Obama declared to his Chicago audience that we ought to resist the urge to "fall back on the same partisanship and pettiness and immaturity that has poisoned our politics for so long." Obama urged us to recall that it was "a man from this state who first carried the banner of the Republican Party to the White House—a party founded on the values of self-reliance and individual liberty and national unity." We all share these values, Obama claimed, but it is the Democratic Party, with a "measure of humility and determination," that will "heal the divides that have held back our progress." Obama drove the idea home by suggesting that we must remember Lincoln's words, offered to "a nation far more divided than ours: 'We are not enemies, but friends—though passion may have strained it must not break our bonds of affection."⁹ Obama is surely correct to note that the nation was "far more divided" when Lincoln uttered these famous words in his First Inaugural Address, as the nation was descending into civil war. Obama suggested that, while we may not be as divided as the nation was in 1861, we are a divided nation desperately in need of unification, in need of a leader—a second Lincoln—to unite us, just like Lincoln. Yet, do not Lincoln's words arguably lose some of their import and forcefulness when used in this manner? Statements like these might lead some observers to conclude that Obama's use of Lincoln is little more than an unreflective appeal to authority or a simple attempt to dress up speeches without much intellectual seriousness or content.

However, there is in fact something serious about Obama's appeal to Lincoln. His appeal to the language of the Gettysburg Address in his victory speech illustrates a serious claim. Simply put, Obama claims to have inherited the Lincoln legacy. Like many before him, Obama claims to follow in Lincoln's footsteps, as the embodiment of Lincoln's understanding of popular government. This compels us to consider carefully Obama's Lincoln, rather than dismiss it as "mere" rhetoric. Similar to that of his progressive and modern liberal progenitors, Obama's appeal to Lincoln forces us to consider fundamental questions about the nature and purpose of American democracy.

Perhaps the most serious and illuminating of Obama's reflections on Lincoln's legacy appears in his 2006 best seller, *The Audacity of Hope: Thoughts on Reclaiming the American Dream*. Here Obama suggests that Lincoln's political thought is central to his own understanding of the purposes and practice of American democracy. To understand Obama's Lincoln, one must see how Lincoln is situated in Obama's narrative of American political history. This prompts us, necessarily, first to examine Obama's discussion of the American Founding, in a chapter entitled "Values":

> "We hold these truths to be self-evident, that all men are created equal, that they are endowed by their Creator with certain unalienable Rights, that among these are Life, Liberty, and the pursuit of Happiness." Those simple words are our starting point as Americans; they describe not only the foundation of our government but the substance of our common creed. Not every American may be able to recite them; few, if asked, could trace the genesis of the Declaration of Independence to its roots in eighteenth-century liberal and republican thought. But the essential idea behind the Declaration—that we are born into this world free, all of us; that each of us arrives with a bundle of

rights that can't be taken away by any person or any state without just cause; that through our own agency we can, and must, make our lives what we will—is one that every American understands. It orients us, sets our course, each and every day.[10]

Immediately shifting from the Declaration's language of self-evident truths, Obama condenses the "essential idea" behind the Declaration to the "value of individual freedom." He claims that this value is engrained so deeply in Americans that we take it for granted and we often forget how radical this idea was at the time of the nation's Founding. He suggests that, at the most elemental level, we commonly understand our liberty in a "negative sense," that is, as the right to be left alone; we are suspicious of those "who want to meddle in our business." But we also understand our liberty in a "more positive sense as well, in the idea of opportunity and the subsidiary values that help realize opportunity." We believe in the "values of self-reliance and self-improvement and risk-taking . . . drive, discipline, temperance, and hard work . . . thrift and personal responsibility." Americans possess a confidence that, so long as individuals are free to pursue their own interests, society will prosper. Obama argues that the "legitimacy of our government and our economy depend on the degree to which these values are rewarded, which is why the values of equal opportunity and nondiscrimination complement rather than impinge on our liberty."[11]

Obama suggests, however, that our individualism is necessarily tempered by a "set of communal values" such as family and cross-generational obligations, patriotism, and the obligations of citizenship. Our individualism is moderated by a "faith in something bigger than ourselves, whether that something expresses itself in formal religion or ethical precepts," and our value of a "constellation of behaviors that express our mutual regard for one another: honesty, fairness, humility, kindness, courtesy, and compassion." Obama thoughtfully suggests that our individualistic and communal values stand in constant tension, and most of American politics is an attempt to navigate these tensions as best we can. In rhetoric reminiscent of Lincoln, Obama suggests that we cannot entirely avoid these tensions in our political life, and finding the right balance is often difficult.[12]

According to Obama, navigating these persistent tensions requires deliberation and compromise, and there is a danger in doctrinairism. There is a danger in expecting to remake the world in light of abstractions. A thoughtful politics, for Obama, appears to begin with a preference for the notion of "values" over the certainty of "ideology." He suggests that "Values are faithfully applied to the facts before us, while ideology overrides whatever facts call theory into question."[13] Part of the genius of the American Founders, Obama claims, resides in their "rejection of absolute truth," implied in the structure of the Constitution and the "very idea of ordered liberty." In a chapter entitled "Our Constitution," Obama suggests that the Founders were practical statesmen who rejected the "infallibility of any idea or ideology or theology or 'ism,' any tyrannical consistency that might lock future generations into a single, unalterable course, or drive both majorities and minorities into the cruelties of the Inquisition, the pogrom, the gulag, or the jihad." Suspicious of abstraction, the Founders preferred "fact and necessity" to "theory" at nearly every turn in the early history of the republic.[14]

This view of the Founders' political thought, however, is not Obama's last word on the principles and practice of the American Founding. According to Obama, the Founders envisioned a deliberative government in which to marry reason and passion, individual freedom and the demands of the community. Only once, Obama reminds us, has the conversation broken down completely, and that was over the one subject the Founders "refused to talk about." The spirit of liberty, Obama suggests, did not extend, "in the minds of the Founders, to the slaves who worked their fields, made their beds, and nursed their children." Deliberation alone could not free the slave. Ultimately, "it was the sword that would sever his chains."[15] Here Obama offers what seems to be a candid admission of his struggle in thinking about the principles of the American Founding, and he asks us to consider what this says about our democracy. We are familiar with the alternative opinions.

There are some, Obama explains, who would simply label the Founders hypocrites and the Constitution a betrayal of the noble principles of the Declaration. Others might take the "safer, more conventional wisdom" that constitutional compromises with slavery were an unfortunate necessity in forming the Union and framing a Constitution that left room for the ultimate abolition of slavery and the Reconstruction Amendments. If asked to choose sides in this debate, Obama candidly admits that, as "an American with the blood of Africa coursing through my veins, . . I can't." Obama states that he loves America too much to focus entirely on the "circumstances of its birth," yet neither can he "brush aside the magnitude of the injustice done, or ignore the ghosts of generations past, or ignore the open wound, the aching spirit, that ails this country still." Obama admits that the best he can do, in the face of America's past, is to recognize that it has not always been the pragmatist, the voice of reason, or the force of compromise that has created the conditions for liberty.[16]

Rather, sometimes liberty and justice have been the result of "unbending idealists" such as William Lloyd Garrison, Frederick Douglass, or John Brown, "the cranks, the zealots, the prophets, the agitators, and the unreasonable—in other words, the absolutists—that have fought for a new order." Obama claims that he cannot summarily dismiss those possessed of similar certainty in today's politics, from the antiabortion activist to the animal rights activist. Obama summarizes his position in suggesting that "I am robbed even of the certainty of uncertainty—for sometimes absolute truths may well be absolute." In the face of this dilemma, Obama concludes:

> I'm left then with Lincoln, who like no man before or since understood both the deliberative function of our democracy and the limits of such deliberation. We remember him for the firmness and depth of his convictions—his unyielding opposition to slavery and his determination that a house divided could not stand. But his presidency was guided by a practicality that would distress us today, a practicality that led him to test various bargains with the South in order to maintain the Union without war. . . . I like to believe that for Lincoln, it was never a matter of abandoning conviction for the sake of expediency. Rather, it was a matter of maintaining within himself the balance between two contradictory ideas—that we must talk and reach for common understandings, precisely because all of us are imperfect and can never act with the certainty that God is on our side; and yet at times we must act nonetheless, as if we are certain, protected from error only by providence.[17]

Obama suggests that Lincoln's humility led him to advance his principles through the framework of American democracy, through reason, speeches, and debate. And when the war came, this humility allowed Lincoln to resist the temptation to demonize the South, or to diminish the horror of war. According to Obama, the "blood of slaves reminds us that our pragmatism can sometimes be moral cowardice. Lincoln, and those buried at Gettysburg, remind us that we should pursue our own absolute truths only if we acknowledge that there may be a terrible price to pay."[18]

Now, there is clearly much to consider here. Obama's turn to Lincoln is sophisticated and thoughtful, and he appears to understand that Lincoln's thoughts and deeds illustrate the tension between idealism and political necessity. Yet it is interesting—and I think instructive—to consider Obama's turn to Lincoln in light of his discussion on the American idea of liberty and the principles of the American Founding. Here, we should remind ourselves of just why Obama suggests he is "left with Lincoln." Obama is left with

Lincoln in response to what he presents as an intractable dilemma posed by the Founders' constitutional compromises with the institution of slavery. He is left with Lincoln while being robbed of the "certainty of uncertainty" and afforded the insight that "absolute truths may well be absolute."

If I understand Obama correctly, he seems to suggest that Lincoln did not abandon his "conviction" but, rather, recognized that a healthy respect for the practical demands of politics necessarily tempers any attempt to realize perfection in politics. Thus, it appears that, for Obama, Lincoln represents a middle ground between the Founders, who compromised with slavery out of either hypocrisy or necessity, and abolitionists such as Garrison and Brown, who would destroy the Constitution in the name of equality and justice. But Obama's discussion is hard to follow here for a few reasons, not the least of which is the seeming contradiction between his statement that the Founders "refused to talk" about slavery and his recognition of the constitutional compromises on the institution. Compromise would seem to suggest that the Founders did talk about the issue and we see the fruits of those compromises in the Constitution itself.

The slavery provisions in the Constitution do not just illustrate a "compromise" in the sense that antislavery forces merely accommodated the institution of slavery in order to get the document ratified by the southern states. Rather, provisions such as the three-fifths compromise, the ability of Congress ultimately to abolish the importation of slaves, and the absence of explicit references to "race" and "slave" in the original, un-amended Constitution and the Bill of Rights, suggest that the Founders did indeed talk about slavery. Despite Obama's references to his Lincolnian guidance in this matter, Lincoln understood this fact, as any reading of the Lincoln-Douglas debates would suggest. Moreover, to suggest that the Founders refused to include the slave in the "spirit of liberty" contradicts Lincoln's forceful argument to the contrary in those debates, his speech on the *Dred Scott* decision, and elsewhere.[19] In this Obama sounds more like Stephen Douglas, Roger Taney, or a contemporary historian or law professor than he does Abraham Lincoln.

Obama's struggle with the Founding and slavery is less apparent in his powerful 2008 speech on race, "To Form a More Perfect Union." Responding to the firestorm of controversy over his association with Revered Jeremiah Wright, Obama began his address by suggesting that the Founders' Constitution "was eventually signed but ultimately unfinished. It was stained by this nation's original sin of slavery, a question that divided the colonies and brought the convention to a stalemate until the founders chose to allow the slave trade to continue for at least twenty more years, and to leave any final resolution to future generations." In Lincolnian-sounding language Obama suggested, "the answer to the slavery question was already embedded within our Constitution—a Constitution that had at its very core the ideal of equal citizenship under the law; a Constitution that promised its people liberty, and justice, and a union that could be and should be perfected over time."[20]

Nevertheless, in *The Audacity of Hope,* Obama's discussion of the principles of the American Founding is curious. He is surely correct to note that the Founders understood there is a necessary disjunction between theory and practice that ought to guide statesmen in their actions. But to suggest that the Founders rejected the notion of absolute truth is simply mistaken. Even a cursory reading of the Founders on the first principles of American government would suggest this is the case. Obama's assertion here is just plain odd, and one wonders what he is suggesting. One would assume that Obama is not ignorant of the facts here. Assuming this, is he suggesting that the Founders might have deliberately said one thing but believed another? That might be tantamount to a charge of hypocrisy, which is of course not uncommon. Or is Obama suggesting that the Founders professed a belief in absolute truth, but that they unknowingly rejected this position in their design of the Constitution? If this is the case, then Obama claims to understand the Founders better than they understood themselves, and better than they were understood by Lincoln. There remains, of course, the possibility that Obama simply appeals to the Founders to support his own positions, purposefully misleading his audience in his discussion of the Founders and "absolute truth."

In any event, Obama's discussion here seems to equate a respect for the messiness of practice with a rejection of principles that might be true everywhere and always. But a statesmanlike suspicion of abstraction surely does not necessitate the rejection of absolute truth. Are we somehow to conclude that the Founders did not believe the self-evident truth that all men are created equal was "absolutely" true? By denying the place of abstract truth in the political theory of the Founding, Obama seems to do to the Founders what Woodrow Wilson did to Abraham Lincoln. As Kesler has argued, Obama appears to suggest that one of the great merits of the American Founders is that they had principles, but they did not believe in those principles too strongly.[21]

Part of the problem here seems to reside in Obama's overall presentation of the principles of the Declaration of Independence. We recall that, in *The*

Audacity of Hope, Obama refers to the words of the Declaration: "We hold these truths to be self-evident, that all men are created equal, that they are endowed by their Creator with certain unalienable Rights, that among these are Life, Liberty, and the pursuit of Happiness." However, Obama offers little discussion of the fact that Lincoln and the Founders held these truths to be inferences from the Laws of Nature and Nature's God, applicable to all human beings, in all places, at all times. Despite Obama's claim to follow Lincoln, no one has summed up the Founders' understanding here better than Lincoln himself, who routinely praised the Founders' dedication to an "abstract truth, applicable to all men and all times."[22] Despite his various claims to carry on Lincoln's legacy, Obama departs significantly from Lincoln's understanding of the Founders and their principles.

It is important to note that, rather than focus on Lincoln and the Founders' understanding of natural rights as self-evident truths, Obama repeatedly refers to the "values" of American democracy rather than to its "truths." Although he does quote the self-evident truths of the Declaration, his discussion quickly turns toward the "values" of the Declaration.[23] For Obama, "values" are part of the language of tolerance and consensus while "truth" is the language of intolerance and conflict. Indeed, we recall that Obama presents the language of absolute truth as the language of "the Inquisition, the pogrom, the gulag, or the jihad." Despite much discussion of rights in *The Audacity of Hope,* Obama pays little attention to the idea of natural rights. By ignoring the crucial importance of natural rights to the political thought of the Founders, Obama ignores the real root of their understanding—and of Lincoln's understanding—of the phrase "all men are created equal." Indeed, despite his claim to follow Lincoln, Obama robs any discussion he might offer on Lincoln of the core elements of Lincoln's own understanding of free government. One cannot help but be reminded of previous attempts in progressive political rhetoric to invoke Lincoln while ignoring or recasting the substance of his political thought.

We should also note the absence of the term *prudence* in Obama's discussion here. While Obama refers to Lincoln's "practicality," to the best of my knowledge he does not refer to Lincoln as "prudent." Perhaps the reason is revealed in Obama's discussion of "values." Obama suggests that values are distinct from ideology. Values, he argues, are applied to the facts before them. Ideology is associated with a rigid doctrinairism. Obama's chosen rhetoric of values is post-Founding and post-Lincoln, but it is the stock and trade of today's political rhetoric. Lincoln and the Founders would have relied on prudence, or practical wisdom, in applying political principles to the facts before them. In their way of thinking, prudence would consist in applying abstract principles of natural right to the practical circumstances at hand. For example, as we have seen, for Lincoln the natural equality of all men in their natural and inalienable rights is true everywhere and always, but how that truth might be applied in practice is not always so clear. Obama's discussion of values would appear to imply a certain flexibility in the principles themselves.

Obama does eventually suggest in his discussion of slavery that "absolute truths may well be absolute." But his discussion ends with a reference to Lincoln's handling of the slavery crisis and the claim that we "pursue our own absolute truths only if we acknowledge that there may be a terrible price to pay." We might ask what this means—*our own* absolute truths. Is the standard by which we judge the "absoluteness" of truth the strength of our belief? Is Obama suggesting that new truths come into being that did not apply to other generations? Is "truth" simply relative? Obama leaves all of this unclear. Even in the face of his brief consideration of the thought that "absolute truths may well be absolute," perhaps for Obama, the principles of the Declaration—Lincoln's principles—are a matter of "truth" only insofar as they are a matter of "conviction." As we have seen in examining Lincoln's staunch defense of human equality, his defense of an abstract truth applicable to all men at all times, Lincoln clearly would not have agreed. After all, many in the South believed deeply in their denial of natural equality, and they showed just as much "conviction" as Lincoln did in affirming that equality.

There is something admirable and insightful about Obama's appreciation for a sensible mean between a fanatical doctrinairism and a simple expediency in politics. But, despite his attempt to praise Lincoln's "values" and the "values" of the Declaration, on the basis of Obama's discussion it appears difficult to distinguish why we should prefer these values to other, opposing values that would threaten them. The language of values springs from a modern moral relativism that Obama seems careful to court in his political rhetoric, but this tradition rejects any objective standard, any "absolute truth," by which to distinguish the higher from the lower, the better from the worse, in the face of practical circumstances. Obama's professed struggle with absolute truth, his struggle in maintaining his well-meant "certainty of uncertainty," illustrates the inherent difficulty in attempting to defend something as right or just in the face of the modern values rhetoric of moral relativism. This values rhetoric not only confuses Obama's discussion of the Founders but it distances him from his professed example of statesmanship, Abraham Lincoln.

Obama, Lincoln, and "Equality of Opportunity"

Obama revisits Lincoln in *The Audacity of Hope* in a chapter entitled "Opportunity." Here, he reminds us of Lincoln's support for federal investment in railroads, canals, and other internal improvements, land grant colleges, the Homestead Act, science, and technology. Such investments helped to integrate the national economy and extend "the ladders of opportunity downward to reach more and more people." Obama rightly recognizes that Lincoln embraced internal improvements and technological and scientific innovation as part of his broader support for free labor and equality of opportunity. Obama suggests that, for Lincoln, "the resources and power of the national government can facilitate, rather than supplant, a vibrant free market."[24]

Lincoln's politics is presented, once again, as a kind of compromise between two strands of thought, between free markets and governmental regulation of the national economy. According to Obama, we do not "have to choose between an oppressive, government-run economy and a chaotic and unforgiving capitalism . . . we should be asking ourselves what mix of policies will lead to a dynamic free market and widespread economic security, entrepreneurial innovation and upward mobility." Recalling Lincoln's 1854 Fragments on Government, Obama suggests that we can be guided by "Lincoln's simple maxim: that we will do collectively, through our government, only those things that we cannot do as well or at all individually and privately. In other words, we should be guided by what works."[25] One is reminded of Franklin Roosevelt's appeal to the same fragments. But, in case the connection does not spring readily to mind, Obama makes the Lincoln-FDR-Obama connection for us. He suggests that, by following Lincoln, we might "rebuild the social contract that FDR first stitched together in the middle of the last century." While Lincoln had laid "the groundwork for a fully integrated national economy" during the Civil War, it was only "during the stock market crash of 1929 and the subsequent Depression that the government's vital role in regulating the marketplace became fully apparent."[26]

As Thomas Krannawitter shrewdly observes, for Obama it seems that while Lincoln first envisioned the principles of the New Deal's pragmatic liberalism, Franklin Roosevelt first put them into practice. Obama, Krannawitter suggests, follows in the tradition of FDR and the New Deal while "ignoring altogether the natural rights social contract that the Founders established and Lincoln defended."[27] Krannawitter's observation here helps us again to see the real indebtedness of Obama's politics to the political thought of FDR and his predecessor Woodrow Wilson. FDR, we recall, had followed Wilson in redefining the "social contract" of the Declaration by claiming that our most essential rights are the result of a bargain struck between the governed and their rulers. For Wilson and FDR, the liberty of the Declaration is the liberty to redefine continually the terms of the social contract in light of growing and changing circumstances, and the task of statesmanship is the continual redefinition of rights in light of those circumstances.[28]

Wilson and FDR had sought to redefine the Declaration's social contract, denaturing the rights professed therein, so as to render the Declaration consistent with progressive and pragmatic liberal principles. However, as Krannawitter observes, Obama simply ignores the Declaration's natural rights social contract. Indeed, in *The Audacity of Hope,* while Obama quotes the first sentence of the Declaration in his discussion of its "values," nowhere does he mention the description of the social contract that follows. Rather, he chooses to discuss FDR's social contract and the redefinition of rights in light of a growing and changing social order. Rather than explicitly reinterpret the Declaration's social contract himself, Obama merely stands upon and presumes the persuasiveness of FDR's reinterpretation of the social contract and the legitimacy of FDR's bill of economic rights.

Here, it is useful to note that Obama returned to Lincoln's Fragments on Government in "What the People Need Done," his highly anticipated speech in Springfield for the Bicentennial of Lincoln's birth in February 2009:

> Possibly in his law office, his feet on a cluttered desk, his sons playing around him, his clothes a bit too small to fit his uncommon frame . . . [Lincoln] put some thoughts on paper, and for what purpose we do not know: "The legitimate object of government," he wrote, "is to do for the people what needs to be done, but which they can not, by individual effort, do at all, or do so well, by themselves." To do for the people what needs to be done but which they cannot do on their own. It's a simple statement. But it answers a central question of Abraham Lincoln's life. Why did he land on the side of union? What was it that made him so unrelenting in pursuit of victory that he was willing to test the Constitution he ultimately preserved? What was it that led this man to give his last full measure of devotion so that our nation might endure?

Although Obama said he cannot answer these questions with certainty, he claimed to suspect that Lincoln's devotion to union did not come from a belief that government is the answer to all problems. Nor did it stem from a lack of appreciation for the rights and responsibilities of individual citizens. Rather, Obama claimed, Lincoln's devotion to union came from his understanding that there are simply things that we cannot achieve through individual effort or initiative. There are certain things only a union can do.[29]

Only a union, Obama argued, could have harnessed the courage of the western pioneers, which is why Lincoln passed the Homestead Act. Only a union could truly foster the ingenuity of American farmers, and Lincoln set up land grant colleges to give "their children an education that let them dream the American dream." Only a union could speed westward expansion, and Lincoln fostered this expansion by building railroads. Lincoln fueled new enterprises with a national currency, technological innovations, and a national academy of sciences. According to Obama, only a union could "serve the hopes of every citizen—to knock down the barriers to opportunity and give each and every person the chance to pursue the American dream." According to Obama, Lincoln understood what Washington, FDR, and Kennedy all understood, that "[t]here isn't any dream beyond our reach . . . any obstacle that can stand in our way, when we recognize that our individual liberty is served, not negated, by a recognition of the common good."[30]

For Obama, it is this recognition, this "spirit" that must be reinvigorated if we are to face the problems of the current day—two wars, an economic crisis, unemployment, lost pensions, rising health care costs, failing schools, and an energy crisis. But Obama suggests that, while these challenges are new, they did not spring up overnight. Rather, "they result from a failure to meet the test that Lincoln set." Obama conceded that there have been times in our history when government "misjudged what we can do by individual effort alone, and what we could only do together." But he argued that in recent years we have seen the "pendulum swing too far in the opposite direction." In recent years, we have witnessed a "knee-jerk disdain for government," a "constant rejection of any common endeavor." Such an attitude, Obama claimed, cannot help us live up to Lincoln's charge. Apparently suggesting that in our recent past we have ceased to be a union, or that we are dangerously on the brink of ceasing to be a union, Obama proclaimed that only a union can meet the challenges of today. According to Obama, only by "coming together to do what people need done" will we, "in Lincoln's words, 'lift artificial weights from all shoulders [and give] an unfettered start, and a fair chance, in the race of life.'"[31]

Obama's appeal to the race of life metaphor and his call for greater equality of opportunity is characteristic of the progressive and modern liberal appeal to the Lincoln image. His appeals to Lincoln's Fragments on Government should again remind one of FDR's attempts to invoke Lincoln's authority during the New Deal. Indeed, the bulk of Obama's reading of Lincoln appears especially indebted to FDR's rhetorical use and abuse of Lincoln.[32]

We have observed in previous chapters that Lincoln surely understood that the common good might necessitate that government sometimes help people provide for themselves. With the obvious exceptions of Obama's call for nationwide access to broadband lines and solutions to the twenty-first-century energy crisis, the political goods to be secured in Obama's understanding of good government are, in many respects, the standard listing of goods espoused by progressives and modern liberals. For the most part, throughout *The Audacity of Hope*, in his presidential campaign rhetoric, and in his speeches as president, Obama urges something approaching the second, or "economic," bill of rights put forth in FDR's Commonwealth Club address and 1944 State of the Union Address.[33] Obama's rhetoric here reminds us of FDR's claim that necessitous men are not free men. For Obama, as for FDR, if men are to be free, they must live beyond necessity. Following in the tradition of Wilson, Dewey, and FDR, government must provide for the necessities of life so that citizens can concentrate on fulfilling their potential for individual self-development.[34]

Obama has often been careful to suggest that a hasty or unexamined endorsement of government entitlements and spending is just as dangerous as a hasty or unexamined reaction against government entitlements and spending. He consistently suggests that government is not the answer to every problem we might confront. On this point, he often claims to be guided by Lincoln's "practicality," what might elsewhere be termed prudence. Like Lincoln, Obama would seem to understand that there is no theoretical solution that neatly solves such questions; rather, government's role in helping to secure the conditions for citizens' well-being might depend upon the nature of the times, and upon the particular circumstances confronting us. Obama would famously suggest in the 2008 presidential debates with John McCain that health care should be a right for every American. However, as Kesler rightly suggests, in *The Audacity of Hope* Obama seems careful to avoid referring to FDR's socioeconomic goods as "rights." Rather, such goods are referred to as part of "opportunity." Since there are very few guarantees in life, people ought to be able to count on a job that pays the bills, on health care when they get sick, on a pension when they retire, and on an education for their children. As Kesler argues, while these things do not appear to be "rights," Obama does refer to them as guarantees, or at least as goods that government will help guarantee. Such goods are thought to allow one to take advantage of opportunities or at least to provide one with security when those opportunities do not work out. For Kesler, the difficulty here is that the logic of these provisions is not very different—in fact it is hard to distinguish—from the logic of FDR's socioeconomic rights. This might help us to understand Obama's ambiguity on this matter. On the one hand, Obama knows that politically there is sometimes a backlash against the language of entitlements, but when asked by moderator Tom Brokaw in the presidential debates if health care should be a right, Obama responded in the affirmative.[35]

Now, Obama's distance from Lincoln here is worth observing, although we admittedly cover familiar territory in doing so. Obama's attempt to invoke Lincoln mirrors FDR's attempt to do the same, and as such it encounters similar difficulties. Despite his occasional calls for the need to balance our aspirations with the realities of political practice, in his rhetoric Obama no less than FDR runs the risk of conflating the ends of government with the means of government, at least as these things were understood by Lincoln and the Founders. For Lincoln, the ends of government—securing natural and inalienable rights—were clear and non-negotiable. The means by which those rights are best secured were understood, by Lincoln, to be subject to deliberation and the dictates of prudence.[36]

In his Lincoln Bicentennial Address, Obama's take on Lincoln's thoughts on the purpose of government is directly tied to the idea that Lincoln sought to lift artificial weights from all shoulders, to afford all citizens a fair and unfettered chance in the race of life. Similar to FDR, Obama seems to suggest that equality of opportunity is not secured unless the results of the exercise of our rights are equalized among individuals. But as we have observed, nothing in Lincoln's political thought appears to suggest such a view. Again, we should recognize that Lincoln's equality is best understood as an equality of opportunity that accepts, indeed necessitates, an inequality of outcomes or results among individuals. By removing artificial weights, men are afforded equal liberty to express diverse and unequal talents in pursuing their interests, with the expectation that there will be unequal results among individuals in that pursuit.[37] In the immediate context facing Lincoln, this largely meant removing the artificial weights of slavery in favor of a free labor system. One can read Obama's treatment of Lincoln and almost forget that Lincoln's thoughts on equality of opportunity were voiced primarily against slavery. This is similar to previous attempts on the part of progressives to incorporate Lincoln's equality rhetoric, and we have seen that the relatively narrow focus of Lincoln's understanding of equality often served as an obstacle to those attempts.

Previous progressive and modern liberal presidents also employed the race of life metaphor to suggest their kinship with Lincoln's vision of American government, and Obama stands on their shoulders. Teddy Roosevelt sought to invoke Lincoln's legacy in arguing for a "practical equality of opportunity." Woodrow Wilson appealed to Lincoln to argue for an equalization of the "conditions of opportunity for self-development." FDR used the Lincoln image to call for "equality in the pursuit of happiness" through a new economic bill of rights. Lyndon Johnson called on Lincoln's American promise in his efforts explicitly to redefine the pursuit of equality from an equality of opportunity to an equality of results. In each of these instances, Lincoln's individual-regarding equality of opportunity under the rule of law either was transformed into an argument for equality of results or was gutted of the natural rights and limited government principles necessary to defend it from such a transformation. Obama follows in this tradition as he appeals to Lincoln's rhetoric of equal opportunity only to argue for ideas that depart from Lincoln's understanding of natural rights, limited government, and the standard maxim of equality.

However desirable or necessary goods such as health care, living wages, pensions, and education might be, these things were simply not understood by Abraham Lincoln as being fundamental rights in and of themselves, nor did he understand such goods as "guarantees" that must necessarily be provided by government. Lincoln did think that government ought to help secure goods that the people cannot secure in their separate and individual capacities. But, as we have observed, this concerns the means rather than the ends of government. Following FDR, this distinction is blurred in Obama's rhetoric, as are the distinctions between equality of rights and equality of results—and between natural inalienable rights and entitlements. Moreover, we must reiterate that nowhere does Lincoln present the security of such goods by government as a necessary imperative of the pursuit of equality of opportunity under the rule of law. It might often be difficult to conclude how Lincoln might have responded to our current day challenges. But to imply, as Obama does, that Lincoln's support of federal investments in infrastructure, science and technology, or education is necessarily equivalent to a support for every spending or entitlement program he advocates is simply unpersuasive.

Conclusion

In the concluding passages of *The Audacity of Hope,* Obama notes that, in his work in Washington, DC, he sometimes feels useful to his family and to those who elected him. Sometimes, he feels as if he might leave behind a legacy that will make our children's lives more hopeful than our own. Yet, other times, Obama suggests, it seems as if this goal "recedes from me, and all the activity I engage in—the hearings and speeches and press conferences and position papers—are an exercise in vanity, useful to no one."[38] Obama claims that when he is in such moods, he takes a run along the Mall early in the evening. He usually stops at the Washington Monument, sometimes at the National World War II Memorial, continues along the reflecting pool, and eventually up the stairs of the Lincoln Memorial. On such evenings he stands between the marble columns of the often empty memorial and reads the Gettysburg Address and Lincoln's Second Inaugural. Imagining the immense crowd of people listening to Martin Luther King, Obama looks out over the Reflecting Pool, across the way to the Washington Monument and the Capitol Dome.[39] Obama concludes this passage, and *The Audacity of Hope,* with the following statement:

> And in that place, I think about America and those who built it. This nation's founders, who somehow rose above petty ambitions and narrow calculations to imagine a nation unfurling across a continent. And those like Lincoln and King, who ultimately laid down their lives in the service of perfecting an imperfect union. And all the faceless, nameless men and women, slaves and soldiers and tailors and butchers, constructing lives for themselves and their children and grandchildren, brick by brick, rail by rail, calloused hand by calloused hand, to fill in the landscape of our collective dreams. It is that process I wish to be a part of. My heart is filled with love for this country.[40]

Obama chooses to end *The Audacity of Hope* with beautiful and inspirational language. One can imagine him, like many other Americans, standing on the steps of the Lincoln Memorial looking out over Washington with feelings of awe, reverence, and noble ambition.

Barack Obama is indeed a master of political rhetoric and his frequent appeals to Lincoln are often inspiring to many. Whether or not one agrees with his conclusions, his analysis of Lincoln in *The Audacity of Hope* illustrates a depth of thought that some might say is uncommon among many contemporary politicians. But Obama's Lincoln is ambiguous. He gives serious attention to Lincoln's understanding of the principles of American democracy, and he often appears to understand that Lincoln's standard maxim of equality calls for an equality of opportunity for individuals to express their individual talents in pursuit of their interests. Moreover, he sometimes seems to recognize that, according to Lincoln's thinking, this pursuit is necessarily limited by the necessities of political practice. But this only serves to highlight the degree to which Obama departs from Lincoln when, in other instances, he equates Lincoln's political thought with the principles of the progressives and modern liberalism. He is able to do this by selectively abstracting away from the natural rights constitutionalism that guided Lincoln's politics. In this Obama is treading on familiar territory, reusing and repackaging a Lincoln offered years ago in the writings and speeches of previous presidents. Obama's Lincoln, in many ways, is prepared by those who came before him. The progressives and FDR redefined Lincoln, recast him in the progressive mold, and offered a version well suited for Obama's use. But Obama's professed struggle with the political thought of the Founding also seems to find expression as a struggle with Lincoln. In each case, the problem resides in an attempt to square the circle, to reconcile progressive political principles with the natural right principles held by the Founders and by Abraham Lincoln. The ease with which Obama has managed to incorporate the Lincoln image into his political rhetoric and the degree to which academics, politicians, and journalists have enthusiastically accepted this incorporation without much question or criticism suggest that the progressives' Lincoln is still very much with us.

Conclusion

WHEN DAVID DONALD DESCRIBED the attempt within the American political tradition to "get right" with Lincoln, he recounted an effort on the part of American politicians to square their policies and ideas, indeed their understandings of what American democracy should be, with Abraham Lincoln's legacy.[1] Politically, the peak of that effort might have occurred during the Progressive Era and the New Deal. But the echoes of that effort and the debate it created still resonate today in academia, especially among historians and political scientists. For some, Donald's account might suggest nothing more than the simple fact that U.S. presidents and presidential candidates tend to appeal to common sources of authority, to common themes and objects of veneration, in order to get elected and gain support for their respective policy agendas, whatever those might be. Among such objects of veneration is the example of Abraham Lincoln; among such themes is the idea of equality as a goal to be secured in American society.

One might, of course, be tempted to stop there. One might suggest that the various appeals to the Lincoln example, wherever or whomever they may come from, are of no real consequence. One could argue that such rhetorical appeals are just that—mere rhetoric, in the most pejorative sense of the term. However, I believe this would be a mistake. In the foregoing discussion we have encountered fundamental questions concerning the nature and purpose of American democratic government. Lincoln, the progressives, FDR and the New Dealers, and Lyndon Johnson, all wrestled with fundamental problems and questions that cut to the heart of our core assumptions about what American democracy is and what it ought to be. The political rhetoric of Lincoln, and those after him who take up these questions, is instructive. Their rhetoric points us toward larger questions about human nature, the nature and basis of rights, the potentialities and limitations of human wisdom, and the nature and purpose of government. Among such concerns are what it means to suggest we are a nation dedicated to the proposition that all men are created equal and just what this dedication might entail as to the legitimate ends and means of American democracy. We confront these questions frequently in American political life today. President Obama's appeal to the Lincoln inheritance prompts us yet again to consider these questions in light of the lessons Lincoln might provide.

As I have attempted to demonstrate, Lincoln sought to secure individuals' equal liberty to exercise diverse and necessarily unequal talents and abilities in the pursuit of happiness, under rule of law. This dedication to equal liberty expects an inequality of results or outcomes among individuals in pursuit of their interests. Lincoln showed in both word and deed that this pursuit of equality ought to recognize the necessity of various political and constitutional goods in moderating democracy and the pursuit of equality itself. Lincoln's pursuit of equality recognized the worth of the constitutional forms and institutions that help to structure and shape a measured and sober popular government. A large measure of the duty of democratic statesmanship is to foster a moderate love of equality rather than to allow the passion for equality to prompt us to pursue equality at all costs, destroying the institutions that help to make free government possible.

Beginning in the Progressive Era, many who invoked Lincoln's name in the pursuit of modern egalitarian principles nevertheless rejected this Lincolnian understanding of equality. The progressives and their heirs argued consistently that the pursuit of new and expanded notions of egalitarianism necessitated an overcoming of the institutions that Lincoln believed fostered a healthy republican government. This pursuit was guided, above all, by a self-conscious and deliberate turning away from the natural rights principles and constitutionalism that lay beneath the Lincolnian notion of equality in favor of a push for equality under the rubric of progressive history. Appealing to the Lincoln image in their writings and speeches, the progressives and their heirs must reject, revise, or reinterpret Lincoln in order to incorporate the Lincoln image into the rhetoric of progress and modern egalitarianism.

Teddy Roosevelt moved away from the natural rights principles informing Lincoln's idea of equality to argue for devices of direct democracy that were aimed at securing progressive, egalitarian reforms, including the redistribution of wealth. Roosevelt rejected Lincoln's principles in favor of a historicist understanding of the American political tradition, in which majority faction was no longer seen as a danger in democratic government. Likewise, Woodrow Wilson's rhetorical use and abuse of Lincoln was necessarily intertwined with his Hegelian rejection of the natural rights basis of Lincolnian political thought. Wilson's Lincoln was no longer tied to natural rights principles that were held to be true everywhere and always. Rather, in Wilson's political rhetoric, Abraham Lincoln became a symbol and a personification of the doctrine of progress and the overcoming of those principles through the rhetorical leadership of the plebiscitary presidency.

In seeking to consolidate this new progressive vision of executive leadership for the American presidency, Franklin Roosevelt associated his Lincoln with the idea that the task of statesmanship is continually to redefine our most fundamental rights in light of a growing and changing social order. Roosevelt's Lincoln was not dedicated to the natural and inalienable rights of the Declaration as they had traditionally been understood. Rather, Roosevelt's Lincoln was dedicated to transfusing those rights with new meaning in light of change and progress. Although Roosevelt's redefinition of rights was limited mainly to the discovery, or creation, of certain economic rights, we have seen that this redefinition had far-reaching consequences.

Roosevelt's notion of statesmanship as the redefinition of rights took on new life in the political rhetoric of Lyndon Johnson's Great Society. Again, the 1964 Civil Rights Act and 1965 Voting Rights Act, as passed and construed by Congress, were compatible with Lincoln's notion of equality, but Johnson's rhetoric, in which the appeal to Lincoln played a very large role, pointed well beyond Lincoln's pursuit of equality. Expanding and building upon Roosevelt's notion of statesmanship, Johnson denied that Lincoln's equality of rights among individuals was still a sufficient goal for American society. Rather, Johnson departed from Lincoln's principles to call for an equality of results among groups. Whatever one might think as to the desirability or reasonableness of Johnson's policies, one must be skeptical of his claim that they follow in a Lincolnian tradition. The same is true today of President Obama's recurrent attempts to claim the Lincoln inheritance. Obama's understanding of the first principles of American democracy owes much to the progressives and FDR, which only serves to distance him from Lincoln, despite his repeated claims to carry on Lincoln's unfinished business.

We have seen that many academics and other observers on both the American left and right fundamentally agree that Lincoln was at least partly responsible for the rise of modern egalitarianism in twentieth-century American politics. Yet this agreement downplays or even misunderstands the real differences between Lincoln's notion of the standard maxim of equality and the modern egalitarianism of many who claim Lincoln's legacy. Before we assess Lincoln's contribution to the rise of modern egalitarianism, we ought first to try to understand Lincoln as he understood himself. That is to say, we should hesitate to agree with Lyndon Johnson that the importance of the Lincoln example resides exclusively in what he has "come to mean." We should refuse to follow in Herbert Croly's attempt to sum up Lincoln's contribution to American political development "whatever his [Lincoln's] theories were."[2] Surely, to assess Lincoln's contribution to the American political tradition might well require that we recognize the influence his rhetoric had on subsequent generations of politicians. And it is certainly worthwhile to consider how Lincoln's thought has been interpreted, and reinterpreted, over time. But in order to do this we must first attempt as best we can to understand Lincoln as he understood himself, and to do this through a direct engagement with Lincoln's words and deeds. Indeed, part of what this study has attempted to demonstrate is that what Lincoln has "come to mean" and what Lincoln actually said are often not at all the same thing.

The progressive and modern liberal appropriation of the Lincoln image begins with a rejection of the first principles of Lincoln's political thought. Nowhere is this more evident than in the progressive reinterpretation, in the denaturing, of the Declaration of Independence, illustrated in the political rhetoric of presidents such as Wilson and FDR.[3] In this progressive spin on the Declaration, our most fundamental rights—rights once claimed to be natural and inalienable—became rights "accorded" to us as the result of a deal struck between the people and their rulers. However, in Lincoln's political thought, the natural and equal possession of inalienable rights establishes the theoretical basis of the people's original right to give or withhold their consent to government and defines the rightful ends of that government. Absent this standard, the ends of government are open to perpetual redefinition, and any principled limits placed upon the means to which we might consent in pursuit of those ends no longer have any objective basis. This is the heart of Lincoln's defense of the principles of the Declaration against the Southern slave interest and the root of his understanding of limited, constitutional government.

Progressivism and modern liberalism's rejection of modern natural right thinking leads to an indifference to constitutionalism, separation of powers, and limited government. Again, the choice-worthiness of such institutional arrangements follows from the assumption that there is an enduring and necessarily imperfect human nature that we can comprehend through human reason. Our reason tells us that all men are born with inalienable rights, which by definition place limits upon government. Moreover, given the imperfections of human nature, our reason suggests that political power ought to be constitutionally balanced and limited. Insofar as these principles are rejected in light of historical progress, it is probable that limited constitutional government would be deemed obsolete. The modern pursuit of equality is severed from the Lincolnian idea that, rightly understood, the pursuit of equality is necessarily limited and tempered by these principles. The denial of an enduring and imperfect human nature, the rejection of the principle that all human beings are equally endowed with natural and inalienable rights, the radicalization of the pursuit of equality, and the willingness to alter constitutional forms and structures in this pursuit, are all intimately related.

Progressives and modern liberals have tried to appropriate the Lincoln image, but we must recognize the unavoidable fact that they believe Lincoln was fundamentally wrong in his understanding of the political world. Triumphantly standing at the end of history, progressives and modern liberals hold that Lincoln's natural rights principles have been superseded by progress. The only way to incorporate Lincoln into the rhetoric of modern egalitarianism is thus to ignore, misrepresent, or reinterpret his true principles. Often the method used is to claim to understand Lincoln better than he understood himself, historicizing Lincoln's thought. This historicizing of Lincoln is a consequence of the historicizing of ideas more generally, which always begs the ultimate question of how we might be so confident as to suggest that our own theories are somehow exempt from the historicism we use to survey and interpret all that has come before us.

Such thinking is in large measure because of the lasting influence of the progressive movement, in both its intellectual and its political components. The political movement produced lasting changes in our national institutions, and the intellectual movement continues to thrive today, particularly in the realm of the social sciences. An unqualified faith in progressive history still seems to prevail. We generally find an assumption that, in the grandest and most encompassing sense, hindsight is always 20/20. Thus, whatever Lincoln or any other figure might have thought they understood about the nature and purpose of government, we today in our historically enlightened state simply know more or better.

We have seen that this way of thinking is applied not only to Lincoln but to the equality he espoused. Like Lincoln himself, the idea of equality has come to be understood historically, as a progressive force marching through time, changing and shifting not merely in the particular expressions of equality but in its very meaning and foundation. Insofar as Lincoln's equality is rooted in the notion of natural rights that government is to secure, or in a belief in an enduring human nature, or in any other supposedly outmoded or anachronistic holdover from a bygone era, it must be subsumed by the historical development of the idea of equality. Insofar as Lincoln held that the pursuit of equal rights must be tempered by the demands of constitutionalism, separation of powers, representation, limited government, and government by consent of the governed, this belief is transcended in light of the progress of history. Such institutions are deemed unnecessary, serving only to frustrate genuine democracy and the pursuit of real equality. However, if we question the coherence of the historicist's claim to wisdom, if we are at least open to the possibility that Lincoln's principles really are true, then Lincoln might still have something to teach us about the principle of equality in a limited constitutional government.

Notes

Introduction

1. David H. Donald, *Lincoln Reconsidered* (1955; reprint, New York: Vintage Books, 1961), 3–18.

2. Abraham Lincoln, "Address delivered at the dedication of the Cemetery at Gettysburg," November 19, 1863, in *The Collected Works of Abraham Lincoln*, ed. Roy P. Basler, 9 vols. (New Brunswick, NJ: Rutgers University Press, 1953), 7:23.

3. On modern egalitarianism, see Martin Diamond, *As Far as Republican Principles Will Admit: Essays by Martin Diamond*, ed. William A. Schambra (Washington, DC: American Enterprise Institute Press, 1992), 241–57, 326–29; Harry V. Jaffa, *How to Think About the American Revolution: A Bicentennial Cerebration* (Durham, NC: Carolina Academic Press, 1978), 13–48; Thomas Sowell, *A Conflict of Visions* (New York: Basic Books, 2002), 129–50; Walter Berns, "Does the Constitution 'Secure These Rights'?" in *How Democratic Is the Constitution?* ed. Robert A. Goldwin and William A. Schambra (Washington, DC: American Enterprise Institute Press, 1980), 76–78; cf. Michael Parenti, "The Constitution as an Elitist Document," in Goldwin and Schambra, *How Democratic?* 39–58.

4. See Theodore Roosevelt, "The Heirs of Abraham Lincoln," speech at the Lincoln Day Banquet, New York City, February 12, 1913, in *The Works of Theodore Roosevelt*, National Edition, ed. Hermann Hagedorn, 20 vols. (New York: Charles Scribner's Sons, 1926), 17:364; cf. Abraham Lincoln, "Message to Congress in Special Session," July 4, 1861, in *Collected Works*, 4:438.

5. Franklin D. Roosevelt (hereafter FDR), "'A Tribute to Abraham Lincoln,' to Be Read on His Birthday," letter to the Lincoln Association of Cleveland, Ohio, January 25, 1936, in *The Public Papers and Addresses of Franklin D. Roosevelt*, ed. Samuel I. Rosenman, 13 vols. (New York: Random House, 1938–1950), 5:68 (emphasis added).

6. Lyndon B. Johnson, "Commencement Address at Howard University: 'To Fulfill These Rights,'" June 4, 1965, in *Public Papers of the Presidents of the United States: Lyndon B. Johnson, 1965*, 2 books (Washington, DC: United States Government Printing Office, 1966), 2:636.

1—Lincoln and the Idea of Equality

1. George P. Fletcher, *Our Secret Constitution: How Abraham Lincoln Redefined American Democracy* (New York: Oxford University Press, 2001), 2.

2. Ibid., 2, 3, 9.

3. James M. McPherson, *Abraham Lincoln and the Second American Revolution*

(New York: Oxford University Press, 1990), 64, 137. Also see Otto H. Olsen, "Abraham Lincoln as Revolutionary," *Civil War History* 25, no. 3 (September 1978): 213–24.

4. See Steven Hayward, "The Children of Abraham," *Reason* 23 (May 1991): 24–31. Fields's remarks are found in *The Civil War*, directed by Ken Burns, Florentine Films and WETA-TV, 1990, episode 9. Also see Mario M. Cuomo, *Why Lincoln Matters, Today More than Ever* (New York: Harcourt, 2004), 32–39, 99–115.

5. Burns is quoted in Hayward, "Children of Abraham," 26; cf. Ken Burns, interview by Charles McDowell, PBS, September 1990; Bernard A. Weisberger, "The Great Arrogance of the Present Is to Forget the Intelligence of the Past," *American Heritage* (September/October 1990): 97–102.

6. Thomas J. DiLorenzo, *The Real Lincoln: A New Look at Abraham Lincoln, His Agenda, and an Unnecessary War* (New York: Three Rivers Press, 2002), 2, 162, 163.

7. Ibid., 163. See Garry Wills, *Lincoln at Gettysburg: The Words That Remade America* (New York: Simon and Schuster, 1992), 38–39, 145–47.

8. See Wills, *Lincoln at Gettysburg*, 38–39, 145–47.

9. Joseph R. Fornieri, "Abraham Lincoln and the Declaration of Independence: The Meaning of Equality," in *Abraham Lincoln: Sources of Style and Leadership*, ed. Frank J. Williams, William J. Pederson, and Vincent Marsala (Westport, CT: Greenwood Press, 1994), 60; Garry Wills, *Inventing America: Jefferson's Declaration of Independence* (New York: Doubleday, 1978), xiii–xxvi. Also see Harry V. Jaffa, "Inventing the Gettysburg Address," *Intercollegiate Review* 28 (Fall 1992): 51–56.

10. Frank S. Meyer, "Lincoln without Rhetoric," *National Review*, August 24, 1965, 725; Frank S. Meyer, "Again on Lincoln," *National Review*, January 25, 1966, 71, 85. The latter of these articles is a response to Jaffa's rejoinder to the former. See Harry V. Jaffa, "Lincoln and the Cause of Freedom," *National Review*, September 21, 1965, 827–28, 842.

11. Meyer, "Again on Lincoln," 71, 85.

12. Meyer, "Lincoln without Rhetoric," 725.

13. M. E. Bradford, "The Heresy of Equality: Bradford Replies to Jaffa," *Modern Age* 20, no. 1 (Winter 1976): 62. As Bradford explains, this piece is a response to Harry V. Jaffa, "Equality as a Conservative Principle," *Loyola of Los Angeles Law Review* 8 (June 1975): 471–505, which is itself a critique of Willmoore Kendall and George W. Carey, *The Basic Symbols of the American Political Tradition* (Baton Rouge: Louisiana State University Press, 1970). Jaffa's "Equality as a Conservative Principle" is reprinted in Jaffa, *How to Think*, 13–48. Also see the response to Bradford in Jaffa, *How to Think*, 141–61.

14. Bradford, "Heresy of Equality," 69, 74, 75. Also see M. E. Bradford, "The Lincoln Legacy: A Long View," *Modern Age* 24, no. 4 (Fall 1980): 355–63.

15. See Kendall and Carey, *Basic Symbols*; Willmoore Kendall, "Equality and the American Political Tradition," in *Willmoore Kendall: Contra Mundum*, ed. Nellie D. Kendall (New Rochelle, NY: Arlington House, 1971), 347–61; Willmoore Kendall, "Equality: Commitment or Ideal?" *Phalanx* 1, no. 3 (Fall 1967): 95–103; Willmoore Kendall, *The Conservative Affirmation* (Chicago: Henry Regnery, 1963), 249–52.

16. Kendall, *Conservative Affirmation*, 252.

17. George W. Carey, "New Preface," *The Basic Symbols of the American Political Tradition*, by Willmoore Kendall and George W. Carey, paperback ed. (Washington, DC: Catholic University of America Press, 1995), ix.

18. Ibid., xv. In many respects, most of the preface might be read as a response to Jaffa's account of Lincoln and his reaction to Kendall and Carey's derailment thesis. See

Jaffa, *How to Think*, 13–48; Hayward, "Children of Abraham," 24–31; Fornieri, "Lincoln and the Declaration of Independence," 46–69. For a solid account of the differences—and the similarities—between Kendall and Jaffa, see John A. Murley, "On the 'Calhounism' of Willmoore Kendall," in Murley and Alvis, *Willmoore Kendall*, 99–139.

19. Carey, "New Preface," xvi. Carey cites Jaffa's work as representative of the first part of the rejoinder. See Harry V. Jaffa, *Crisis of the House Divided: An Interpretation of the Issues in the Lincoln-Douglas Debates* (1959; reprint, Chicago: University of Chicago Press, 1982); Harry V. Jaffa, *Equality and Liberty: Theory and Practice in American Politics* (New York: Oxford University Press, 1965); Harry V. Jaffa, *The Conditions of Freedom: Essays in Political Philosophy* (Baltimore: Johns Hopkins University Press, 1975); Jaffa, *How to Think*.

20. Carey, "New Preface," xv. Hayward is one of the few to question the progressive claim to Lincoln, and he rightly argues that Lincoln's equality is not to be confused with the views of equality espoused by the progressives and their heirs. Although he briefly discusses the appeal to Lincoln in Franklin Roosevelt and Mario Cuomo, he does not go into great detail regarding the progressive and modern liberal rhetorical appropriation of Lincoln. See Hayward, "Children of Abraham," 24–31. Likewise, without pointing to any specific instances, Kesler asserts that, invoking the Gettysburg Address, modern liberals often attribute non-Lincolnian notions of equality to Lincoln himself. See Charles R. Kesler, "Introduction," in *Keeping the Tablets: Modern American Conservative Thought*, ed. William F. Buckley, Jr., and Charles R. Kesler (New York: Harper and Row, 1988), 11. Recently, Thomas Krannawitter has taken up this topic and shares the thesis argued here, suggesting that, while the progressives indeed celebrated Lincoln, they did not celebrate his principles, which were the same principles as were held by the American Founders. See Thomas L. Krannawitter, *Vindicating Lincoln: Defending the Politics of Our Greatest President* (Lanham, MD: Rowman and Littlefield, 2008), esp. chapter 8, "The Father of Big Government?" 289–316.

21. Carey, "New Preface," xvi.

22. Ibid., xvi–xvii. See Abraham Lincoln, "Speech at Springfield, Illinois," June 26, 1857, in *Collected Works*, 2:406.

23. Carey, "New Preface," xix–xx. See Lincoln, "Speech at Springfield," June 26, 1857, 2:406; Lincoln, "Message to Congress in Special Session," 4:438.

24. Carey, "New Preface," xxi.

25. Leo Paul S. de Alvarez, "The Missing Passage of the Vanderbilt Lectures," in Murley and Alvis, *Willmoore Kendall*, 141–42; cf. Kesler, "Introduction," 11.

26. See Murley, "'Calhounism' of Willmoore Kendall," 122 (emphasis added). Also see Hayward, "Children of Abraham," 24–31; Fornieri, "Lincoln and the Declaration of Independence," 65–66.

27. Lincoln, "Speech at Springfield," June 26, 1857, 2:406.

28. Abraham Lincoln, "Speech at Peoria, Illinois," October 16, 1854, in *Collected Works*, 2:266 (original emphasis); Abraham Lincoln, "Speech at Chicago, Illinois," July 10, 1858, ibid., 2:499.

29. See John Locke, *The Second Treatise of Government: An Essay Concerning the True Original, Extent, and End of Civil Government*, in *Two Treatises of Government*, ed. Peter Laslett (Cambridge: Cambridge University Press, 1988), esp. §54: "Though I have said . . . That all men by nature are equal, I cannot be supposed to understand all sorts of equality: age or virtue may give men a just precedency: excellency of parts and merit may place others above the common level: birth may subject some, and alliance or benefits

others, to pay an observance to those to whom nature, gratitude, or other respects, may have made it due: and yet all this consists with the equality, which all men are in, in respect of jurisdiction or dominion one over another; which was the equality I there spoke of, as proper to the business in hand, being that equal right, that every man hath, to his natural freedom, without being subjected to the will or authority of any other man."

30. See Harry V. Jaffa, *A New Birth of Freedom: Abraham Lincoln and the Coming of the Civil War* (Lanham, MD: Rowman and Littlefield, 2000), 300.

31. Abraham Lincoln, "Fragment on Slavery," July 1, 1854, in *Collected Works*, 2:222–23.

32. Fornieri, "Lincoln and the Declaration of Independence," 57; Jaffa, *New Birth*, 300.

33. Abraham Lincoln, "To George B. Ide, James R. Doolittle, and A. Hubbell," May 30, 1864, in *Collected Works*, 7:368; Lincoln, "Fragment on Slavery," 2:222 (original emphasis); Abraham Lincoln, "Speech at Springfield, Illinois," October 4, 1854, in *Collected Works*, 2:245, 246 (original emphasis); cf. Lincoln, "Speech at Peoria," 2:264–65. Here I follow Larry Arnhart, *Darwinian Natural Right: The Biological Ethics of Human Nature* (Albany: State University of New York Press, 1998), 196–97.

34. James W. Ceaser, *Nature and History in American Political Development: A Debate* (Cambridge: Harvard University Press, 2006), 6, 24.

35. George Anastaplo, *Abraham Lincoln: A Constitutional Biography* (Lanham, MD: Rowman and Littlefield, 1999), 234, 330n473; Jaffa, *How to Think*, 45. See Locke, *Second Treatise*, chapter 5, 285–302.

36. Abraham Lincoln, "Speech at Springfield, Illinois," July 17, 1858, in *Collected Works*, 2:520; Abraham Lincoln, "Reply: First Debate with Stephen A. Douglas at Ottawa, Illinois," August 21, 1858, 3:16 (original emphasis); Abraham Lincoln, "Speech at Hartford, Connecticut," March 5, 1860, 4:9. See also Lincoln, "Speech at Peoria," 2:265–66, 270–71; "Fragment on Pro-slavery Theology," October 1, 1858, 3:204–5; and "Address before the Wisconsin State Agricultural Society, Milwaukee, Wisconsin," September 30, 1859, 3:479–80.

37. Abraham Lincoln, "Speech at New Haven, Connecticut," March 6, 1860, in *Collected Works*, 4:24.

38. See McPherson, *Second American Revolution*, 62–63, 137; Herman Belz, *Abraham Lincoln, Constitutionalism, and Equal Rights in the Civil War Era* (New York: Fordham University Press, 1998), 96. According to Belz, the Founders, Lincoln, and the framers of the Fourteenth Amendment all thought of equality "in relation to basic rights of person, property, and access to the legal system that enabled individuals to pursue their interests within the framework of ordered liberty." Ibid., 185.

39. Fornieri, "Lincoln and the Declaration of Independence," 55.

40. Jaffa, *How to Think*, 43–45; Kendall, *Conservative Affirmation*, 252.

41. Jaffa, *How to Think*, 43–45.

42. Abraham Lincoln, "Reply to New York Workingmen's Democratic Republican Association," March 21, 1864, in *Collected Works*, 7:259–60. One should note the difference on this point between Lincoln and modern historians such as Burns and Fields. As Hayward suggests, to imply as Fields does that Lincoln would regard the standard maxim of equality as "meaningless" as long as "some citizens live in houses and others live on the street" is surely incorrect. See Hayward, "Children of Abraham," 26, 29; Jaffa, *How To Think*, 45.

43. James Madison, "Federalist 10," in Alexander Hamilton, James Madison, and John Jay, *The Federalist*, ed. Jacob E. Cooke (Hanover, NH: Wesleyan University Press, 1982), 58. As Martin Diamond notes, this passage is not simply protective of existing patterns of wealth distribution, as it may appear to some contemporary readers. "Madison," Diamond claims, "is in fact concerned not to protect established wealth as such, but rather the process by which the 'faculties' continuously receive their due outcome." See Diamond, *Republican Principles*, 241–57, 386n6; Jaffa, *How to Think*, 45.

44. Lincoln, "Message to Congress in Special Session," 4:438. Also see Lincoln, "Speech at New Haven," 4:24; Abraham Lincoln, "Speech in Independence Hall, Philadelphia, Pennsylvania," February 22, 1861, in *Collected Works*, 4:240; Abraham Lincoln, "Speech to the One Hundred Sixty-Sixth Ohio Regiment," August 22, 1864, in *Collected Works*, 7:512.

45. Jaffa, *How to Think*, 148–49. Also see Krannawitter, *Vindicating Lincoln*, 311–12.

46. Diamond, *Republican Principles*, 255–57.

47. Richard J. Hofstadter, *The American Political Tradition and the Men Who Made It* (New York: Knopf, 1954), 16–17. Here I follow Hayward, "Children of Abraham," 26–27; Krannawitter, *Vindicating Lincoln*, 116–19.

48. Anastaplo, *Abraham Lincoln*, 234, 330n473.

49. Lincoln, "Speech at Springfield," June 26, 1857, 2:406; Lincoln, "Message to Congress in Special Session," 4:438; Abraham Lincoln, "Speech at a Republican Banquet, Chicago, Illinois," December 10, 1856, in *Collected Works*, 2:385.

50. Abraham Lincoln, "Reply: Seventh and Last Debate with Stephen A. Douglas at Alton, Illinois," October 15, 1858, in *Collected Works*, 3:303.

51. Abraham Lincoln, "Speech to the One Hundred Sixty-Fourth Ohio Regiment," August 18, 1864, in *Collected Works*, 7:505. According to Basler, the August 19, 1864, *New York Tribune* recorded this sentence as "There may be some *inequalities* in the practical working of our system" (emphasis added). Quoted in Lincoln, *Collected Works*, 7:505n2.

52. Lincoln, "One Hundred Sixty-Fourth Ohio Regiment," 505.

53. Abraham Lincoln, "Opinion on the Draft," September 14, 1863, in *Collected Works*, 6:448–49.

54. Ethan Fishman, "On Professor Donald's Lincoln," in *Lincoln's American Dream*, ed. Kenneth L. Deutsch and Joseph R. Fornieri (Washington, DC: Potomac Books, 2005), 233. Also see Ethan Fishman, "Under the Circumstances: Abraham Lincoln and Classical Prudence," in *Abraham Lincoln: Sources of Style and Leadership*, ed. Frank J. Williams, William J. Pederson, and Vincent Marsala (Westport: Greenwood Press, 1994), 3–15; Aristotle, *Nicomachean Ethics* VI.4–8 (1140a25–1142a30) in *The Basic Works of Aristotle*, ed. Richard McKeon (New York: Random House, 1941), 1026–30; St. Thomas Aquinas, *Summa Theologica* II.II.Q.47, A.2–3, in St. Thomas Aquinas, *Summa Theologica, Literally Translated by Fathers of the English Dominican Province* (New York: Benziger Brothers, 1947), 1390–91.

55. Joseph Fornieri, "Lincoln and the Emancipation Proclamation: A Model of Prudent Leadership," in *Tempered Strength: Studies in the Nature and Scope of Prudential Leadership*, ed. Ethan Fishman (Lanham, MD: Lexington Books, 2002), 127.

56. Abraham Lincoln, "Speech in the United States House of Representatives on Internal Improvements," June 20, 1848, in *Collected Works*, 1:484.

57. Lincoln, "Speech at Chicago," 2:501.

58. Lincoln asks "Why did those old men, about the time of the adoption of the Constitution, decree that Slavery should not go into the new Territory, where it had not

already gone? Why declare that within twenty years the African Slave Trade, by which slaves are supplied, might be cut off by Congress? Why were all these acts? I might enumerate more of these acts—but enough. What were they but a clear indication that the framers of the Constitution intended and expected the ultimate extinction of that institution?" See ibid., 492.

59. See, for example, Hofstadter, *American Political Tradition*, 93–136; Lerone J. Bennett, Jr., "Was Abe Lincoln a White Supremacist?" *Ebony* 23 (February 1968): 35–42; Lerone J. Bennett, Jr., *Forced into Glory: Abraham Lincoln's White Dream* (Chicago: Johnson Publishing, 2000); DiLorenzo, *The Real Lincoln*, 10–32; Michael Lind, *What Lincoln Believed: The Values and Convictions of America's Greatest President* (New York: Doubleday, 2004), 1–27, 191–232.

60. Fornieri, "Lincoln and the Emancipation Proclamation," 130–31, 139.

61. Ibid., 139–43. Also see Krannawitter, *Vindicating Lincoln*, 271–82.

62. Lincoln, "Speech at Peoria, Illinois," 2:256.

63. Fornieri, "Lincoln and the Emancipation Proclamation," 143–44; Jaffa, *Crisis*, 375–77. Also see Jaffa, *New Birth*, 228; Anastaplo, *Abraham Lincoln*, 197–227; Krannawitter, *Vindicating Lincoln*, 13–45. Lincoln's efforts toward black suffrage in Louisiana served as a model for the extension of voting rights for freed slaves during Reconstruction. In a private letter to Louisiana governor Michael Hahn, Lincoln recommended that some qualified blacks be granted the elective franchise. Lincoln is often criticized for deferring to the state of Louisiana on this matter, but prior to the Fifteenth Amendment, the elective franchise had always been left to the discretion of the states and beyond the authority of the federal government. To have demanded more than he did, Lincoln would have acted beyond the legitimate authority of the federal government at the time. See Fornieri, "Lincoln and the Emancipation Proclamation," 143–44; Abraham Lincoln, "To Michael Hahn," March 13, 1864, in *Collected Works*, 7:243.

64. Alexis de Tocqueville, *Democracy in America*, ed. J. P. Mayer, trans. George Lawrence (New York: HarperCollins, 1988).

65. See Abraham Lincoln, "Address Before the Young Men's Lyceum of Springfield, Illinois," January 27, 1838, and "Temperance Address: An Address, Delivered before the Springfield Washington Temperance Society," February 22, 1842, in *Collected Works*, 1:108–15, 271–79. See Jaffa, *How to Think*, 21; Jaffa, *Crisis*, 181–272.

66. For a thoughtful commentary on the absence of the Declaration in Tocqueville's *Democracy in America*, see Thomas G. West, "Misunderstanding the American Founding," in *Interpreting Tocqueville's Democracy in America*, ed. Ken Masugi (Savage, MD: Rowman and Littlefield, 1991), 155–77.

67. See Tocqueville, *Democracy in America*, 57.

68. See Murley, "'Calhounism' of Willmoore Kendall," 125–26.

69. See Carey, "New Preface," xiv. In support of this view, Carey refers to progressive academics such as Smith, Beard, and Parrington. See J. Allen Smith, *The Spirit of American Government* (1919; reprint, Cambridge, MA: Harvard University Press, 1965); Charles A. Beard, *An Economic Interpretation of the Constitution of the United States* (1913; reprint, New York: Free Press, 1986); Vernon L. Parrington, *Main Currents in American Thought: An Interpretation of American Literature from the Beginnings to 1920*, 2 vols. (New York: Harcourt Brace, 1927).

70. Murley, "'Calhounism' of Willmoore Kendall," 100. As Murley suggests, the progressive opinion was succinctly captured in Carl Becker's claim that "To ask whether

the natural rights philosophy of the Declaration of Independence is true or false is essentially a meaningless question." For Becker, history has demonstrated that the natural rights language of the Declaration was nothing more than the temporary expression of the mind of men in a particular historic era. See Carl L. Becker, *The Declaration of Independence: A Study in the History of Political Ideas* (1922; reprint, New York: Vintage Books, 1942), 277. On Becker, the Declaration, and historicism, see Jaffa, *New Birth*, 73–152; Krannawitter, *Vindicating Lincoln*, 115–19; Hayward, "Children of Abraham," 27.

71. For solid accounts of Lincoln's image during the progressive era, see Merrill D. Peterson, *Lincoln in American Memory* (New York: Oxford University Press, 1994); Barry Schwartz, *Abraham Lincoln and the Forge of National Memory* (Chicago: University of Chicago Press, 2000). Also see Krannawitter, *Vindicating Lincoln*, 298–302.

72. Krannawitter, *Vindicating Lincoln*, 301.

2—Theodore Roosevelt's Lincoln

1. Theodore Roosevelt, *An Autobiography* (New York: MacMillan, 1913), in *Works*, 20:375–76. See William F. Hanna, "Theodore Roosevelt and the Lincoln Image," *Lincoln Herald* 94, no. 4 (Spring 1992): 2; Peterson, *Lincoln in American Memory*, 164; Schwartz, *Forge of National Memory*, 127–28.

2. For general accounts of Roosevelt and the progressive appeals to the Lincoln image, see Peterson, *Lincoln in American Memory*, 141–94; Schwartz, *Forge of National Memory*; Hanna, "Roosevelt and the Lincoln Image," 2–9; Donald, *Lincoln Reconsidered*, 3–18.

3. On the Progressive platform, see Theodore Roosevelt, "A Confession of Faith," address before the National Progressive Party Convention, Chicago, Illinois, August 6, 1912, in *Works*, 17:254–99. On the argument that the Progressive platform anticipated FDR's New Deal and the development of "economic rights," see Sidney M. Milkis, "Progressivism, Then and Now," in *Progressivism and the New Democracy*, ed. Sidney M. Milkis and Jerome M. Mileur (Amherst: University of Massachusetts Press, 1999), 9; Jerome M. Mileur, "The Legacy of Reform: Progressive Government, Regressive Politics," in Milkis and Mileur, *Progressivism and the New Democracy*, 259–64.

4. See Roosevelt, *Autobiography*, 20:347–48, cf. 455.

5. Lyn Ragsdale, *Presidential Politics* (Boston: Houghton Mifflin, 1993), 44–47, 62–63.

6. See Jaffa, *How to Think*, 25–26; David H. Donald, "Abraham Lincoln: Whig in the White House," in *The Enduring Lincoln*, ed. Norman A. Graebner (Urbana: University of Illinois Press, 1959), 47–66; cf. Stephen B. Oates, "Abraham Lincoln: Republican in the White House," in *Abraham Lincoln and the American Political Tradition*, ed. John L. Thomas (Amherst: University of Massachusetts Press, 1986), 98–110.

7. See Ragsdale, *Presidential Politics*, 62–63; Hanna, "Roosevelt and the Lincoln Image," 4–6; Clinton Rossiter, *The American Presidency* (1956; reprint, New York: Harcourt, Brace, and World, 1960), 102–4. On Roosevelt's relationship to the rise of the modern presidency, see Jean M. Yarbrough, "Theodore Roosevelt and the Stewardship of the American Presidency," in *History of American Political Thought*, ed. Bryan-Paul Frost and Jeffrey Sikkenga (Lanham, MD: Lexington Books, 2003), 541ff.; Ronald J. Pestritto, "Why Progressivism Is Not, and Never Was, a Source of Conservative Values," Claremont

Institute, August 2005, at http://www.claremont.org/publications/ pubid.439/ pub_detail. asp (accessed September 21, 2010); Jeffrey K. Tulis, "The Two Constitutional Presidencies," in *The Presidency and the Political System*, ed. Michael Nelson (Washington, DC: Congressional Quarterly Press, 1995), 91–123; Jeffrey K. Tulis, *The Rhetorical Presidency* (Princeton, NJ: Princeton University Press, 1987), 95–116.

8. Roosevelt, "Heirs of Abraham Lincoln," 17:364; cf. Abraham Lincoln, "Message to Congress in Special Session," 4:438.

9. Theodore Roosevelt, "Progressive Democracy," a review of Herbert Croly's *Progressive Democracy* and Walter Lippmann's *Drift and Mastery*, November 18, 1914, in *Works*, 12:232–39. See Herbert Croly, *Progressive Democracy* (1914; reprint, New Brunswick: Transaction Publishers, 1998); Walter Lippmann, *Drift and Mastery* (1914; reprint, Madison: University of Wisconsin Press, 1986); Walter Lippmann, *A Preface to Politics* (1914; reprint, Amherst, MA: Prometheus Books, 2005).

10. Schwartz, *Forge of National Memory*, 132–33. See "Abraham Lincoln, 1809–1909," *Chicago Daily Tribune*, February 7, 1909; "Lincoln at Gettysburg," *The Nation*, July 10, 1913, 27.

11. Roosevelt, "Heirs of Abraham Lincoln," 359–78 (360, 373); cf. Theodore Roosevelt, "The Recall of Judicial Decisions," address at Philadelphia, Pennsylvania, April 10, 1912, in *Works*, 195.

12. Roosevelt, "Heirs of Abraham Lincoln," 359–60, 362. One of the best accounts of Lincoln and the formation of the Republican Party remains Don E. Fehrenbacher, *Prelude to Greatness: Lincoln in the 1850s* (Stanford, CA: Stanford University Press, 1962), esp. 19–47. Also see Eric Foner, *Free Soil, Free Labor, Free Men* (1970; reprint, Oxford: Oxford University Press, 1995).

13. Roosevelt, "Heirs of Abraham Lincoln," 363; cf. Lincoln, "Seventh and Last Debate," 3:315.

14. Roosevelt, "Heirs of Abraham Lincoln," 364; cf. Abraham Lincoln, "Annual Message to Congress," December 3, 1861, in *Collected Works*, 5:35–53.

15. Theodore Roosevelt, "A Charter of Democracy," address before the Ohio State Constitutional Convention at Columbus, Ohio, February 21, 1912, in *Works*, 17:121.

16. Roosevelt, "Heirs of Abraham Lincoln," 359–60.

17. Ibid., 359–60 (emphasis added).

18. See Yarbrough, "Stewardship," 542, 545. Will Morrisey sees an "ambiguity" in Roosevelt's understanding of rights. While Roosevelt did talk of fundamental rights, human rights, or rights that no other man should be allowed to take away, it is unclear if he believed in any notion of natural rights as the Founders (or Lincoln) would have understood them. While the Founders and Lincoln would have seen nature as the ultimate ground for rights, for Roosevelt rights were apparently grounded in "the eternal forces of human growth." If pressed, Morrisey argues, this might lead to a kind of historicism, although Roosevelt does not develop this thought. See Will Morrisey, "Theodore Roosevelt on Self-Government and the Administrative State," in *The Progressive Revolution in Politics and Political Science*, ed. John Marini and Ken Masugi (Lanham: Rowman and Littlefield, 2005), 55–56.

19. Roosevelt, *Autobiography*, 20:463–64.

20. Roosevelt, "Heirs of Abraham Lincoln," 359 (emphasis added).

21. Lincoln, "Speech at Springfield," June 26, 1857, 2:406 (emphasis added).

22. Roosevelt, "Heirs of Abraham Lincoln," 360, 361.

23. Ibid., 361.
24. Ibid., 361–62.
25. Yarbrough, "Stewardship," 546, 547 (emphasis added).
26. Ibid. Also see Hayward, "Children of Abraham," 24–31; Ceaser, *Nature and History*, 59–70.
27. Roosevelt, "Heirs of Abraham Lincoln," 362.
28. Lincoln, "Seventh and Last Debate," 3:315; Roosevelt, "Heirs of Abraham Lincoln," 362–63. Cf. Theodore Roosevelt, "Washington and Lincoln: The Great Examples," in *Works*, 19:56; Lincoln, "Address before the Wisconsin State Agricultural Society," 3:481.
29. See Lincoln, "Message to Congress in Special Session," 4:438; Roosevelt, "Heirs of Abraham Lincoln," 364.
30. Theodore Roosevelt, "The New Nationalism," speech at Osawatomie, Kansas, August 31, 1910, in *Works*, 17:8–9.
31. Ibid., 9.
32. Ibid., 9–10.
33. Ibid., 17.
34. Roosevelt, "Heirs of Abraham Lincoln," 360.
35. Ibid., 362–66.
36. Roosevelt, "Washington and Lincoln," 48–61 (55–56).
37. Lincoln, "Speech at New Haven," 4:24; Roosevelt, "Washington and Lincoln," 56–57. Cf. Gabor S. Boritt, *Lincoln and the Economics of the American Dream* (Memphis: Memphis State University Press, 1978), 178–79; Foner, *Free Soil*, 31–39.
38. Lincoln, "Annual Message," December 3, 1861, 52; Lincoln, "Address before the Wisconsin State Agricultural Society," 3:478.
39. See George Fitzhugh, *Sociology for the South: or the Failure of Free Society* (1854; reprint, Ithaca, NY: Cornell University Library, 2007); George Fitzhugh, *Cannibals All! or Slaves without Masters*, ed. C. Vann Woodward (1857; reprint, Cambridge: Belknap Press, 2004); James Henry Hammond, "Speech on the Admission of Kansas," U.S. Senate, March 4, 1858, in *Slavery Defended: The Views of the Old South*, ed. Eric L. McKitrick (Englewood Cliffs, NJ: Prentice-Hall, 1963), 121–25. See Foner's discussion of Fitzhugh in *Free Soil*, 66–68; cf. Boritt, *American Dream*, 138, 180, 184. Lincoln's law partner William Herndon once claimed that Fitzhugh's *Sociology* "aroused the ire of Lincoln more than most proslavery books." Herndon to Weik, October 28, 1885, quoted in Boritt, *American Dream*, 184, and Foner, *Free Soil*, 66.
40. See Lincoln, "Annual Message," December 3, 1861, 52; cf. Lincoln, "Address before the Wisconsin State Agricultural Society," 3:479. Lincoln did sometimes refer to "money kings" and "land kings," although such references are few. Thomas Schneider suggests that Lincoln faced a rhetorical difficulty in addressing white audiences on the problem of Negro slavery, an audience who had no fear of being enslaved. To make the danger of slavery to American institutions real for white Americans, "Lincoln drew out the similarities between slavery and economic oppression." However, Schneider argues that it is wrong to suggest Lincoln simply equated the institution of chattel slavery and economic oppression. Lincoln never lost sight of the fundamental distinction between true slavery and economic oppression—only "slavery" was literal enslavement. See Thomas E. Schneider, *Lincoln's Defense of Politics* (Columbia: University of Missouri Press, 2006), 147–48. On the view that Lincoln held to a belief in "economic slavery," see Allen C. Guelzo, *Abraham Lincoln, Redeemer President* (Grand Rapids, MI: William B. Eerdmans, 1999), 9, 121, 184, cited in Schneider, *Defense of Politics*, 184–85.

41. Roosevelt, "Washington and Lincoln," 57–58 (original emphasis).
42. Ibid., 59.
43. See Lind, *What Lincoln Believed*, 258–59; Hofstadter, *American Political Tradition*, 105–7. Foner makes a similar argument in his review of Boritt's *American Dream*. See Eric Foner, "A New Abraham Lincoln?" *Reviews in American History* 7, no. 3 (September 1979): 375–79.
44. Boritt, *American Dream*, 178.
45. Lincoln, "Address before the Wisconsin State Agricultural Society," 3:479; Boritt, *American Dream*, 178. Despite the fact that Lincoln saw no permanent laboring class in America, Boritt reminds us that he saw the potential for a tension between capital and labor. Lincoln publicly supported the right of wage laborers to organize and strike, however temporary their position. See Boritt, *American Dream*, 178, 182–84; Lincoln, "Speech at New Haven," 4:24–26; Lincoln, "Speech at Hartford," 4:7–8; Lincoln, "New York Workingmen's Democratic Republican Association," 7:259.
46. Abraham Lincoln, "Address on Colonization to a Deputation of Negroes," August 14, 1862, in *Collected Works*, 5:374 (emphasis added).
47. Abraham Lincoln, "Fragments on Government," July 1, 1854, in *Collected Works*, 2:220–22.
48. For representative examples, see Lincoln, "Address before the Wisconsin State Agricultural Society," 3:478–80; Lincoln, "Speech at New Haven," 4:24–25; Lincoln, "Annual Message," December 3, 1861, 51–52; Lincoln, "New York Workingmen's Democratic Republican Association," 259–60.
49. Boritt, *American Dream*, 184. Lincoln's standard answer to the problem of urban poverty was homestead legislation, his support of which was firmly rooted in his praise of free labor. The argument was that if Eastern wage-earners were encouraged to move west and turn to agriculture, labor competition in the East would be reduced, thereby raising wages and improving the quality of life for both new farmers in the West, and wage-earners in the East. See, for example, Abraham Lincoln, "Speech to Germans at Cincinnati, Ohio," February 12, 1861, in *Collected Works*, 4:201–3; Foner, *Free Soil*, 27–29; Lind, *What Lincoln Believed*, 259–62.
50. Roosevelt, "Heirs of Abraham Lincoln," 364.
51. Roosevelt, "New Nationalism," 13–14.
52. Ibid., 9. See Yarbrough, "Stewardship," 545; Pestritto, "Progressivism."
53. See Theodore Roosevelt, "The Right of the People to Rule," address at Carnegie Hall, New York City, March 20, 1912, in *Works*, 151–71.
54. Roosevelt, "Recall of Judicial Decisions," 202. Roosevelt cited James Bryce's famed commentary *The American Commonwealth*, in which Bryce asserts that American society as of 1888 had progressed beyond the problem of majority tyranny. This "once dreaded danger," Bryce wrote, had disappeared from American life. James Bryce, *The American Commonwealth*, 3 vols. (London: MacMillan and Company, 1888), 3:143. This sentiment pervades all of Roosevelt's progressive writings. His argument was not that the problem of tyranny as such had disappeared. Rather, the problem had become exclusively the minority tyranny of wealthy and powerful special interests over the common man.
55. On the debased taste for equality versus the legitimate passion for equality, see Tocqueville, *Democracy in America*, 57; cf. Diamond, *Republican Principles*, 241–57.
56. Roosevelt, "Heirs of Abraham Lincoln," 364–65.
57. Roosevelt, "Charter of Democracy," 120–21(emphasis added); Roosevelt is quoting Abraham Lincoln, "First Inaugural Address," March 4, 1861, in *Collected Works*, 4:269.

58. See "Federalist Papers" 10, 39, and 63 in Hamilton et al., *The Federalist*, 61–62, 251–52, 428.

59. Roosevelt, "Heirs of Abraham Lincoln," 364. William Howard Taft was especially critical of Roosevelt's call for initiative, referendum, and recall. As just one illustration of the extremes to which the debate over "pure" and "representative" democracy went, consider the following: As president, Taft vetoed an act to create the states of Arizona and New Mexico, publicly condemning the fact that the Arizona constitution would permit the recall of judges. Taft engaged Roosevelt in this rhetoric of "pure democracy" versus "representative government," perhaps going too far in the other direction by claiming that "The *rule of the people* [emphasis added] would . . . degenerate into anarchy and revert to despotism as the only way of escape." "An Untrammeled Judiciary," *New York Times*, August 16, 1911. The Progressive press responded in kind, claiming that Taft had not just vetoed the recall of judges; he had vetoed the "basic principles of popular government." *Philadelphia North American*, November 17, 1911, quoted in George E. Mowry, *Theodore Roosevelt and the Progressive Movement* (Madison: University of Wisconsin Press, 1946), 171.

60. Roosevelt, "Charter of Democracy," 120–21.

61. Lincoln, "Annual Message," December 3, 1861, 51.

62. Lincoln, "First Inaugural Address," 270. Lincoln did not mention impeachment in this passage. See Judd Stewart, "Abraham Lincoln on Present-day Problems and Abraham Lincoln as Represented by Theodore Roosevelt," letter to the Members of the Ohio State Constitutional Convention, Columbus, Ohio, February 1912 (Illinois State Historical Society), 8. See Schwartz, *Forge of National Memory*, 128.

63. Roosevelt, "Heirs of Abraham Lincoln," 364–65; cf. Lincoln, "Annual Message," December 3, 1861, 51.

64. James Madison, "Federalist 39," in Hamilton et al., *The Federalist*, 251–52 (emphasis added).

65. Roosevelt, "Heirs of Abraham Lincoln," 367; cf. Abraham Lincoln, "Speech at Cincinnati, Ohio," September 17, 1859, in *Collected Works*, 3:460, and Roosevelt, "Right of the People to Rule," 164.

66. Lincoln, "Speech at Cincinnati, Ohio," 3:460–61 (emphasis added).

67. Roosevelt, "Heirs of Abraham Lincoln," 367.

68. Roosevelt, "Recall of Judicial Decisions," 193.

69. Roosevelt, "Heirs of Abraham Lincoln," 375–76.

70. Ibid., 370; cf. Theodore Roosevelt, "The Future of the Progressive Party," speech at Chicago, Illinois, December 10, 1912, in *Works*, 17:355–56. See "Offers Recall Amendment; Senator Bristow also Proposes to Embody the Initiative in Constitution," *New York Times*, December 5, 1912 (the first paragraph for this article is not available in the *New York Times* electronic archives).

71. Roosevelt, "Heirs of Abraham Lincoln," 370; Roosevelt, "Recall of Judicial Decisions," 195.

72. Roosevelt, "Heirs of Abraham Lincoln," 367–68. See Stephen Douglas's reply in the Sixth Debate with Lincoln, at Quincy, Illinois, October 13, 1858, in Lincoln, *Collected Works*, 3:266–67.

73. See Yarbrough, "Stewardship," 547.

74. Roosevelt, "Heirs of Abraham Lincoln," 369. See Lincoln, "Speech at Springfield," July 17, 1858, 2:516.

75. Roosevelt, "Charter of Democracy," 139 (emphasis added).
76. Ibid., 121 (emphasis added).
77. Roosevelt, "Progressive Democracy," 233.
78. Ibid., 233–34. See Croly, *Progressive Democracy*, 230–31, 237, 243–44.
79. Roosevelt, "Heirs of Abraham Lincoln," 375–76.
80. Ibid., 370; cf. Lincoln, "First Inaugural Address," 268.
81. Roosevelt, "Heirs of Abraham Lincoln," 369.
82. Lincoln, "Speech at Chicago," 2:495 (emphasis added).
83. Roosevelt, "Heirs of Abraham Lincoln," 377 (emphasis added); Herbert Croly, *The Promise of American Life* (1909; reprint, New York: Capricorn Books, 1964), 38–41. David Alvis and I explore Croly's analysis of Lincoln in greater detail, in David Alvis and Jason R. Jividen, "Distaining the Beaten Path: Herbert Croly and the Hundredth Anniversary of Lincoln's Birth" (paper presented at the annual meeting of the American Political Science Association, Toronto, Canada, September 3, 2009).
84. Yarbrough, "Stewardship, 537.
85. Croly, *Promise*, 28–38; see ibid., 27–51, on the Jeffersonian and the Hamiltonian traditions, and ibid., 52–71, on the Democrats and Whigs. See also David Alvis, "Herbert Croly's Transformation of the American Regime," Claremont Institute, 2003, at http://www.claremont.org/publications/pubid.247/pub_detail.asp (accessed May 4, 2007); Alvis and Jividen, "Distaining the Beaten Path," 4–7; David Levy, *Herbert Croly of the New Republic: The Life and Thought of an American Progressive* (Princeton, NJ: Princeton University Press, 1985), 98.
86. See Croly, *Promise*, 170, 172, 17, 100–105, 182–83; also Levy, *Herbert Croly*, 99–101.
87. Croly, *Promise*, 207, 400; cf. 454; see also Alvis and Jividen, "Distaining the Beaten Path," 31; Croly, *Promise*, 89, 92.
88. Croly, *Promise*, 94 (emphasis added); cf. Herbert Croly, "The Paradox of Lincoln," *New Republic*, February 18, 1920, 350–53.
89. Lincoln, "Speech at Peoria," 2:272.
90. Ibid., 271 (emphasis added). Also see Lincoln's address at Cooper Institute: "Human action can be modified to some extent, but human nature cannot be changed. There is a judgment and a feeling against slavery in this nation, which cast at least a million and a half of votes. You cannot destroy that judgment and feeling—that sentiment—by breaking up the political organization which rallies around it." Abraham Lincoln, "Address at Cooper Institute, New York City," February 27, 1860, in *Collected Works*, 3:541–42.
91. Abraham Lincoln, "Response to a Serenade," November 10, 1864, in *Collected Works*, 8:101 (emphasis added).
92. See Alvis and Jividen, "Distaining the Beaten Path," 33–36. On Hegelian idealism in Croly's political thought, see David Noble, "Herbert Croly and American Progressive Thought," *Western Political Quarterly* 7 (December 1954): 537–53; David Noble, *The Paradox of Progressive Thought* (Minneapolis: University of Minnesota Press, 1958), 34–77; cf. Levy, *Herbert Croly*, 117–31.
93. Recall Hamilton's famous declaration that "The sacred rights of mankind are not to be rummaged for, among old parchments, or musty records. They are written, as with a sun beam, in the whole *volume* of human nature, by the hand of the Divinity itself; and can never be erased or obscured by mortal power." Alexander Hamilton, "The Farmer Refuted," February 23, 1775, in *Selected Speeches and Writings of Alexander Hamilton*, ed. Morton J.

Frisch (Washington, DC: American Enterprise Institute Press, 1985), 21. On the natural rights basis of Hamilton's political theory, see Gerald Stourzh, *Alexander Hamilton and the Idea of Republican Government* (Stanford, CA: Stanford University Press, 1970); Mackubin Thomas Owens, Jr., "Alexander Hamilton on Natural Rights and Prudence," *Interpretation* 14 (1986): 331–51.

94. Ronald J. Pestritto, *Woodrow Wilson and the Roots of Modern Liberalism* (Lanham, MD: Rowman and Littlefield, 2005), 238; "Federalist Papers" 1, 26, 37, in Hamilton et al., *The Federalist*, 1–4, 5–6, 231–39.

95. Madison, "Federalist Papers" 10, 51, in Hamilton et al., *The Federalist*, 56–65, 347–53.

96. In Hamilton's formulation, it is a "just observation" that the people "commonly *intend* the PUBLIC GOOD. . . . But their good sense would despise the adulator, who should pretend that they always *reason right* about the *means* of promoting it." Hamilton, "Federalist 71," ibid., 482. Also see "Federalist 63," ibid., 424–25.

97. Yarbrough, "Stewardship," 548. See Roosevelt, "New Nationalism," 5–22.

98. Lincoln, "Response to Serenade," November 10, 1864, 8:101; Lincoln, "Speech at Peoria," 2:271.

99. See Alvis and Jividen, "Distaining the Beaten Path," 33–36.

3—Woodrow Wilson's Lincoln

1. Here I follow Pestritto, *Woodrow Wilson*, 1–7, 253–71. There is a debate as to whether or how Wilson should be seen as a progressive. Some argue that Wilson was a consistent Jeffersonian states-rights democrat. See, for example, Mowry, *Roosevelt and the Progressive Movement*, 277. Eisenach argues that Wilson was a constitutional conservative, emphasizing his support for the traditional party system and his opposition to the expansion of national power through the interstate commerce clause. For Eisenach, Wilson's election to the presidency was a crushing blow to the progressive movement. See Eldon J. Eisenach, *The Lost Promise of Progressivism* (Lawrence: University Press of Kansas, 1994), 122–29. Others argue that Wilson began as a Jeffersonian only to move eventually toward progressivism. See Harry Clor, "Woodrow Wilson," in *American Political Thought: The Philosophic Dimension of American Statesmanship*, ed. Morton J. Frisch and Richard G. Stevens (Itasca, IL: F. E. Peacock, 1983), 282–84; George W. Ruiz, "The Ideological Convergence of Theodore Roosevelt and Woodrow Wilson," *Presidential Studies Quarterly* 1 (Winter 1989): 159–77. However, Pestritto ably demonstrates the real continuity between the philosophic historicism of Wilson's academic writings, his progressive politics, and his efforts to redefine the ends and means of American government.

2. See Pestritto, *Woodrow Wilson*, 1–7, 253–71.

3. Woodrow Wilson, *The State: Elements of Historical and Practical Politics* (1898; reprint, Boston: D. C. Heath, 1918), 62.

4. Woodrow Wilson, "An Address in Chicago to Democrats on Lincoln's Birthday," February 12, 1912, in *The Papers of Woodrow Wilson*, ed. Arthur S. Link, 69 vols. (Princeton, NJ: Princeton University Press, 1966–1993), 24:152–53.

5. Woodrow Wilson, *The New Freedom: A Call for the Emancipation of the Generous Energies of a People* (1913; reprint, Englewood Cliffs, NJ: Prentice-Hall, 1961), 19–20.

6. Wilson, *New Freedom*, 41; Woodrow Wilson, *Constitutional Government in the United States* (1908; reprint, New York: Columbia University Press, 1961), 55, 57.

7. Wilson, *New Freedom*, 42; cf. Wilson, *Constitutional Government*, 56–57. On the influence of Wilson's understanding of the "living constitution" on constitutional interpretation and the U.S. Supreme Court, see Paul Carrese, "Montesquieu, the Founders, and Woodrow Wilson: The Evolution of Rights and the Eclipse of Constitutionalism," in Marini and Masugi, *Progressive Revolution*, 149–57; Christopher Wolfe, "Woodrow Wilson: Interpreting the Constitution," *Review of Politics* 41, no. 1 (January 1979): 121–42.

8. Wilson, *Constitutional Government*, 57; also Tulis, *Rhetorical Presidency*, 121.

9. See Wolfe, "Woodrow Wilson," 121–42; Tulis, *Rhetorical Presidency*, 117–32; Charles R. Kesler, "Woodrow Wilson and the Statesmanship of Progress," in *Natural Right and Political Right: Essays in Honor of Harry V. Jaffa*, ed. Thomas B. Silver and Peter W. Schramm (Durham, NC: Carolina Academic Press, 1984), 103–27.

10. Wilson, *New Freedom*, 42. That the Founders understood "separation of powers" in this supposedly mechanistic manner is contradicted by *The Federalist*, in which the separation of the departments of government is strictly based upon the assumption that the boundaries between the departments cannot be reduced to a theory but must rather depend upon practical experience. See especially "Federalist Papers" 47–51, in Hamilton et al., *The Federalist*, 323–53.

11. Wilson, *New Freedom*, 39. My primary concern here is to discuss the manner in which Wilson's historicism frustrates his attempt to invoke Lincoln's legacy. In order not to detract from this purpose, rather than attempt to offer an exhaustive account of Wilson's political thought using his speeches and writings, I have relied heavily on several secondary works on Wilson's historicism. See Pestritto, *Woodrow Wilson*, especially 33–65; Scott J. Zentner, "Liberalism and Executive Power: Woodrow Wilson and the American Founders," *Polity* 26, no. 4 (Summer 1994): 579–99; Scott J. Zentner, "President and Party in the Thought of Woodrow Wilson," *Presidential Studies Quarterly* 26, no. 3 (Summer 1996): 676n12; Charles R. Kesler, "The Public Philosophy of the New Freedom and the New Deal," in *The New Deal and Its Legacy: Critique and Reappraisal*, ed. Robert Eden (New York: Greenwood Press, 1989), 155–66; Kesler, "Statesmanship of Progress," 103–27; Paul Eidelberg, *A Discourse on Statesmanship: The Design and Transformation of the American Polity* (Urbana: University of Illinois Press, 1974), 279–362; Wolfe, "Woodrow Wilson," 121–42; Clor, "Woodrow Wilson," 267–94; Robert Eden, *Political Leadership and Nihilism* (Tampa: University Presses of Florida, 1983), 1–35; John Marini, "Progressivism, Modern Political Science, and the Transformation of American Conservatism," in Marini and Masugi, *Progressive Revolution*, 221–51.

12. Woodrow Wilson, "The Study of Administration," November 1, 1886, in *Papers*, 5:357–58. See Pestritto, *Woodrow Wilson*, 221–52.

13. Kesler, "Statesmanship of Progress," 115–18; Kesler, "New Freedom and the New Deal," 157.

14. Wilson, *Constitutional Government*, 4; cf. Wilson, *New Freedom*, 42–43.

15. Wilson, *Constitutional Government*, 5; Kesler, "Statesmanship of Progress," 115–16; Kesler, "New Freedom and the New Deal," 157–58.

16. Abraham Lincoln, "To Henry L. Pierce and Others," April 6, 1859, in *Collected Works*, 3:376; Woodrow Wilson, "A Calendar of Great Americans," February 1894, in *Papers*, 8:373–74. See Pestritto, *Woodrow Wilson*, 57.

17. Woodrow Wilson, "An Address to the Los Angeles Jefferson Club," May 12, 1911, in *Papers*, 23:34. See Pestritto, *Woodrow Wilson*, 54–55.

18. Kesler, "Statesmanship of Progress," 115–16; Kesler, "New Freedom and the New Deal," 157–58.

19. Peterson, *Lincoln in American Memory*; Schwartz, *Forge of National Memory*; Anthony Gaughan, "Woodrow Wilson and the Legacy of the Civil War," *Civil War History* 43, no. 3 (September 1997): 225–42.

20. Pestritto, *Woodrow Wilson*, 57, 209–10; Croly, *Promise*, 94. See also Eden, *Political Leadership*, 11, 27–28; Krannawitter, *Vindicating Lincoln*, 298; Woodrow Wilson, "'Abraham Lincoln: A Man of the People,' An Address in Chicago on Lincoln's Birthday," February 12, 1909, in *Papers*, 19:39.

21. Clor, "Woodrow Wilson," 277–80. As Clor suggests, these themes run throughout the speeches collected in Wilson, *New Freedom*. See, for example, 19–33, 36, 50–51, 78–80.

22. Wilson, *The State*, 62; Wilson, *New Freedom*, 131. Also see Woodrow Wilson, "An Inaugural Address," March 4, 1913, in *Papers*, 27:150–51. On the relationship between Wilson's politics of individuality and the modern democratic state, see Zentner, "Liberalism and Executive Power," 581–83.

23. Compare Clor, "Woodrow Wilson," 275–84, and Eidelberg, *Discourse on Statesmanship*, 290–91, 324ff.

24. Woodrow Wilson, "A Campaign Address in Asbury Park, New Jersey," October 15, 1910, in *Papers*, 21:329–30.

25. "A News Report of Four Campaign Speeches in Monmouth County New Jersey," *Newark Evening News*, October 12, 1911, reprinted in Wilson, *Papers*, 23:445–46. On Lincoln and the idea of "economic slavery," compare Schneider, *Defense of Politics*, 147–48, and Guelzo, *Redeemer President*, 9, 121, 184.

26. Wilson, "Address in Chicago to Democrats," 152–53. Cf. Wilson, *New Freedom*, 169.

27. Woodrow Wilson, "Remarks in Springfield, Illinois, on the Main Issue of the Campaign," October 9, 1912, in *Papers*, 25:392.

28. Woodrow Wilson, "Lessons from Lincoln," address delivered at the Coliseum, State Fair Grounds, Springfield, Illinois, October 9, 1912, in *A Crossroads of Freedom: The 1912 Campaign Speeches of Woodrow Wilson*, ed. John Wells Davidson (New Haven: Yale University Press, 1956), 397–98; cf. Croly, *Promise*, 278–79.

29. Kesler, "Statesmanship of Progress," 115–16; Kesler, "New Freedom and the New Deal," 157–58.

30. Kesler, "Statesmanship of Progress," 104.

31. Kesler, "New Freedom and the New Deal," 155–56; Belz, *Lincoln, Constitutionalism, and Equal Rights*, 232.

32. Wilson, "Man of the People," 33–34.

33. Ibid., 35–36.

34. Wilson, "Calendar of Great Americans," 378–79.

35. Wilson, "Man of the People," 39 (emphasis added).

36. Cf. Woodrow Wilson, "Leaders of Men," June 17, 1890, in *Papers*, 6:662. See Kesler, "Statesmanship of Progress," 119–20.

37. Pestritto, *Woodrow Wilson*, 57.

38. Wilson, "Lessons from Lincoln," 395–96. Also see Woodrow Wilson, "Human Rights," address delivered at the Parade Grounds, Minneapolis, Minnesota, on September 18, 1912, in *Crossroads*, 185–95.

39. Lincoln, "Speech at Springfield," June 26, 1857, 2:407; also Lincoln, "Speech at a Republican Banquet," 2:385. See Jaffa, *Crisis*, 271–72, 408–9; also Hayward's attempt to distance progressive thought from Lincoln in Hayward, "Children of Abraham," 24–31.

40. Ceaser, *Nature and History*, 28, 20–21. Also see Arthur M. Melzer, Jerry Weinberger, and Richard Zinman, "Introduction" in *History and the Idea of Progress*, ed. Arthur M. Melzer, Jerry Weinberger, and Richard Zinman (Ithaca, NY: Cornell University Press, 1995), 3.

41. Ceaser, *Nature and History*, 28.

42. Lincoln, "Speech at Peoria," 2:275, 276 (emphasis added).

43. See Lincoln, "Speech at Springfield," June 26, 1857, 2:398–410; Lincoln, "Reply: Fifth Debate with Stephen A. Douglas, at Galesburg, Illinois," October 7, 1858, 3:220; *Dred Scott v. Sanford*, 60 U.S. 393.

44. See Woodrow Wilson, *Division and Reunion, 1829–1909* (1893; reprint, New York: Longmans, Green, 1916), 119; Pestritto, *Woodrow Wilson*, 109–10.

45. Pestritto, *Woodrow Wilson*, 109–10. Also see Krannawitter, *Vindicating Lincoln*, 58–61.

46. John C. Calhoun, "Speech on the Importance of Domestic Slavery," U.S. Senate, January 10, 1838, in *Slavery Defended: The Views of the Old South*, ed. Eric L. McKitrick (Englewood Cliffs, NJ: Prentice-Hall, 1963), 18–19. See also John C. Calhoun, "Speech on the Reception of Abolition Petitions," February 6, 1837, in *Union and Liberty: The Political Philosophy of John C. Calhoun*, ed. Ross M. Lence (Indianapolis: Liberty Fund, 1992), 461–76.

47. Alexander Stephens, "Cornerstone Speech," Savannah, Georgia, March 21, 1861, at http://www.historicaldocuments.com/ CornerstoneSpeech.htm (accessed May 4, 2007).

48. Pestritto, *Woodrow Wilson*, 109–10.

49. Anastaplo, for example, suggests that Lincoln seems to have been "dedicated to the hope, if not the expectation, of continuous and unlimited progress." The last lines of the Gettysburg Address, Anastaplo claims, dimly reflect a "faith in progress that is rooted in the Enlightenment, and perhaps in the technology that the Enlightenment depended upon and promoted." Anastaplo, *Abraham Lincoln*, 328n468, cf. 348n492.

50. Abraham Lincoln, "First Lecture on Discoveries and Inventions," April 6, 1858, and "Second Lecture on Discoveries and Inventions," February 11, 1859, in *Collected Works*, 2:437–42, 3:356–63.

51. See esp. Lincoln, "Address before the Wisconsin State Agricultural Society," 3:471–82.

52. See Eugene F. Miller, "Democratic Statecraft and Technological Advance: Abraham Lincoln's Reflections on 'Discoveries and Inventions,'" *Review of Politics* 63, no. 3 (Summer 2001): 485–515.

53. Lincoln, "Second Lecture on Discoveries and Inventions," 356–63 (356, 357).

54. Ibid., 357 (original emphasis).

55. See Miller, "Democratic Statecraft and Technological Advance," 491–94.

56. Ibid., esp. 488n3. Miller here rightly takes issue with Guelzo, who misses the critical side of Lincoln's lectures when he suggests Lincoln "unreflectively" describes a "history cast in terms of ever-mounting stages of progress, culminating unapologetically in joint creation of the steam engine and the American republic." Guelzo, *Redeemer President*, 173–74.

57. Ceaser, *Nature and History*, 49; Miller, "Democratic Statecraft and Technological Advance," 491–94.

58. See Lincoln's statements that Douglas had come to place slavery on the "cotton gin basis," suggesting that, if there ever were any "natural limits" to slavery expansion,

technological "progress" had shattered them. Abraham Lincoln, "Rejoinder: Sixth Debate with Stephen A. Douglas, at Quincy, Illinois," October 13, 1858, and "Seventh and Last Debate," in *Collected Works*, 3:275–83, 316. On Douglas, Manifest Destiny, and the use of technology to overcome the supposed "natural limits of slavery," see Jaffa, *Crisis*, 65–71; and Harry V. Jaffa, "Abraham Lincoln," in Frisch and Stevens, *American Political Thought*, 209–12.

59. Lincoln, "Address at Cooper Institute," 3:535 (emphasis added).

60. Wilson, "Man of the People," 41, 43, 45.

61. Ibid., 40.

62. Ibid., 41–42 (emphasis added).

63. Pestritto, *Woodrow Wilson*, 209–10. Also see Krannawitter, *Vindicating Lincoln*, 299–301.

64. Wilson, "Man of the People," 45–46. Note that Wilson here rejects the political theory of Madison's "Federalist 10" and multiplicity of interests as the primary feature of free, republican government.

65. See Wilson, "Leaders of Men," 6:644–71 (659).

66. See Woodrow Wilson, "Leaderless Government," September 1897, in *Papers*, 10:288–305; Wilson, "Leaders of Men," 6:644–71. As Robert Eden has pointed out, the term *leadership* is mentioned twelve times in *The Federalist*, and of those, eleven times the term is used disparagingly. In the one instance when the term is used favorably, it is in reference to the leaders of the American Revolution. Leadership, for the Founders, was associated with the problem of demagoguery and faction. Insofar as the danger of demagoguery is a permanent problem for popular government, then "leadership" is a potentially dangerous problem. See Eden, *Political Leadership*, 5; also James W. Ceaser, *Presidential Selection: Theory and Development* (Princeton, NJ: Princeton University Press, 1979), 192–97; James W. Ceaser, Glen E. Thurow, Jeffrey Tulis, and Joseph M. Bessette, "The Rise of the Rhetorical Presidency," *Presidential Studies Quarterly* 11 (Spring 1981): 158–71; Tulis, *Rhetorical Presidency*, 130.

67. See Woodrow Wilson, "Cabinet Government in the United States," *International Review* 7 (August 1879): 146–63; Woodrow Wilson, *Congressional Government: A Study in American Politics* (1884; reprint, New York: Meridian Books, 1956). See Sidney M. Milkis and Michael Nelson, *The American Presidency: Origins and Development, 1776–2002*, 4th ed. (Washington, DC: Congressional Quarterly Press, 2003), 231–35.

68. Wilson, *Constitutional Government*, 68. See Milkis and Nelson, *American Presidency*, 231–35; Ceaser, *Presidential Selection*, 170–212.

69. Wilson, *Constitutional Government*, 57.

70. See ibid., 54–81; Ceaser, *Presidential Selection*, esp. 192–97; Tulis, *Rhetorical Presidency*, 117–44.

71. See Tulis, *Rhetorical Presidency*, esp. 25–57, 117–44; Tulis, "Two Constitutional Presidencies," 91–123; Ceaser, *Presidential Selection*, 5, 17, 214; Theodore J. Lowi, *The Personal President: Power Invested, Promise Unfulfilled* (Ithaca, NY: Cornell University Press, 1985), 97–175.

72. Milkis and Nelson suggest that some (most notably Fred Greenstein) look to Franklin Roosevelt as the first modern president. It is arguable, however, that the roots of the modern presidency might be seen in Wilson and the progressives. See Milkis and Nelson, *American Presidency*, 304n4; Fred I. Greenstein, "Change and Continuity in the Modern Presidency," in *The New American Political System*, ed. Anthony King (Washington,

DC: American Enterprise Institute Press, 1978), 45–85; Fred I. Greenstein, "Introduction: Toward a Modern Presidency," in *Leadership in the Modern Presidency*, ed. Fred I. Greenstein (Cambridge, MA: Harvard University Press, 1988), 1–6. On Wilson's role in the development of the modern presidency, see Ceaser et al., "Rhetorical Presidency"; Tulis, *Rhetorical Presidency*, 117–44; Ceaser, *Presidential Selection*, 170–212; Eidelberg, *Discourse on Statesmanship*, 4, 279, 286; Kesler, "Statesmanship of Progress," 103–27; Kesler, "New Freedom and the New Deal," 155–66; Zentner, "Liberalism and Executive Power," 579–99; Pestritto, *Woodrow Wilson*, 163–97 (esp. 172–76). Against this view, see Terri Bimes and Stephen Skowronek, "Woodrow Wilson's Critique of Popular Leadership: Reassessing the Modern–Traditional Divide in Presidential History," *Polity* 29 (Fall 1996): 27–63; David K. Nichols, *The Myth of the Modern Presidency* (University Park: Pennsylvania State University Press, 1994).

73. Willmoore Kendall, "The Two Majorities," in Kendall, *Contra Mundum*, 205–6; Kendall, *Conservative Affirmation*, 251–52; Kendall and Carey, *Basic Symbols*, 84.

74. See Gottfried Dietze, *America's Political Dilemma* (Baltimore: Johns Hopkins University Press, 1968), 57–58 (cf. 185–90, 175–205 more generally).

75. Belz, *Lincoln, Constitutionalism, and Equal Rights*, 91.

76. Lincoln, "Message to Congress in Special Session," 4:429. See Larry Arnhart, "'The God-like Prince': John Locke, Executive Prerogative, and the American Presidency," *Presidential Studies Quarterly* 11 (Spring 1979): 121–30.

77. See Locke, *Second Treatise*, §160, 168, pp. 375, 380; Arnhart, "God-like Prince," 123–25.

78. Arnhart, "God-like Prince," 125, 127; also Harvey C. Mansfield, Jr., *Taming the Prince* (New York: Free Press, 1989), 202, 258–61 (more generally, 189–284, 290–97, on the problem of prerogative and constitutional government).

79. Arnhart, "God-like Prince," 125; cf. Arthur M. Schlesinger, Jr., *The Imperial Presidency* (Boston: Houghton Mifflin, 1973).

80. Belz, *Lincoln, Constitutionalism, and Equal Rights*, 42–43; Krannawitter, *Vindicating Lincoln*, 332, 293–94; Jaffa, *How to Think*, 25–26.

81. According to Dietze, "in the end, the state of emergency possibly could become the rule rather than the exception." *America's Political Dilemma*, 57–58. Also see Rossiter, *American Presidency*, 99–101. On the prevalence and implications of "crisis" language in American presidential rhetoric, see Tulis, *Rhetorical Presidency*, 181.

82. See Lincoln, "Message to Congress in Special Session," 4:429; Benjamin A. Kleinerman, "Lincoln's Example: Executive Power and the Survival of Constitutionalism," *Perspectives on Politics* 3, no. 4 (December 2005), 805–8; also Belz, *Lincoln, Constitutionalism, and Equal Rights*, 91–95; Krannawitter, *Vindicating Lincoln*, 322–34.

83. See Lincoln, "Message to Congress in Special Session," 4:429. Kleinerman argues that Lincoln's letter to General Butler late in the war is representative of his views here. Lincoln advises Butler to discard openly "all reliance for what you do, on any election." The discretionary judgment of the military commander must rest upon a determination of military necessity and "not a popular vote." Kleinerman, "Lincoln's Example," 805–8. See Abraham Lincoln, "To Benjamin F. Butler," August 9, 1864, in *Collected Works*, 7:488; cf. Abraham Lincoln, "Speech in the U.S. House of Representatives on the Presidential Question," July 27, 1848, in *Collected Works*, 1:501–15. On public opinion and the enforcement of the Emancipation Proclamation, see Abraham Lincoln, "Annual Message to Congress," December 6, 1864, in *Collected Works*, 8:152.

84. Woodrow Wilson, "Address in the Williams Grove Auditorium, Williams Grove, Pennsylvania," August 29, 1912, in *Crossroads*, 53 (emphasis added).

85. Kendall, "Two Majorities," 205–6.

86. Kendall, *Conservative Affirmation*, 251–52; Kendall and Carey, *Basic Symbols*, 84n10. On the relevance of the plebiscitary presidency to Kendall's quarrel with Jaffa over Lincoln, see Murley, "'Calhounism' of Willmoore Kendall," 122 ff.

87. See George Anastaplo, *The Constitution of 1787: A Commentary* (Baltimore: Johns Hopkins University Press, 1989), 318n85; Bimes and Skowronek, "Woodrow Wilson's Critique"; Nichols, *Myth of the Modern Presidency*.

88. See Richard J. Ellis and Stephen Kirk, "Presidential Mandates in the Nineteenth Century: Conceptual Change and Institutional Development," *Studies in American Political Development* 9 (Spring 1995): 117–86; Richard J. Ellis and Stephen Kirk, "Jefferson, Jackson, and the Origins of the Presidential Mandate," in *Speaking to the People: The Rhetorical Presidency in Historical Perspective*, ed. Richard J. Ellis (Amherst: University of Massachusetts Press, 1998), 35–65; Robert A. Dahl, "Myth of the Presidential Mandate," *Political Science Quarterly* 105, no. 3 (Autumn 1990): 355–72.

89. Ellis and Kirk, "Presidential Mandates," 178–79. See Thomas Jefferson, "To Elias Shipman and Others, a Committee of the Merchants of New Haven," July 12, 1801, in Thomas Jefferson, *Writings*, ed. Merrill D. Peterson (New York: Library of America, 1984), 497–500.

90. Ellis and Kirk, "Presidential Mandates," 137–51. See Andrew Jackson, "Removal of the Public Deposits," September 18, 1833, and Andrew Jackson, "Veto Message—Bank of the United States," July 10, 1832, in *The Statesmanship of Andrew Jackson as Told in His Writings and Speeches*, ed. Francis Newton Thorpe (New York: Tandy-Thomas, 1909), 262–64, 154–76.

91. Ellis and Kirk, "Presidential Mandates," 156.

92. Ibid., 163–65; Lincoln, "On the Presidential Question," 1:505.

93. Ellis and Kirk, "Presidential Mandates," 165, 166–67.

94. See ibid., 168; Lincoln, "On the Presidential Question," 505; Abraham Lincoln, "Reply to Committee Notifying Lincoln of his Renomination," June 9, 1864, "Response to a Serenade," October 19, 1864, "Response to a Serenade," November 8, 1864, and "Response to Serenade," November 10, 1864, in *Collected Works*, 7:380, 8:52–53, 8:96, 100–102.

95. Ellis and Kirk, "Presidential Mandates," 175. See Lincoln, "Annual Message," December 6, 1864, 8:136–52.

96. Lincoln, "Annual Message," December 6, 1864, 149.

4—Franklin Roosevelt's Lincoln

1. See Kesler, "Statesmanship of Progress," 115–16; Kesler, "New Freedom and the New Deal," 157–58.

2. Quoted by Hayward, "Children of Abraham," 26; cf. Ken Burns, interview by Charles McDowell, PBS, September, 1990; Weisberger, "The Great Arrogance," 97–102.

3. Fields's remarks are found in *The Civil War*, directed by Ken Burns, Florentine Films and WETA-TV, 1990, episode 9; cf. McPherson, *Second American Revolution*, 64, 137; Cuomo, *Why Lincoln Matters*, 32–39, 99–115.

4. Again, I follow Hayward, "Children of Abraham," 26.

5. Lincoln, "Speech at Springfield," June 26, 1857, 2:406.
6. See Hayward, "Children of Abraham," 26.
7. FDR, "'Unless There Is Security at Home, There Cannot Be Lasting Peace in the World,' Message to the Congress on the State of the Union," January 11, 1944, in *Public Papers*, 13:40.
8. Burns is quoted in Hayward, "Children of Abraham," 26; Roosevelt, "Tribute to Abraham Lincoln," 5:68 (emphasis added).
9. In addition to my own look at Roosevelt's *Public Papers and Addresses*, I have relied on several key secondary works, most of which make reference to the specific instances of FDR's use of Lincoln that I discuss below. In particular, I have relied heavily on Ronald D. Rietveld, "Franklin D. Roosevelt's Abraham Lincoln," in *Franklin D. Roosevelt and Abraham Lincoln: Competing Perspectives on Two Great Presidencies*, ed. William D. Pederson and Frank J. Williams (Armonk: M. E. Sharpe, 2003), 10–60, and Alfred Haworth Jones, *Roosevelt's Image Brokers: Poets, Playwrights, and the Use of the Lincoln Symbol* (Port Washington, NY: Kennikat Press, 1974). Also see Donald, *Lincoln Reconsidered*, 3–18; Philip Abbott, *The Exemplary Presidency: Franklin D. Roosevelt and the American Political Tradition* (Amherst: University of Massachusetts Press, 1990); Peterson, *Lincoln in American Memory*, 311–52; Barry Schwartz, *Abraham Lincoln in the Post-Heroic Era: History and Memory in Late Twentieth-Century America* (Chicago: University of Chicago Press, 2008).
10. Mario M. Cuomo and Harold Holzer, "Lincoln as Political Scripture," in Cuomo, *Why Lincoln Matters*, 18–19; Donald, *Lincoln Reconsidered*, 13, 14; Lind, *What Lincoln Believed*, 10–12. See also Michael Kammen, *Mystic Chords of Memory: The Transformation of Tradition in American Culture* (New York: Alfred A. Knopf, 1991), 294, 452; Peterson, *Lincoln in American Memory*, 320; Krannawitter, *Vindicating Lincoln*, 302–13.
11. FDR is quoted in Jones, *Roosevelt's Image Brokers*, 65, and Donald Day, *Franklin D. Roosevelt's Own Story* (Boston: Little, Brown, 1951), 120.
12. Herbert Hoover, "Dangers from Centralization and Bureaucracy to Liberty and Individual Initiative if National Government Assumes Responsibility for Local Relief," February 12, 1931, in *The State Papers and Other Public Writings of Herbert Hoover*, ed. William Starr Myers, 2 vols. (Garden City: Doubleday, Doran, 1934), 1:500–505. See Rietveld, "Roosevelt's Abraham Lincoln," 12.
13. See FDR, "The Forgotten Man Speech," radio address, Albany, New York, April 7, 1932, in *Public Papers*, 1:625; FDR, "A Concert of Action Based on Fair and Just Concert of Interests," address at Jefferson Day Dinner, Saint Paul, Minnesota, April 18, 1932, ibid., 1:629–30, 639; FDR, "We Are Through with 'Delay'; We Are Through with 'Despair'; We Are Ready and Waiting for Better Things," campaign address on a program for unemployment and long-range planning, Boston, Massachusetts, October 31, 1932, ibid., 1:845; FDR, "We Are Moving toward a Greater Freedom, to Greater Security for the Average Man," Second Fireside Chat of 1934, September 30, 1934, ibid., 3:422.
14. Roosevelt, "Tribute to Abraham Lincoln," 5:68 (emphasis added).
15. Sidney M. Milkis, "Franklin D. Roosevelt, the Economic Constitutional Order, and the New Politics of Presidential Leadership," in *The New Deal and the Triumph of Liberalism*, ed. Sidney M. Milkis and Jerome M. Mileur (Amherst: University of Massachusetts Press, 2002), 34–35; Milkis and Nelson, *American Presidency*, 276.
16. FDR, "Campaign Address at Wilmington, Delaware on 'Liberty,'" October 29, 1936, in *Public Papers*, 5:557; Abraham Lincoln, "Address at Sanitary Fair, Baltimore, Maryland," April 18, 1864, 7:301–3.

17. Roosevelt, "On 'Liberty,'" 5:557; Lincoln, "Address at Sanitary Fair," 7:301–3.

18. Roosevelt, "On 'Liberty,'" 5:557–58. Rosenman provides a useful note here: Wilmington was the home of the DuPont corporations and affiliate companies, the owners of which had formed the American Liberty League with top conservative Democrats in order to oppose and defeat the New Deal.

19. See Rietveld, "Roosevelt's Abraham Lincoln," 20.

20. See John Dewey, *The Public and Its Problems* (1927; reprint, New York: Henry Holt, 1946); John Dewey, *Individualism Old and New* (New York: Milton, Balch, 1930); John Dewey, *Liberalism and Social Action* (New York: G. P. Putnam's Sons, 1935). On FDR and the New Deal's indebtedness to Dewey, see Milkis, "New Politics of Presidential Leadership," 37–40; Sidney M. Milkis, *The President and the Parties: The Transformation of the American Party System since the New Deal* (Oxford: Oxford University Press, 1993), 38–51.

21. FDR, "Introduction," in *Public Papers*, 7:xxviii–xxxi; Roosevelt, "Moving toward a Greater Freedom," 422; FDR, "In 1776 the Fight Was for Democracy in Taxation. In 1936 That Is Still the Fight," campaign address at Worcester, Massachusetts, October 21, 1936, in *Public Papers*, 5:524; cf. Lincoln, "Fragments on Government," 2:220–22.

22. Milkis, "New Politics of Presidential Leadership," 38. See Dewey, *The Public and Its Problems*, 208, 211 (cf. 87, 95, 102, on natural rights); also Milkis, *The President and the Parties*, 38–51.

23. FDR, "We in Turn Are Striving to Uphold the Integrity of the Moral of Our Democracy," address at the Jackson Day Dinner, Washington, DC, January 8, 1938, in *Public Papers*, 7:38–39.

24. FDR, "Avoiding War, We Seek Our Ends through the Peaceful Processes of Popular Government under the Constitution," address at the dedication of the memorial on the Gettysburg battlefield, Gettysburg, Pennsylvania," July 3, 1938, in *Public Papers*, 7:419–21.

25. FDR, "The Democratic Party Will . . . Continue to Receive the Support of the Majority of Americans Just So Long as It Remains a Liberal Party," address at Denton, Maryland, September 5, 1938, ibid., 7:520. See Rietveld, "Roosevelt's Abraham Lincoln," 23–25.

26. FDR, "On Jackson Day Every True Follower of Jackson Asks that the Democratic Party Continue to Make Democracy Work," address at Jackson Day dinner, January 7, 1939, in *Public Papers*, 8:65.

27. Here I follow Rietveld, "Roosevelt's Abraham Lincoln," 28–31. See "Hoover's Attack on the New Deal at Republicans' Lincoln Day Dinner," *New York Times*, February 14, 1939; Max Lerner, "The Lincoln Image," *New Republic*, March 8, 1939, 135.

28. FDR, "The Future Lies with Those Political Leaders Who Realize That the Great Public Is Interested More in Government than in Politics," address at Jackson Day Dinner, January 8, 1940, in *Public Papers*, 9:29–30.

29. FDR, *Complete Presidential Conferences of Franklin D. Roosevelt*, ed. Jonathan Daniels, 25 vols. (New York: DaCapo Press, 1972), 15:508–9, quoted in Rietveld, "Roosevelt's Abraham Lincoln," 36, and Jones, *Roosevelt's Image Brokers*, 71.

30. See Rietveld, "Roosevelt's Abraham Lincoln," 34, 41ff.

31. Recall Woodrow Wilson's praise of Lincoln's practicality and flexibility in his "Man of the People," 19:33–46.

32. FDR, "New Conditions Impose New Requirements upon Government and Those Who Conduct Government," campaign address on progressive government at the Commonwealth Club, San Francisco, California, September 23, 1932, in *Public Papers*,

1:753; cf. Croly, *Promise*, 89, 99; Roosevelt, "Heirs of Abraham Lincoln," 17:360; Roosevelt, *Autobiography*, 20:375–76; Wilson, "Lessons from Lincoln," 395–96.

33. See, for example, Lincoln, "Speech at Springfield," June 26, 1857, 2:398–410; Lincoln, "Reply: Fifth Debate," 3:220.

34. Robert Eden, "On the Origins of the Regime of Pragmatic Liberalism: John Dewey, Adolf A. Berle, and FDR's Commonwealth Club Address of 1932," *Studies in American Political Development* 7 (Spring 1993): 74–150. See Roosevelt, "New Conditions," 1:742–56; Milkis, *The President and the Parties*, 38–51.

35. See esp. Dewey, *Individualism Old and New*.

36. Sidney M. Milkis, "New Deal Party Politics, Administrative Reform, and the Transformation of the American Constitution," in Eden, *The New Deal and Its Legacy*, 138–39. See John Dewey, "The Future of Liberalism," *Journal of Philosophy* 32 (April 25, 1935): 225–30.

37. Arthur M. Schlesinger, Jr., *The Age of Roosevelt: The Coming of the New Deal* (Boston: Houghton Mifflin, 1958), 257; Arthur M. Schlesinger, Jr., *The Age of Roosevelt: The Politics of Upheaval* (Boston: Houghton Mifflin, 1958), 155, 654. See also James MacGregor Burns, *Roosevelt: The Lion and the Fox* (New York: Harcourt, Brace, and World, 1956), 375, 380; Hofstadter, *American Political Tradition*, 315–16.

38. Milkis, "New Deal Party Politics," 136–37; cf. Morton J. Frisch, "Franklin Delano Roosevelt," in Frisch and Stevens, *American Political Thought*, 319–35.

39. Eden, "Regime of Pragmatic Liberalism, 76–77. See Dewey, *Liberalism and Social Action*; Charles W. Anderson, *Pragmatic Liberalism* (Chicago: University of Chicago Press, 1990), x; Harvey C. Mansfield, Jr., *America's Constitutional Soul* (Baltimore: Johns Hopkins University Press, 1991), 1–17, 193–208 (sources cited by Eden, in "Regime of Pragmatic Liberalism," 76–77).

40. Eden, "Regime of Pragmatic Liberalism," 77. See John Dewey, *Freedom and Culture* (1939; reprint, New York: G. P. Putnam's Sons, 1979), 4–5; Dewey, *The Public and Its Problems*, 102; Dewey, *Liberalism and Social Action*, 39–41. On Dewey and pragmatism's rejection of the self-evident truths of the Declaration of Independence, see David Fott, "John Dewey's Alternative Liberalism," in Frost and Sikkenga, *History of American Political Thought*, 585–97; James H. Nichols, Jr., "Pragmatism and the U.S. Constitution," in *Confronting the Constitution: The Challenge to Locke, Montesquieu, Jefferson, and the Federalists from Utilitarianism, Historicism, Marxism, Freudianism, Pragmatism, Existentialism . . .* , ed. Allan Bloom and Steven J. Kautz (Washington, DC: American Enterprise Institute Press, 1990), 369–88; cf. Eden, "Regime of Pragmatic Liberalism," 76n10.

41. Eden, "Regime of Pragmatic Liberalism," 132. While it is widely appreciated that the New Deal put classical liberalism on the defensive, Eden suggests, the extent to which the New Deal deliberately transformed the received tradition of pragmatism has received less attention. Eden offers Theodore J. Lowi, *The End of Liberalism: The Second Republic of the United States* (New York: Norton, 1979) as a representative example of the conventional wisdom here. See Eden, "Regime of Pragmatic Liberalism," 75.

42. Thomas Krannawitter has recently echoed Eden's argument, suggesting that FDR departs from earlier progressives by refusing to attack openly the principles of the Founders and Lincoln. Rather, Krannawitter suggests, FDR "opted to praise them, presenting his own politics as a continuation of, and addition to, those earlier principles." Krannawitter, *Vindicating Lincoln*, 302. Also see Milkis, *The President and the Parties*, 42–43; Milkis, "New Politics of Presidential Leadership," 53.

43. See John Dewey, "The House Divided against Itself," *New Republic*, April 24, 1929, 270–71; Dewey, *Individualism Old and New*, 9–18; cf. Wilson, "Address in Chicago to Democrats," 24:152–53; Abraham Lincoln, "A House Divided," speech at Springfield, Illinois, June 16, 1858, in *Collected Works*, 2:461–69.

44. Dewey, *Individualism Old and New*, 17–18.

45. Eden, "Regime of Pragmatic Liberalism," 83.

46. Ibid., 83–88. The extent to which the principles of Lockean liberalism are indeed inadequate or insufficient to meet the demands of the modern industrial economy is a matter of debate. Locke understood that, with the invention of money and the creation of civil society, the commonwealth has both the right and the duty to regulate the laws of property so as to benefit the common good of the whole society, as a careful reading of his *Second Treatise* will reveal. See Locke, *Second Treatise*, esp. sections 27, 31, 39, 45–51, 57, 120, 134, 138; Eden, "Regime of Pragmatic Liberalism," 85–86; Nathan Tarcov, "A 'Non-Lockean' Locke and the Character of Liberalism," in *Liberalism Reconsidered*, ed. Douglas MacLean and Claudia Mills (Totowa: Rowman and Allanheld, 1983), 130–40, esp. 134 ff.

47. Eden, "Regime of Pragmatic Liberalism," 83–84, 87.

48. Ibid., 84–85.

49. Ibid., 105.

50. See Rietveld, "Roosevelt's Abraham Lincoln," 54; Carl Sandburg, "Abraham Lincoln, 1809–1865," in *There Were Giants in the Land: Twenty-eight Historic Americans as Seen by Twenty-eight Contemporary Americans*, ed. Henry J. Morgenthau, Jr., et al. (New York: Farrar and Rinehart, 1942), 232; Jones, *Roosevelt's Image Brokers*, 105; Cuomo, *Why Lincoln Matters*, 26, 89; Stephen Skowronek, *The Politics that Presidents Make: Leadership from John Adams to Bill Clinton* (Cambridge: Belknap Press, 1997), 203–4, 298, 495n12 (more generally, see 288–324); T. Harry Williams, "Abraham Lincoln: Pragmatic Democrat," in *The Enduring Lincoln*, ed. Norman A. Graebner (Urbana: University of Illinois Press, 1959), 23–46; T. Harry Williams, "Abraham Lincoln: Principle and Pragmatism in Politics," *Mississippi Historical Review* 40 (June 1953): 89–106; Donald, *Lincoln Reconsidered*, 70, 128–43; David H. Donald, *Lincoln* (New York: Simon and Schuster, 1995), 15, 332, 452; McPherson, *Second American Revolution*, 41; David J. Siemers, "Principled Pragmatism: Abraham Lincoln's Method of Political Analysis," *Presidential Studies Quarterly* 34, no. 4 (December 2004): 804–27. Against this view, and more generally on the distinction between pragmatism and prudence, see Fornieri, "Lincoln and the Emancipation Proclamation," 125–49; Fishman, "Professor Donald's Lincoln," 232–42; Ethan Fishman, *The Prudential Presidency: An Aristotelian Approach to Presidential Leadership* (Westport, CT: Praeger, 2001); Fishman, "Under the Circumstances," 3–15. Also compare Fishman, "The Prudential FDR," in *FDR and the Modern Presidency*, ed. Mark J. Rozell and William D. Pederson (Westport, CT: Praeger, 1997), 147–65. Here Fishman attempts to defend FDR as a proponent of classical prudence against Schlesinger's and Burns's assessments of FDR as a pragmatist.

51. Eden, "Regime of Pragmatic Liberalism," 105; cf. Mansfield, *America's Constitutional Soul*, 1–17.

52. See Jeffrey Tulis, "The Decay of Presidential Rhetoric," in *Rhetoric and American Statesmanship*, ed. Glen E. Thurow and Jeffrey D. Wallin (Durham: Carolina Academic Press, 1980), 99–110; Tulis, *Rhetorical Presidency*; Eden, "Regime of Pragmatic Liberalism," 109, 129; Glen E. Thurow, "Voice of the People: Speechmaking and the Modern Presidency," an address delivered at Wake Forest University, October 1, 1979, cited in Tulis, "Decay of Presidential Rhetoric," 104; Ceaser et al., "Rhetorical Presidency," 158–71.

53. Milkis notes that book 1, chapter 25, of Machiavelli's *Discourses on Livy* "suggests the significance of Roosevelt's contribution to progressive reform." Machiavelli writes that, should one wish to reform the government of a city, for the reform to be accepted and maintained to the satisfaction of everyone, then one must retain at least the appearance of the old forms so that it seems as if no change has occurred, even if a real change has in fact taken place. See Milkis, "New Politics of Presidential Leadership," 65n29; Niccolo Machiavelli, *Discourses on Livy*, trans. Harvey C. Mansfield, Jr., and Nathan Tarcov (Chicago: University of Chicago Press, 1996), 60.

54. Roosevelt, "New Conditions," 1:742–56. In my account of Roosevelt's political rhetoric and the Commonwealth Club address, I have relied heavily upon Kesler, "New Freedom and the New Deal," 155–66; Eden, "Regime of Pragmatic Liberalism," 74–150; Milkis, "New Politics of Presidential Leadership," 31–72; and Milkis, *The President and the Parties*, 21–51. Kesler, Eden, and Milkis all argue that the Commonwealth Club address illustrates Roosevelt's self-conscious attempt to transform American political thought and institutions. I believe this is a persuasive interpretation of the ends of the New Deal, and one can see the theoretical influence of progressives such as Croly, Dewey, and Wilson here. However, there are other interpretations worth considering. Perhaps most familiar are those that refer to the New Deal as nothing more than mere experimentation or a hodgepodge of ad hoc policies with no clear ideological or theoretical coherence. See Schlesinger, *Coming of the New Deal*, 257; Schlesinger, *Politics of Upheaval*, 155, 654; Burns, *The Lion and the Fox*, 375, 380; Hofstadter, *American Political Tradition*, 315–16. Morton Frisch argues not only that Roosevelt offered a coherent political theory but that it was ultimately consistent with the principles of the American Founding. Frisch argues that Roosevelt's thought was not a rejection of the American political tradition but a farsighted and deliberate reinterpretation of it that moved in a direction to which the Constitution had always pointed. In this sense, Frisch argues, Roosevelt was best seen as a kind of "conservator." See Frisch, "Franklin Delano Roosevelt," 319–35. I would argue, however, that this argument does not attach enough weight to the fact that Roosevelt's recasting of the Declaration denatures the rights professed therein and robs the Declaration and the Constitution of any theoretical, objective defense of limited government.

55. Roosevelt, "Avoiding War," 419.

56. FDR, "'I Pledge You—I Pledge Myself to a New Deal for the American People': The Governor Accepts the Nomination for the Presidency," Chicago, Illinois, July 2, 1932, in *Public Papers*, 1:648.

57. Kesler, "New Freedom and the New Deal," 159–60. Also see Krannawitter, *Vindicating Lincoln*, 303.

58. Roosevelt, "New Conditions," 1:743–44.

59. Kesler, "New Freedom and the New Deal," 161. Also see Krannawitter, *Vindicating Lincoln*, 305–8. Eden, "Regime of Pragmatic Liberalism," 137n204.

60. Kesler, "New Freedom and the New Deal," 161–62.

61. Roosevelt, "Avoiding War," 420.

62. Kesler, "New Freedom and the New Deal," 161–62.

63. Roosevelt, "New Conditions," 1:744–45.

64. Ibid., 746, 747.

65. Ibid., 747–48, 749–50.

66. Ibid., 751–52.

67. Ibid., 752.

68. Ibid., 753 (emphasis added).

69. Ibid., 754. Here I closely follow Kesler, "New Freedom and the New Deal," 161–63. See Wilson, *Constitutional Government*, 4; Wilson, *New Freedom*, 42–43.

70. Roosevelt, "New Conditions," 1:754. See Kesler, "New Freedom and the New Deal," 163–65.

71. Roosevelt, "New Conditions," 1:754, 755, cf. 746. Again, here I closely follow Kesler, "New Freedom and the New Deal," 164.

72. Kesler, "New Freedom and the New Deal," 161–62. Also see Krannawitter, *Vindicating Lincoln*, 303–8.

73. Milkis, *The President and the Parties*, 42–43; Milkis, "New Politics of Presidential Leadership," 53.

74. Eden, "Regime of Pragmatic Liberalism," 132.

75. Ibid., 133–39.

76. Roosevelt, "New Conditions," 1:745.

77. Eden, "Regime of Pragmatic Liberalism," 132. See Thomas Jefferson, "To John C. Breckinridge," August 12, 1803, in Thomas Jefferson, *Writings*, ed. Merrill D. Peterson (New York: Library of America, 1984), 1136–41.

78. Eden, "Regime of Pragmatic Liberalism," 141–42.

79. Eden places a particular spin on New Deal liberalism, which focuses on the exploitation of the first principles of Lockean liberalism. While most Americans had considered the Lockean liberal tradition to be one of limited government and formal constitutionalism, Eden argues that in the Commonwealth Club address, Berle and Roosevelt attempted to exploit Machiavellian elements within the Lockean understanding of natural equality and natural rights. This points far beyond, or beneath, the idea of executive prerogative to consider the very foundation of Locke's doctrine of human equality as rooted in the desire for self-preservation. Berle attempted to reveal that the Lockean principles of equality and majority rule, when pushed to the extreme, are tyrannical principles that sanction all means in the pursuit of self-preservation. Such an account of Locke's Machiavellian roots, and the potential of these foundations for American politics, would seem to hinge upon a particular interpretation of Locke, a particular understanding of the history of political philosophy, and a willingness to describe the principles of the Founding as predominantly Lockean. See ibid., 133–50; Leo Strauss, *Natural Right and History* (Chicago: University of Chicago Press, 1953), esp. 202–51.

80. Eden, "Regime of Pragmatic Liberalism,"139. Also see Dietze, *America's Political Dilemma*, 57–58 (cf. 185–90, 175–205, more generally); Rossiter, *American Presidency*, 99–101. On the prevalence and implications of "crisis" in American presidential rhetoric, see Tulis, *Rhetorical Presidency*, 181.

81. Eden, "Regime of Pragmatic Liberalism," 145. Also see Mansfield, *Taming the Prince*, 202, 258–61. More generally, see 189–284, 290–97 on the problem of prerogative and constitutional government. On the tendency of liberalism to sacrifice constitutional formalism in the pursuit of its desired ends, see Mansfield, *America's Constitutional Soul*, 205–8. Quarrels among political theorists regarding the relationship of Locke, the Founders, and Lincoln sometimes hinge upon varying interpretations of the teaching of Locke's *Second Treatise*. On the question of Lincoln's relationship to Lockean liberalism, compare Eden, "Regime of Pragmatic Liberalism," 81–88, 132, 139–50, and Eden, *Political Leadership*, 240. Also consider the shift in Jaffa's interpretation of Lincoln's statesmanship with regard to the "Lockean" principles of the Declaration of Independence. Compare Jaffa,

Crisis, 211–32, 308–29; Jaffa, *Conditions of Freedom*, 3–8, 149–60; Jaffa, *How to Think*, 13–48; Jaffa, *New Birth*, esp. 73–152. Also see the recent commentary on Jaffa's Lincoln in Catherine Zuckert and Michael Zuckert, *The Truth about Leo Strauss: Political Philosophy and American Democracy* (Chicago: University of Chicago Press, 2006), 217–27, 239–52; cf. Charles R. Kesler, "A New Birth of Freedom: Harry V. Jaffa and the Study of America," in *Leo Strauss, the Straussians, and the American Regime*, ed. Kenneth L. Deutsch and John A. Murley (Lanham: Rowman and Littlefield, 1999), 265–82; Belz, *Lincoln, Constitutionalism, and Equal Rights*, 87n52.

82. Lincoln, "Young Men's Lyceum," 1:108–15; cf. James Madison, "Federalist 49," in Hamilton et al., *The Federalist*, 338–43, esp. 340.

83. Roosevelt, "I Pledge You," 648.

84. Roosevelt, "New Conditions," 1:756 (cf. 744).

85. Kesler, "New Freedom and the New Deal," 159–65. See Roosevelt, "New Conditions," 1:755 (cf. 746).

86. Roosevelt, "Unless There Is Security," 32–42; cf. FDR, "We Are Not Going to Turn the Clock Back," campaign address at Soldiers' Field, Chicago, Illinois, October 28, 1944, in *Public Papers*, 13:369. Also see FDR, "We Are Fighting to Save a Great and Precious Form of Government for Ourselves and the World," acceptance of the renomination for the presidency, June 27, 1936, Philadelphia, Pennsylvania, in *Public Papers*, 5:230–36. The "Second" or "Economic Bill of Rights" had its origins in a report of the National Resources Planning Board, January 14, 1942. See Rosenman's notes in Roosevelt, *Public Papers*, 13:43; Milkis, "New Politics of Presidential Leadership," 57.

87. Roosevelt, "Unless There Is Security," 33.

88. Ibid., 40–41; cf. Roosevelt, "Precious Form of Government," 233–34.

89. Roosevelt, "On 'Liberty,'" 5:557; Lincoln, "Address at Sanitary Fair," 7:301–3.

90. See Kesler, "New Freedom and the New Deal," 162–65.

91. Roosevelt, "Unless There Is Security," 41.

92. See Frisch, "Franklin Delano Roosevelt," esp. 330–34.

93. See Eden, "Regime of Pragmatic Liberalism," 137n204; Krannawitter, *Vindicating Lincoln*, 304–6; Mansfield, *America's Constitutional Soul*, 56–59 (cf. 31–34, 93–95, 185–86, 196–200); Harvey C. Mansfield, Jr., "Responsibility versus Self-Expression," in *Old Rights and New*, ed. Robert A. Licht (Washington, DC: American Enterprise Institute Press, 1993), 96–111.

94. Milkis, "New Politics of Presidential Leadership," 59.

95. Ibid., 60.

96. Cass R. Sunstein, *The Second Bill of Rights: FDR's Unfinished Revolution and Why We Need It More Than Ever* (New York: Basic Books, 2004), esp. 175–92.

97. Kendall and Carey, *Basic Symbols*, 84n10, 144. See also Kendall, *Conservative Affirmation*, 249–52; Willmoore Kendall, "Commitment or Ideal?" 95–103; Meyer, "Lincoln without Rhetoric," 725; Meyer, "Again on Lincoln," 71, 85; Bradford, "Heresy of Equality," 62–77.

98. See Madison's "Federalist 10" in Hamilton et al., *The Federalist*, 56–65.

99. See Lincoln, "Fragments on Government," 2:221–22; also Roosevelt, "Introduction," 7:xxviii–xxxi; Roosevelt, "Moving toward a Greater Freedom," 422.

100. See Harry V. Jaffa, *American Conservatism and the American Founding* (Durham, NC: Carolina Academic Press), 227–29; Harry V. Jaffa et al., *Original Intent and the Framers of the Constitution: A Disputed Question* (Washington, DC: Regnery Gateway,

1994), 261–62 (cf. 28–29, 122–23). Also see Belz, *Lincoln, Constitutionalism, and Equal Rights*, 87n52.

101. See Krannawitter, *Vindicating Lincoln*, 310–11.

102. Here I follow Mansfield, *America's Constitutional Soul*, 56–59 (cf. 31–34, 93–95, 185–86, 196–200); Mansfield, "Responsibility versus Self-Expression," 96–111.

5—Lyndon Johnson's Lincoln

1. Martin Luther King, Jr., "I Have a Dream," August 28, 1963, in *American Political Rhetoric*, ed. Peter Augustine Lawler and Robert Martin Schaefer (Lanham: Rowman and Littlefield, 2005), 277–78.

2. For one of Johnson's earlier statements of his goal to make emancipation a "fact," see his May 30, 1963, speech as vice president at the Memorial Day commemoration of the 150-year anniversary of the battle of Gettysburg. Johnson recounts the significance of this speech in Lyndon B. Johnson (hereafter LBJ), *The Vantage Point: Perspectives of the Presidency, 1963–1969* (New York: Holt, Rinehart, and Winston, 1971), 156–57; cf. Lincoln, "Speech in Independence Hall," 4:240. For further examples of Johnson's promise to "make emancipation a fact" during this period, see LBJ, "Remarks at the Lincoln Memorial," February 12, 1964, in *Public Papers* (hereafter *PP*), *1963–1964*, 1:293; LBJ, "Remarks to New Participants in 'Plans for Progress' Equal Opportunity Appointments," January 16, 1964, in *PP 1963–64*, 1:142; LBJ, "Remarks to New Participants in 'Plans for Progress' Equal Opportunity Appointments," January 22, 1964, in *PP 1963–64*, 1:213; LBJ, "Remarks to a Group of Treasury Department Officials in Equal Employment Opportunity," April 21, 1964, in *PP 1963–64*, 1:504; LBJ, "Remarks to a Group of Civil Rights Leaders," April 29, 1964, in *PP 1963–64*, 1:588; LBJ, "Remarks in New York before the 50th Annual Convention of the Amalgamated Clothing Workers," May 9, 1964, in *PP 1963–64*, 1:657; LBJ, "Remarks at a Meeting of the President's Commission on Equal Employment Opportunity," May 12, 1964, in *PP 1963–64*, 1:684; LBJ, "Remarks in Madison Square Garden at a Rally of the Liberal Party of New York," October 15, 1964, in *PP 1963–64*, 2:1349; LBJ, "Remarks at the National Urban League's Community Action Assembly," December 10, 1964, in *PP 1963–64*, 2:1656. Also see LBJ, "Remarks to Students Participating in the U.S. Senate Youth Program," February 5, 1965, in *PP 1965*, 1:150; LBJ, "Special Message to Congress: The American Promise," March 15, 1965, in *PP 1965*, 1:284; LBJ, "Remarks of Welcome at the White House to President Yameogo of Upper Volta," March 29, 1965, in *PP 1965*, 1:339–41.

3. Belz, *Lincoln, Constitutionalism, and Equal Rights*, 96, 185; Herman Belz, *Equality Transformed: A Quarter-Century of Affirmative Action* (New Brunswick, NJ: Transaction Publishers, 1991), 8–9; Jaffa, *Conditions of Freedom*, 149–51; Jaffa, *Crisis*, 11–14.

4. Johnson, *Vantage Point*, 166.

5. Ibid., 167.

6. Ibid.

7. Johnson, "Howard University," 2:636.

8. Johnson, "Lincoln Memorial," 1:293. See Lincoln, "Speech in Independence Hall," 4:240; Abraham Lincoln, "Address delivered at the dedication of the Cemetery at Gettysburg," November 19, 1863, in *Collected Works*, 23.

9. LBJ, "Special Message to the Congress Proposing a Nationwide War on the Sources of Poverty," March 16, 1964, in *PP 1963–64*, 1:376.

10. All remarks by LBJ dated 1964 in *PP 1963-64*: "Remarks on the City Hall Steps, Dayton, Ohio," October 16, 2:1372; "Remarks at the Chicago Stadium," October 30, 2:1545-46; "Remarks at Southwest Texas State College, San Marcos," November 20, 2:1609. Also see "Remarks at the Convention Center Arena in Pittsburgh, Pennsylvania," October 27, 2:1473; "Remarks in Koscinsko Park, Milwaukee," October 30, 2:1539; "Remarks in Madison Square Garden," October 31, 2:1560.

11. See Lincoln, "Fragments on Government," 2:220-22; Lincoln, "Deputation of Negroes," 5:374; Jaffa, *American Conservatism*, 227-29; Jaffa et al, *Original Intent*, 261-62 (cf. 122-23); Boritt, *American Dream*, 178-84.

12. Johnson, "To a Group of Civil Rights Leaders," April 29, 1964, 1:588, 589.

13. See Johnson (all in 1964), "Plans for Progress," January 16, 1:142; "Plans for Progress," January 22, 1:213; "Treasury Department Officials," April 21, 1:504; "Amalgamated Clothing Workers," May 9, 1:657; "President's Commission on Equal Employment Opportunity," May 12, 1:684.

14. See Edward J. Erler, "Still Separate but Equal," Claremont Institute, summer 2004, at http://www.claremont.org/publications/crb/id.1059/article_detail.asp (accessed September 21, 2010).

15. Johnson explains his strategy in *Vantage Point*, 155-79. See especially 161-67, where Johnson explains the mandate conferred upon him by the 1964 presidential election. This notion of the presidential mandate animates many of the most vocal critics of Lincoln's standard maxim of equality. See especially Kendall, "Two Majorities," 202-27; Kendall, *Conservative Affirmation*, 251-52. On the relevance of the idea of the presidential mandate to Kendall's criticism of Lincoln and the standard maxim, see Murley, "'Calhounism' of Willmoore Kendall," 122ff. On the controversial history of the idea of the mandate, see Ellis and Kirk, "Presidential Mandates," 117-86; Dahl, "Myth of the Presidential Mandate," 355-72.

16. Johnson, "National Urban League," December 10, 1964, 2:1653.

17. See Samuel H. Beer, "In Search of a New Public Philosophy," in *The New American Political System*, ed. Anthony King (Washington, DC: American Enterprise Institute Press, 1978), 5-44, for a discussion of the faith in human perfectibility, social engineering, and technocratic administration that animates the thinking of the progressives, New Deal, and Great Society.

18. Lincoln, "Response to Serenade," November 10, 1864, 8:101; Lincoln, "Speech at Peoria," October 16, 1854, 2:271.

19. See Erler, "Still Separate but Equal."

20. Johnson, "National Urban League," December 10, 1964, 1656.

21. Johnson, *Vantage Point*, 166.

22. Johnson, "American Promise," March 15, 1965, 1:282.

23. Ibid., 282, 283.

24. Ibid., 283.

25. Ibid., 284. See also Abraham Lincoln, "To James C. Conkling," August 26, 1863, and "To Charles D. Robinson," August 17, 1864, in *Collected Works*, 6:409, 7:500. Also see Johnson's 1965 remarks to the U.S. Senate Youth Program. Here Johnson would again employ the Lincoln image as part of his appeal to the idea of equal opportunity and human dignity, suggesting that "A hundred years ago Abraham Lincoln was signing the Emancipation Proclamation. And it was a proclamation but it wasn't a fact. . . . We all are working today," Johnson claims, "to see that it is a fact—to see that regardless of our religion, or the color of our skin, or where we live, or what State we come from, or how we spell our name,

we have the protection of our Bill of Rights and our Constitution . . . the dignity of man is uppermost in our thoughts—and the freedom of the individual is the basic requirement of every American, and fair and equal opportunities under our laws." Johnson, "U.S. Senate Youth Program," 150.

26. On the distinction between political and civil rights, the privileges and immunities clause of the Fourteenth Amendment, and the right of suffrage, see Akhil Reed Amar, *The Bill of Rights: Creation and Reconstruction* (New Haven: Yale University Press, 1998), 217–18.

27. Johnson, "American Promise," March 15, 1965, 1:286.

28. LBJ, "Remarks at the University of Michigan," May 22, 1964, in *PP 1963–64*, 1:704, 706.

29. Beer, "New Public Philosophy," 15–37. One should also consider Mansfield's discussion of the new rights rooted in the idea of the Nietzschean creative self, which came to dominate the New Left and the "Black Power" movement. See Mansfield, "Responsibility versus Self-Expression," 96–111; Mansfield, *America's Constitutional Soul*, 56–59 (cf. 31–34, 93–95, 185–86, 196–200).

30. Fornieri, "Lincoln and the Emancipation Proclamation," 143–44. On voting rights, see Lincoln, "To Michael Hahn," 7:243; Abraham Lincoln, "Last Public Address," April 11, 1865, in *Collected Works*, 8:403.

31. Johnson, "Lincoln Memorial," 1:293.

32. LBJ, "Remarks at the White House on Lincoln's Birthday," February 12, 1965, in *PP 1965*, 1:180 (emphasis added). See also Johnson, "Lincoln Memorial," 1:293; Lincoln, "Speech in Independence Hall," 4:240.

33. On the tendency of some modern commentators to denigrate Lincoln's measured approach to emancipation and the extension of citizenship and suffrage to the freedmen, see Fornieri, "Lincoln and the Emancipation Proclamation," 125–49; Fishman, "Under the Circumstances," 3–15; Krannawitter, *Vindicating Lincoln*, 13–45; Anastaplo, *Abraham Lincoln*, 197–227; Allen C. Guelzo, "How Abe Lincoln Lost the Black Vote: Lincoln and Emancipation in the African American Mind," *Journal of the Abraham Lincoln Association* 25, no. 1 (Winter 2004): 20. One should also consider Jaffa's discussion of the Kantian absolutism of many modern observers in his *New Birth*, 292–303, esp. 301–3; cf. Jaffa, *Crisis*, 327, and Zuckert and Zuckert, *Leo Strauss*, 217–27.

34. Richard J. Hofstadter, "Abraham Lincoln and the Self-Made Myth," in Hofstadter, *American Political Tradition*, 93–136; Bennett, "Was Abe Lincoln a White Supremacist?"; Bennett, *Forced into Glory*; Julius Lester, *Look Out, Whitey! Black Power's Gon' Get Your Mama!* (New York: Dial Press, 1968), 58, 63. On the history of the ambiguity of black opinion on Lincoln and the Emancipation Proclamation, see Guelzo, "How Abe Lincoln Lost the Black Vote," 1–22.

35. Likewise, in his "Great Society" speech at the University of Michigan in 1964, Johnson suggests that the current generation of students "has been *appointed by history*" to "lead America toward a *new age* . . . a society where the demands of morality, and the needs of the spirit, can be realized in the life of the Nation," where every citizen is given "full equality" and a chance to "escape from the crushing weight of poverty," where it is possible for "all nations to live in enduring peace" (emphasis added). See Johnson, "University of Michigan," 1:706.

36. Cf. Croly, *Promise*, 89, 94; Roosevelt, *Works*, 17:195, 360, 369, 373, 19:57–60.

37. Johnson, "Howard University," 2:635–40.

38. Daniel Patrick Moynihan, *The Negro Family: The Case for National Action*

(Washington, DC: Office of Policy Planning and Research, U.S. Department of Labor, 1965). The report was released in March 1965 and published in August. Moynihan urged that his thesis was not novel, and he drew upon others who had voiced variations on the same concerns. In particular see E. Franklin Frazier, *The Negro Family in the United States* (Chicago: University of Chicago Press, 1939), and Stanley M. Elkins, *Slavery: A Problem in American Institutional and Intellectual Life* (New York: Grosset and Dunlap, 1959).

39. Moynihan, *Negro Family*, i (emphasis added).

40. Ibid., 48–50; cf. Bayard Rustin, "From Protest to Politics: The Future of the Civil Rights Movement," *Commentary* 39 (February 1965), 27.

41. See Johnson, "Howard University," 2:635–40. On the relationship between the Moynihan Report and Johnson's Howard address and the immediate political context surrounding them, see Lee Rainwater and William L. Yancey, *The Moynihan Report and the Politics of Controversy* (Cambridge: MIT Press, 1967); David Zarefsky, "Lyndon Johnson Redefines 'Equal Opportunity': The Beginnings of Affirmative Action," *Central States Speech Journal* 31, no. 2 (Summer 1980): 85–94; David Zarefsky, "Presidential Rhetoric and the Power of Definition," *Presidential Studies Quarterly* 34, no. 3 (September 2004): 607–19.

42. Johnson, "Howard University," 2:636.

43. See Beer, "New Public Philosophy," 12, 29–30.

44. See Sowell, *Conflict of Visions*, 131–33; Richard J. Ellis, "Rival Visions of Equality in American Political Culture," *Review of Politics* 54, no. 2 (Spring 1992): 275–80; Belz, *Equality Transformed*, 236–37.

45. Zarefsky, "Johnson Redefines 'Equal Opportunity,'" 90, 93. See Moynihan, *Negro Family*, 3, where this argument is made explicit.

46. See Robert A. Goldwin, *Why Blacks, Women, and Jews Are Not Mentioned in the Constitution, and Other Unorthodox Views* (Washington, DC: American Enterprise Institute Press, 1990), 9–20.

47. On the early history of this transformation, see Belz, *Equality Transformed*. This new understanding of equality also had a significant influence on the issue of voting rights, given voice in the reinterpretation of the Voting Rights Act of 1965 and the equal protection clause in the apportionment cases of the Warren Court. The Warren Court argued that the principle of equality demanded equal voting power above all other concerns, despite the fact that apportionment was traditionally regarded as a political question, subject to the dictates of legislative prudence. See Alfred H. Kelly, Winfred A. Harbison, and Herman Belz, *The American Constitution: Its Origins and Development*. 2 vols. (New York: W. W. Norton, 1991), 2:607–19. One should note that just two years before the Howard address in *Gray v. Sanders* (1963), the Court would suggest that the equality principle of the Gettysburg Address necessitates "one person–one vote."

48. For example, see Croly, *Promise*, 178–82; Garry Wills, *Nixon Agonistes: The Crisis of the Self-Made Man* (Boston: Houghton Mifflin, 1970), 234–43; Bradford, "Heresy of Equality," 64; Ellis, "Rival Visions," 275–80.

49. Jaffa, *Crisis*, 376.

6—Barack Obama's Lincoln

1. Barack Obama, "Announcement for President," speech at Springfield, Illinois, February 10, 2007, at http://www.nytimes.com/2007/02/10/us/politics/11obama-text.htm (accessed September 21, 2010).

2. Obama, "Announcement for President." See Lincoln, "House Divided," June 16, 1858, 2:468.

3. Obama, "Announcement for President."

4. See Evan Thomas and Richard Wolffe, "Obama's Lincoln," *Newsweek*, November 24, 2008, 29–31.

5. Barack Obama, "What I See in Lincoln's Eyes," *Time*, June 26, 2005, at http://timeinc8-sd11.websys.aol.com/time/magazine/article/0,9171,1077287,00.html (accessed April 20, 2009); cf. Peggy Noonan, "Conceit of Government: Why Are Our Politicians So Full of Themselves?" *Wall Street Journal*, June 29, 2005; Barack Obama, *The Audacity of Hope: Thoughts on Reclaiming the American Dream* (New York: Three Rivers Press, 2006), 123–24.

6. Doris Kearns Goodwin, *Team of Rivals: The Political Genius of Abraham Lincoln* (New York: Simon and Schuster, 2005). See Philip Rucker, "A Familiar Precedent for a President-elect," *Washington Post*, November 19, 2008; Michael Beschloss, "The Great Inspirer," *Newsweek*, November 24, 2008, 33.

7. Barack Obama, "Victory Speech," speech at Grant Park, Chicago, Illinois, November 4, 2008, at http://www.nytimes.com/2008/11/04/us/politics/04text-obama.html (accessed September 21, 2010).

8. Charles R. Kesler, "The Audacity of Barack Obama," Claremont Institute, January 19, 2009, at http://www.claremont.org/publications/crb/id.1579/article_detail.asp (accessed September 21, 2010).

9. Obama, "Victory Speech." See Lincoln, "First Inaugural Address," 4:271.

10. Obama, *Audacity of Hope*, 53.

11. Ibid., 54–55.

12. Ibid., 55.

13. Ibid., 59.

14. Ibid., 93.

15. Ibid., 95–96.

16. Ibid., 96–97.

17. Ibid., 97–98.

18. Ibid., 98.

19. For just a few examples (all in *Collected Works*), see Lincoln, "Speech at Peoria," 2:266; Lincoln, "Speech at Springfield," June 26, 1857, 2:499; Lincoln, "Speech at Chicago," 2:501; Lincoln, "Speech at Springfield," July 17, 1858, 2:520; Lincoln, "Reply: First Debate," 3:16. See Kesler, "Audacity of Barack Obama."

20. See Barack Obama, "To Form a More Perfect Union," speech at Philadelphia, Pennsylvania, March 18, 2008, at http://www.nytimes.com/2008/03/18/us/politics/18text-obama.html (accessed September 21, 2010).

21. Kesler, "Audacity of Barack Obama."

22. Lincoln, "To Henry L. Pierce and Others," April 6, 1859, 3:376.

23. See Kesler, "Audacity of Barack Obama."

24. Obama, *Audacity of Hope*, 152.

25. Ibid., 158–59; cf. Lincoln, "Fragments on Government," 2:220–22.

26. Obama, *Audacity of Hope*, 159, 152, 153.

27. Krannawitter, *Vindicating Lincoln*, 293–94, 308. Also see Thomas L. Krannawitter, "Obama as Lincoln," *Washington Times*, December 19, 2008; Kesler, "Statesmanship of Progress," 103–27; Kesler "New Freedom and the New Deal," 155–66.

28. See Wilson, *Constitutional Government*, 4–5; Wilson, *New Freedom*, 42–43; Roosevelt, "New Conditions," 1:742–56.

29. Barack Obama, "What the People Need Done," Remarks at the 102nd Abraham Lincoln Association Annual Banquet, Springfield, Illinois, February 12, 2009, at http://www.whitehouse.gov/the_press_office/Remarks-of-President-Barack-Obama-What-the-People-Need-Done-Abraham-Lincoln-Bicentennial-Springfield-Illinois (accessed April 20, 2009).

30. Ibid.

31. Ibid.; cf. Lincoln, "Message to Congress in Special Session," 4:438.

32. Roosevelt, "Introduction," 7:xxviii–xxxi. Also see Roosevelt, "Moving toward a Greater Freedom," 3:422; Lincoln, "Fragments on Government," 2:220–22. Compare Hayward, "Children of Abraham," 24–31; Cuomo, *Why Lincoln Matters*, 32–39, 99–115; Krannawitter, *Vindicating Lincoln*, 310, 312, 318.

33. See Roosevelt, "New Conditions," 1:742–56; Roosevelt, "Unless There Is Security," 13:32–44.

34. See Kesler, "New Freedom and the New Deal," 159–65. See Roosevelt, "New Conditions," 1:755 (cf. 746).

35. See Kesler, "Audacity of Barack Obama."

36. See Jaffa, *American Conservatism*, 227–29; Jaffa et al., *Original Intent*, 261–62 (cf. 122–23); Mansfield, *America's Constitutional Soul*, 56–59 (cf. 31–34, 93–95, 185–86, 196–200); Mansfield, "Responsibility versus Self-Expression," 96–111; Krannawitter, *Vindicating Lincoln*, 304–6.

37. Lincoln, "Speech at a Republican Banquet," 2:385.

38. Obama, *Audacity of Hope*, 361.

39. Ibid., 361–62.

40. Ibid.; cf. Obama, "Victory Speech."

Conclusion

1. Donald, *Lincoln Reconsidered*, 3–18.

2. Croly, *Promise*, 94; also Johnson, "Lincoln's Birthday," 1:180–811.

3. See especially Wilson, *Constitutional Government*, 4; Wilson, *New Freedom*, 42–43; Roosevelt, "New Conditions," 1:752.

Bibliography

Abbott, Philip. *The Exemplary Presidency: Franklin D. Roosevelt and the American Political Tradition*. Amherst: University of Massachusetts Press, 1990.
"Abraham Lincoln, 1809–1909." *Chicago Daily Tribune*, February 7, 1909.
Alvis, David. "Herbert Croly's Transformation of the American Regime." Claremont Institute, 2003, at http://www.claremont.org/publications/pubid.247/pub_detail.asp (accessed May 4, 2007).
Alvis, David, and Jason R. Jividen. "Distaining the Beaten Path: Herbert Croly and the Hundredth Anniversary of Lincoln's Birth." Paper presented at the annual meeting of the American Political Science Association, Toronto, Canada, September 3, 2009.
Amar, Akhil Reed. *The Bill of Rights: Creation and Reconstruction*. New Haven: Yale University Press, 1998.
Anastaplo, George. *The Constitution of 1787: A Commentary*. Baltimore: Johns Hopkins University Press, 1989.
———. *Abraham Lincoln: A Constitutional Biography*. Lanham, MD: Rowman and Littlefield, 1999.
Anderson, Charles W. *Pragmatic Liberalism*. Chicago: University of Chicago Press, 1990.
Aristotle. *Nicomachean Ethics*. In *The Basic Works of Aristotle*, ed. Richard McKeon. New York: Random House, 1941.
Arnhart, Larry. "'The God-like Prince': John Locke, Executive Prerogative, and the American Presidency." *Presidential Studies Quarterly* 11 (Spring 1979): 121–30.
———. *Darwinian Natural Right: The Biological Ethics of Human Nature*. Albany: State University of New York Press, 1998.
Beard, Charles A. *An Economic Interpretation of the Constitution of the United States*. 1913. Reprint, New York: Free Press, 1986.
Becker, Carl L. *The Declaration of Independence: A Study in the History of Political Ideas*. 1922. Reprint, New York: Vintage Books, 1942.
Beer, Samuel H. "In Search of a New Public Philosophy." In *The New American Political System*, ed. Anthony King, 5–44. Washington, DC: American Enterprise Institute Press, 1978.
Belz, Herman. *Equality Transformed: A Quarter-Century of Affirmative Action*. New Brunswick, NJ: Transaction Publishers, 1991.
———. *Abraham Lincoln, Constitutionalism, and Equal Rights in the Civil War Era*. New York: Fordham University Press, 1998.
Bennett, Lerone J., Jr. "Was Abe Lincoln a White Supremacist?" *Ebony* 23 (February 1968): 35–42.

Bibliography

———. *Forced into Glory: Abraham Lincoln's White Dream*. Chicago: Johnson Publishing, 2000.
Berns, Walter. "Does the Constitution 'Secure These Rights'?" In *How Democratic Is the Constitution?* ed. Robert A. Goldwin and William A. Schambra, 59–78. Washington, DC: American Enterprise Institute Press, 1980.
Beschloss, Michael. "The Great Inspirer." *Newsweek*, November 24, 2008.
Bimes, Terri, and Stephen Skowronek. "Woodrow Wilson's Critique of Popular Leadership: Reassessing the Modern–Traditional Divide in Presidential History." *Polity* 29 (Fall 1996): 27–63.
Boritt, Gabor S. *Lincoln and the Economics of the American Dream*. Memphis: Memphis State University Press, 1978.
Bradford, M. E. "The Heresy of Equality: Bradford Replies to Jaffa." *Modern Age* 20, no. 1 (Winter 1976): 62–77.
———. "The Lincoln Legacy: A Long View." *Modern Age* 24, no. 4 (Fall 1980): 355–63.
Bryce, James. *The American Commonwealth*. 3 vols. London: MacMillan and Company, 1888.
Burns, James MacGregor. *Roosevelt: The Lion and the Fox*. New York: Harcourt, Brace, and World, 1956.
Calhoun, John C. "Speech on the Reception of Abolition Petitions," February 6, 1837. In *Union and Liberty: The Political Philosophy of John C. Calhoun*, ed. Ross M. Lence, 461–76. Indianapolis: Liberty Fund, 1992.
———. "Speech on the Importance of Domestic Slavery." U.S. Senate, January 10, 1838. In *Slavery Defended: The Views of the Old South*, ed. Eric L. McKitrick, 16–19. Englewood Cliffs, NJ: Prentice-Hall, 1963.
Carey, George, W. "New Preface." In *The Basic Symbols of the American Political Tradition*, by Willmoore Kendall and George W. Carey, ix–xxiii. Washington, DC: The Catholic University of America Press, 1995, ix–xxiii.
Carrese, Paul. "Montesquieu, the Founders, and Woodrow Wilson: The Evolution of Rights and the Eclipse of Constitutionalism." In *The Progressive Revolution in Politics and Political Science*, ed. John Marini and Ken Masugi, 149–57. Lanham, MD: Rowman and Littlefield, 2005.
Ceaser, James W. *Presidential Selection: Theory and Development*. Princeton, NJ: Princeton University Press, 1979.
———. *Nature and History in American Political Development: A Debate*. Cambridge: Harvard University Press, 2006.
Ceaser, James W., Glen E. Thurow, Jeffrey Tulis, and Joseph M. Bessette. "The Rise of the Rhetorical Presidency." *Presidential Studies Quarterly* 11 (Spring 1981): 158–71.
Clor, Harry. "Woodrow Wilson." In *American Political Thought: The Philosophic Dimension of American Statesmanship*, ed. Morton J. Frisch and Richard G. Stevens, 267–94. Itasca, IL: F. E. Peacock, 1983.
Croly, Herbert. *The Promise of American Life*. 1909. Reprint, New York: Capricorn Books, 1964.
———. *Progressive Democracy*. 1914. Reprint, New Brunswick, NJ: Transaction Publishers, 1998.
———. "The Paradox of Lincoln." *New Republic*, February 18, 1920.

Cuomo, Mario, M. *Why Lincoln Matters, Today More than Ever.* New York: Harcourt, 2004.
Dahl, Robert A. "Myth of the Presidential Mandate." *Political Science Quarterly* 105, no. 3 (Autumn 1990): 355–72.
Day, Donald. *Franklin D. Roosevelt's Own Story.* Boston: Little, Brown, 1951.
de Alvarez, Leo Paul S. "The Missing Passage of the Vanderbilt Lectures." In *Willmoore Kendall: Maverick of American Conservatives,* ed. John A. Murley and John E. Alvis, 141–55. Lanham, MD: Lexington Books, 2002.
Dewey, John. *The Public and Its Problems.* 1927. Reprint, New York: Henry Holt, 1946.
———. "The House Divided against Itself." *New Republic,* April 24, 1929.
———. *Individualism Old and New.* New York: Milton, Balch, 1930.
———. "The Future of Liberalism." *Journal of Philosophy* 32 (April 25, 1935): 225–30.
———. *Liberalism and Social Action.* New York: G. P. Putnam's Sons, 1935.
———. *Freedom and Culture.* 1939. Reprint, New York: G. P. Putnam's Sons, 1979.
Diamond, Martin. *As Far as Republican Principles Will Admit: Essays by Martin Diamond.* Edited by William A. Schambra. Washington, DC: American Enterprise Institute Press, 1992.
Dietze, Gottfried. *America's Political Dilemma.* Baltimore: Johns Hopkins University Press, 1968.
DiLorenzo, Thomas J. *The Real Lincoln: A New Look at Abraham Lincoln, His Agenda, and an Unnecessary War.* New York: Three Rivers Press, 2002.
Donald, David H. *Lincoln Reconsidered.* 1955. Reprint, New York: Vintage Books, 1961.
———. "Abraham Lincoln: Whig in the White House." In *The Enduring Lincoln,* ed. Norman A. Graebner, 47–66. Urbana: University of Illinois Press, 1959.
———. *Lincoln.* New York: Simon and Schuster, 1995.
Eden, Robert. *Political Leadership and Nihilism.* Tampa: University Presses of Florida, 1983.
———. "On the Origins of the Regime of Pragmatic Liberalism: John Dewey, Adolf A. Berle, and FDR's Commonwealth Club Address of 1932." *Studies in American Political Development* 7 (Spring 1993): 74–150.
Eidelberg, Paul. *A Discourse on Statesmanship: The Design and Transformation of the American Polity.* Urbana: University of Illinois Press, 1974.
Eisenach, Eldon, J. *The Lost Promise of Progressivism.* Lawrence: University Press of Kansas, 1994.
Elkins, Stanley M. *Slavery: A Problem in American Institutional and Intellectual Life.* New York: Grosset and Dunlap, 1959.
Ellis, Richard J. "Rival Visions of Equality in American Political Culture." *Review of Politics* 54, no. 2 (Spring 1992): 253–80.
Ellis, Richard J., and Stephen Kirk. "Presidential Mandates in the Nineteenth Century: Conceptual Change and Institutional Development." *Studies in American Political Development* 9 (Spring 1995): 117–86.
———. "Jefferson, Jackson, and the Origins of the Presidential Mandate." In *Speaking to the People: The Rhetorical Presidency in Historical Perspective,* ed. Richard J. Ellis, 35–65. Amherst: University of Massachusetts Press, 1998.
Erler, Edward J. "Still Separate but Equal." Claremont Institute, summer 2004, at http://www.claremont.org/publications/crb/id.1059/article_detail.asp (accessed September 21, 2010).

Fehrenbacher, Don. E. *Prelude to Greatness: Lincoln in the 1850s.* Stanford, CA: Stanford University Press, 1962.

Fishman, Ethan. "Under the Circumstances: Abraham Lincoln and Classical Prudence." In *Abraham Lincoln: Sources of Style and Leadership*, ed. Frank J. Williams, William J. Pederson, and Vincent Marsala, 3–15. Westport, CT: Greenwood Press, 1994.

———. "The Prudential FDR." In *FDR and the Modern Presidency: Leadership and Legacy*, ed. Mark J. Rozell and William D. Pederson, 148–65. Westport, CT: Praeger, 1997.

———. *The Prudential Presidency: An Aristotelian Approach to Presidential Leadership.* Westport, CT: Praeger, 2001.

———. "On Professor Donald's Lincoln." In *Lincoln's American Dream*, ed. Kenneth L. Deutsch and Joseph R. Fornieri, 232–42. Washington, DC: Potomac Books, 2005.

Fitzhugh, George. *Sociology for the South: or the Failure of Free Society.* 1854. Reprint, Ithaca, NY: Cornell University Libraries, 2007.

———. *Cannibals All! or Slaves without Masters.* Edited by C. Vann Woodward. 1857. Reprint, Cambridge, MA: Belknap Press, 2004.

Fletcher, George P. *Our Secret Constitution: How Abraham Lincoln Redefined American Democracy.* New York: Oxford University Press, 2001.

Foner, Eric. *Free Soil, Free Labor, Free Men.* 1970. Reprint, Oxford: Oxford University Press, 1995.

———. "A New Abraham Lincoln?" *Reviews in American History* 7, no. 3 (September 1979): 375–79.

Fornieri, Joseph R. "Abraham Lincoln and the Declaration of Independence: The Meaning of Equality." In *Abraham Lincoln: Sources of Style and Leadership*, ed. Frank J. Williams, William J. Pederson, and Vincent Marsala, 45–69. Westport, CT: Greenwood Press, 1994.

———. "Lincoln and the Emancipation Proclamation: A Model of Prudent Leadership." In *Tempered Strength: Studies in the Nature and Scope of Prudential Leadership*, ed. Ethan Fishman, 125–49. Lanham, MD: Lexington Books, 2002.

Fott, David. "John Dewey's Alternative Liberalism." In *History of American Political Thought*, ed. Bryan-Paul Frost and Jeffrey Sikkenga, 585–97. Lanham, MD: Lexington Books, 2003.

Frazier, E. Franklin. *The Negro Family in the United States.* Chicago: University of Chicago Press, 1939.

Frisch, Morton J. "Franklin Delano Roosevelt." In *American Political Thought: The Philosophic Dimension of American Statesmanship*, ed. Morton J. Frisch and Richard G. Stevens, 319–35. Itasca, IL: F. E. Peacock, 1983.

Gaughan, Anthony. "Woodrow Wilson and the Legacy of the Civil War." *Civil War History* 43, no. 3 (September 1997): 225–42.

Goldwin, Robert A. *Why Blacks, Women, and Jews Are Not Mentioned in the Constitution, and Other Unorthodox Views.* Washington, DC: American Enterprise Institute Press, 1990.

Goodwin, Doris Kearns. *Team of Rivals: The Political Genius of Abraham Lincoln.* New York: Simon and Schuster, 2005.

Greenstein, Fred I. "Change and Continuity in the Modern Presidency." In *The New American Political System*, ed. Anthony King, 45–85. Washington, DC: American Enterprise Institute Press, 1978.

———. "Introduction: Toward a Modern Presidency." In *Leadership in the Modern Presidency*, ed. Fred I. Greenstein, 1–6. Cambridge, MA: Harvard University Press, 1988.

Guelzo, Allen C. *Abraham Lincoln, Redeemer President*. Grand Rapids, MI: William B. Eerdmans, 1999.

———. "How Abe Lincoln Lost the Black Vote: Lincoln and Emancipation in the African American Mind." *Journal of the Abraham Lincoln Association* 25, no. 1 (Winter 2004): 1–22.

Hamilton, Alexander. "The Farmer Refuted," February 23, 1775. In *Selected Writings and Speeches of Alexander Hamilton: Writings*, ed. Morton J. Frisch, 19–22. Washington, DC: American Enterprise Institute Press, 1985.

Hamilton, Alexander, James Madison, and John Jay. *The Federalist*. Edited by Jacob E. Cooke. Hanover, NH: Wesleyan University Press, 1982.

Hammond, James Henry. "Speech on the Admission of Kansas," U.S. Senate, March 4, 1858. In *Slavery Defended: The Views of the Old South*, ed. Eric L. McKitrick, 121–25. Englewood Cliffs, NJ: Prentice-Hall, 1963.

Hanna, William F. "Theodore Roosevelt and the Lincoln Image." *Lincoln Herald* 94, no. 4 (Spring 1992): 2–9.

Hayward, Steven. "The Children of Abraham." *Reason* 23 (May 1991): 24–31.

Hofstadter, Richard J. *The American Political Tradition and the Men Who Made It*. New York: Knopf, 1954.

Hoover, Herbert. "Dangers from Centralization and Bureaucracy to Liberty and Individual Initiative if National Government Assumes Responsibility for Local Relief." Radio address, February 12, 1931. In *The State Papers and Other Public Writings of Herbert Hoover*, ed. William Starr Myers, 1:500–505. 2 vols. Garden City, NY: Doubleday, Doran, 1934.

"Hoover's Attack on the New Deal at Republicans' Lincoln Day Dinner." *New York Times*, February 14, 1939.

Jackson, Andrew. "Veto Message—Bank of the United States," July 10, 1832. In *The Statesmanship of Andrew Jackson as Told in his Writings and Speeches*, ed. Francis Newton Thorpe, 154–76. New York: Tandy-Thomas Company, 1909.

———. "Removal of the Public Deposits," September 18, 1833. In *The Statesmanship of Andrew Jackson as Told in his Writings and Speeches*, ed. Francis Newton Thorpe, 261–81. New York: Tandy-Thomas Company, 1909.

Jaffa, Harry V. *Crisis of the House Divided: An Interpretation of the Issues in the Lincoln-Douglas Debates*. 1959. Reprint, Chicago: University of Chicago Press, 1982.

———. *Equality and Liberty: Theory and Practice in American Politics*. New York: Oxford University Press, 1965.

———. "Lincoln and the Cause of Freedom." *National Review*, September 21, 1965.

———. *The Conditions of Freedom: Essays in Political Philosophy*. Baltimore: Johns Hopkins University Press, 1975.

———. "Equality as a Conservative Principle." *Loyola of Los Angeles Law Review* 8 (June 1975): 471–505.

———. *How to Think About the American Revolution: A Bicentennial Cerebration*. Durham, NC: Carolina Academic Press, 1978.

———. "Abraham Lincoln." In *American Political Thought: The Philosophic Dimension of American Statesmanship*, ed. Morton J. Frisch and Richard G. Stevens, 209–12. Itasca, IL: F. E. Peacock, 1983.

———. *American Conservatism and the American Founding.* Durham, NC: Carolina Academic Press, 1984.

———. "Inventing the Gettysburg Address." *Intercollegiate Review* 28 (Fall 1992): 51–56.

———. *A New Birth of Freedom: Abraham Lincoln and the Coming of the Civil War.* Lanham, MD: Rowman and Littlefield, 2000.

Jaffa, Harry V., with Bruce Ledewitz, Robert L. Stone, and George Anastaplo. *Original Intent and the Framers of the Constitution: A Disputed Question.* Washington, DC: Regnery Gateway, 1994.

Jefferson, Thomas. "To Elias Shipman and Others, a Committee of the Merchants of New Haven," July 12, 1801. In Thomas Jefferson, *Writings,* ed. Merrill D. Peterson, 497–500. New York: Library of America, 1984.

———. "To John C. Breckinridge," August 12, 1803. In *Writings,* 1136–41.

———. "To John Adams," October 28, 1813. In *Writings,* 1304–10.

Johnson, Lyndon B. *Public Papers of the Presidents of the United States: Lyndon B. Johnson, 1963–1964.* 2 vols. Washington, DC: United States Government Printing Office, 1965.

———. *Public Papers of the Presidents of the United States: Lyndon B. Johnson, 1965.* 2 vols. Washington, DC: United States Government Printing Office, 1966.

———. "Remarks to New Participants in 'Plans for Progress' Equal Opportunity Appointments," January 16, 1964. In *Public Papers, 1963–64,* 1:139–43.

———. "Remarks to New Participants in 'Plans for Progress' Equal Opportunity Appointments," January 22, 1964. In *Public Papers, 1963–64,* 1:211–15.

———. "Remarks at the Lincoln Memorial," February 12, 1964. In *Public Papers, 1963–64,* 1:293.

———. "Special Message to the Congress Proposing a Nationwide War on the Sources of Poverty," March 16, 1964. In *Public Papers, 1963–64,* 1:375–80.

———. "Remarks to a Group of Treasury Department Officials in Equal Employment Opportunity," April 21, 1964. In *Public Papers, 1963–64,* 1:503–5.

———. "Remarks to a Group of Civil Rights Leaders," April 29, 1964. In *Public Papers, 1963–64,* 1:588–89.

———. "Remarks in New York before the 50th Annual Convention of the Amalgamated Clothing Workers," May 9, 1964. In *Public Papers, 1963–64,* 1:655–59.

———. "Remarks at a Meeting of the President's Commission on Equal Employment Opportunity," May 12, 1964. In *Public Papers, 1963–64,* 1:681–85.

———. "Remarks at the University of Michigan," May 22, 1964. In *Public Papers, 1963–64,* 1:704–7.

———. "Remarks in Madison Square Garden at a Rally of the Liberal Party of New York," October 15, 1964. In *Public Papers, 1963–64,* 2:1348–53.

———. "Remarks on the City Hall Steps, Dayton, Ohio," October 16, 1964. In *Public Papers, 1963–64,* 2:1368–74.

———. "Remarks at the Convention Center Arena in Pittsburgh, Pennsylvania," October 27, 1964. In *Public Papers, 1963–64,* 2:1470–80.

———. "Remarks at the Chicago Stadium," October 30, 1964. In *Public Papers, 1963–64,* 2:1545–47.

———. "Remarks in Koscinsko Park, Milwaukee," October 30, 1964. In *Public Papers, 1963–64,* 2:1535–40.

———. "Remarks in Madison Square Garden," October 31, 1964. In *Public Papers, 1963–64*, 2:1558–61.

———. "Remarks at Southwest Texas State College, San Marcos," November 20, 1964. In *Public Papers, 1963–64*, 2:1606–10.

———. "Remarks at the National Urban League's Community Action Assembly," December 10, 1964. In *Public Papers, 1963–64*, 2:1653–56.

———. "Remarks to Students Participating in the U.S. Senate Youth Program," February 5, 1965. In *Public Papers, 1965*, 1:148–52.

———. "Remarks at the White House on Lincoln's Birthday," February 12, 1965. In *Public Papers, 1965*, 1:180–81.

———. "Special Message to Congress: The American Promise," March 15, 1965. In *Public Papers, 1965*, 1:281–87.

———. "Remarks of Welcome at the White House to President Yameogo of Upper Volta," March 29, 1965. In *Public Papers, 1965*, 1:339–41.

———. "Commencement Address at Howard University: 'To Fulfill These Rights,'" June 4, 1965. In *Public Papers, 1965*, 2:635–40.

———. *The Vantage Point: Perspectives of the Presidency, 1963–1969*. New York: Holt, Rinehart, and Winston, 1971.

Jones, Alfred Haworth. *Roosevelt's Image Brokers: Poets, Playwrights, and the Use of the Lincoln Symbol*. Port Washington, NY: Kennikat Press, 1974.

Kammen, Michael. *Mystic Chords of Memory: The Transformation of Tradition in American Culture*. New York: Alfred A. Knopf, 1991.

Kelly, Alfred H., Winfred A. Harbison, and Herman Belz. *The American Constitution: Its Origins and Development*. 2 vols. New York: W. W. Norton, 1991.

Kendall, Willmoore. *The Conservative Affirmation*. Chicago: Henry Regnery, 1963.

———. "Equality: Commitment or Ideal?" *Phalanx* 1, no. 3 (Fall 1967): 95–103.

———. "Equality and the American Political Tradition." In *Willmoore Kendall: Contra Mundum*, ed. Nellie D. Kendall, 347–61. New Rochelle, NY: Arlington House, 1971.

———. "The Two Majorities." In *Willmoore Kendall: Contra Mundum*, ed. Nellie D. Kendall, 202–27. New Rochelle, NY: Arlington House, 1971.

Kendall, Willmoore, and George W. Carey. *The Basic Symbols of the American Political Tradition*. Baton Rouge: Louisiana State University Press, 1970.

Kesler, Charles, R. "Woodrow Wilson and the Statesmanship of Progress." In *Natural Right and Political Right: Essays in Honor of Harry V. Jaffa*, ed. Thomas B. Silver and Peter W. Schramm, 103–27. Durham, NC: Carolina Academic Press, 1984.

———. "Introduction." In *Keeping the Tablets: Modern American Conservative Thought*, ed. William F. Buckley, Jr., and Charles R. Kesler, 3–18. New York: Harper and Row, 1988.

———. "The Public Philosophy of the New Freedom and the New Deal." In *The New Deal and Its Legacy: Critique and Reappraisal*, ed. Robert Eden, 155–66. New York: Greenwood Press, 1989.

———. "A New Birth of Freedom: Harry V. Jaffa and the Study of America." In *Leo Strauss, the Straussians, and the American Regime*, ed. Kenneth L. Deutsch and John A. Murley, 265–82. Lanham, MD: Rowman and Littlefield, 1999.

———. "The Audacity of Barack Obama." Claremont Institute, January 19, 2009, at http://www.claremont.org/publications/crb/id.1579/article_detail.asp (accessed April 20, 2009).

King, Martin Luther, Jr. "I Have a Dream," August 28, 1963. In *American Political Rhetoric.* ed. Peter Augustine Lawler and Robert Martin Schaefer, 277–80. 5th ed. Lanham, MD: Rowman and Littlefield, 2005.

Kleinerman, Benjamin A. "Lincoln's Example: Executive Power and the Survival of Constitutionalism." *Perspectives on Politics* 3, no. 4 (December 2005): 801–16.

Krannawitter, Thomas L. "Obama as Lincoln." *Washington Times*, December 19, 2008.

———. *Vindicating Lincoln: Defending the Politics of Our Greatest President.* Lanham, MD: Rowman and Littlefield, 2008.

Lerner, Max. "The Lincoln Image." *New Republic*, March 8, 1939.

Lester, Julius. *Look Out, Whitey! Black Power's Gon' Get Your Mama!* New York: Dial Press, 1968.

Levy, David. *Herbert Croly of the New Republic: The Life and Thought of an American Progressive.* Princeton, NJ: Princeton University Press, 1985.

Lincoln, Abraham. *The Collected Works of Abraham Lincoln.* Edited by Roy P. Basler. 9 vols. New Brunswick, NJ: Rutgers University Press, 1953.

———. "Address before the Young Men's Lyceum of Springfield, Illinois," January 27, 1838. In *Collected Works*, 1:108–15.

———. "Temperance Address: An Address, Delivered before the Springfield Washington Temperance Society," February 22, 1842. In *Collected Works*, 1:271–79.

———. "Speech in the United States House of Representatives on Internal Improvements," June 20, 1848. In *Collected Works*, 1:480–90.

———. "Speech in the U.S. House of Representatives on the Presidential Question," July 27, 1848. In *Collected Works*, 1:501–15.

———. "Fragments on Government," July 1, 1854. In *Collected Works*, 2:220–22.

———. "Fragment on Slavery," July 1, 1854. In *Collected Works*, 2:222–23.

———. "Speech at Springfield, Illinois," October 4, 1854. In *Collected Works*, 2:240–47.

———. "Speech at Peoria, Illinois," October 16, 1854. In *Collected Works*, 2:247–83.

———. "Speech at a Republican Banquet, Chicago, Illinois," December 10, 1856. In *Collected Works*, 2:383–86.

———. "Speech at Springfield, Illinois," June 26, 1857. In *Collected Works*, 2:398–410.

———. "First Lecture on Discoveries and Inventions," April 6, 1858. In *Collected Works*, 2:437–42.

———. "A House Divided." Speech at Springfield, Illinois, June 16, 1858. In *Collected Works*, 2:461–69.

———. "Speech at Chicago, Illinois," July 10, 1858. In *Collected Works*, 2:484–502.

———. "Speech at Springfield, Illinois," July 17, 1858. In *Collected Works*, 2:504–21.

———. "Reply: First Debate with Stephen A. Douglas at Ottawa, Illinois," August 21, 1858. In *Collected Works*, 3:12–30.

———. "Fragment on Pro-slavery Theology," October 1, 1858. In *Collected Works*, 3:204–5.

———. "Reply: Fifth Debate with Stephen A. Douglas, at Galesburg, Illinois," October 7, 1858. In *Collected Works*, 3:219–37.

———. "Rejoinder: Sixth Debate with Stephen A. Douglas, at Quincy, Illinois," October 13, 1858. In *Collected Works*, 3:275–83.

———. "Reply: Seventh and Last Debate with Stephen A. Douglas at Alton, Illinois," October 15, 1858. In *Collected Works*, 3:297–318.

———. "Second Lecture on Discoveries and Inventions," February 11, 1859. In *Collected Works*, 3:356–63.

———. "To Henry L. Pierce and Others," April 6, 1859. In *Collected Works*, 3:374–76.

———. "Speech at Cincinnati, Ohio," September 17, 1859. In *Collected Works*, 3:438–62.

———. "Address before the Wisconsin State Agricultural Society, Milwaukee, Wisconsin," September 30, 1859. In *Collected Works*, 3:471–82.

———. "Address at Cooper Institute, New York City," February 27, 1860. In *Collected Works*, 3:522–50.

———. "Speech at Hartford, Connecticut," March 5, 1860. In *Collected Works*, 4:2–13.

———. "Speech at New Haven, Connecticut," March 6, 1860. In *Collected Works*, 4:13–30.

———. "Speech to Germans at Cincinnati, Ohio," February 12, 1861. In *Collected Works*, 4:201–3.

———. "Speech in Independence Hall, Philadelphia, Pennsylvania," February 22, 1861. In *Collected Works*, 4:240.

———. "First Inaugural Address," March 4, 1861. In *Collected Works*, 4:262–71.

———. "Message to Congress in Special Session," July 4, 1861. In *Collected Works*, 4:421–41.

———. "Annual Message to Congress," December 3, 1861. In *Collected Works*, 5:35–53.

———. "Address on Colonization to a Deputation of Negroes," August 14, 1862. In *Collected Works*, 5:370–75.

———. "To James C. Conkling," August 26, 1863. In *Collected Works*, 6:406–10.

———. "Opinion on the Draft," September 14, 1863. In *Collected Works*, 6:444–49.

———. "Address delivered at the dedication of the Cemetery at Gettysburg," November 19, 1863. In *Collected Works*, 7:22–23.

———. "To Michael Hahn," March 13, 1864. In *Collected Works*, 7:243.

———. "Reply to New York Workingmen's Democratic Republican Association," March 21, 1864. In *Collected Works*, 7:259–60.

———. "Address at Sanitary Fair, Baltimore, Maryland," April 18, 1864. In *Collected Works*, 7:301–303.

———. "To George B. Ide, James R. Doolittle, and A. Hubbell," May 30, 1864. In *Collected Works*, 7:368.

———. "Reply to Committee Notifying Lincoln of his Renomination," June 9, 1864. In *Collected Works*, 7:380.

———. "To Benjamin F. Butler," August 9, 1864. In *Collected Works*, 7:487–88.

———. "To Charles D. Robinson," August 17, 1864. In *Collected Works*, 7:499–502.

———. "Speech to the One Hundred Sixty-Fourth Ohio Regiment," August 18, 1864. In *Collected Works*, 7:504–5.

———. "Speech to the One Hundred Sixty-Sixth Ohio Regiment," August 22, 1864. In *Collected Works*, 7:512.

———. "Memorandum Concerning His Probable Failure of Re-election," August 23, 1864. In *Collected Works*, 7:514.

———. "Response to a Serenade," October 19, 1864. In *Collected Works*, 8:52–53.

———. "Response to a Serenade," November 8, 1864. In *Collected Works*, 8:96.

———. "Response to a Serenade," November 10, 1864. In *Collected Works*, 8:100–102.

———. "Annual Message to Congress," December 6, 1864. In *Collected Works*, 8:136–53.

———. "Last Public Address," April 11, 1865. In *Collected Works*, 8:399–405.

"Lincoln at Gettysburg." *The Nation*, July 10, 1913.

Lind, Michael. *What Lincoln Believed: The Values and Convictions of America's Greatest President*. New York: Doubleday, 2004.

Lippmann, Walter. *Drift and Mastery*. 1914. Reprint, Madison: University of Wisconsin Press, 1986.

———. *A Preface to Politics*. 1914. Reprint, Amherst, MA: Prometheus Books, 2005.

Locke, John. *The Second Treatise of Government: An Essay Concerning the True Original, Extent, and End of Civil Government*. In *Two Treatises of Government*, ed. Peter Laslett. Cambridge: Cambridge University Press, 1988.

Lowi, Theodore J. *The End of Liberalism: The Second Republic of the United States*. New York: Norton, 1979.

———. *The Personal President: Power Invested, Promise Unfulfilled*. Ithaca, NY: Cornell University Press, 1985.

Machiavelli, Niccolo. *Discourses on Livy*. Translated by Harvey C. Mansfield, Jr., and Nathan Tarcov. Chicago: University of Chicago Press, 1996.

Mansfield, Harvey C., Jr. *Taming the Prince*. New York: Free Press, 1989.

———. *America's Constitutional Soul*. Baltimore: Johns Hopkins University Press, 1991.

———. "Responsibility versus Self-Expression." In *Old Rights and New*, ed. Robert A. Licht, 96–111. Washington, DC: American Enterprise Institute Press, 1993.

Marini, John. "Progressivism, Modern Political Science, and the Transformation of American Conservatism." In *The Progressive Revolution in Politics and Political Science*, ed. John Marini and Ken Masugi, 221–51. Lanham, MD: Rowman and Littlefield, 2005.

McPherson, James M. *Abraham Lincoln and the Second American Revolution*. New York: Oxford University Press, 1990.

Melzer, Arthur M., Jerry Weinberger, and Richard Zinman. "Introduction." In *History and the Idea of Progress*, ed. Arthur M. Melzer, Jerry Weinberger, and Richard Zinman, 1–9. Ithaca, NY: Cornell University Press, 1995.

Meyer, Frank S. "Lincoln without Rhetoric." *National Review*, August 24, 1965.

———. "Again on Lincoln." *National Review*, January 25, 1966.

Mileur, Jerome M. "The Legacy of Reform: Progressive Government, Regressive Politics." In *Progressivism and the New Democracy*, ed. Sidney M. Milkis and Jerome M. Mileur, 259–87. Amherst: University of Massachusetts Press, 1999.

Milkis, Sidney M. "New Deal Party Politics, Administrative Reform, and the Transformation of the American Constitution." In *The New Deal and Its Legacy: Critique and Reappraisal*, ed. Robert Eden, 123–54. New York: Greenwood Press, 1989.

———. *The President and the Parties: The Transformation of the American Party System since the New Deal*. Oxford: Oxford University Press, 1993.

———. "Progressivism, Then and Now." In *Progressivism and the New Democracy*, ed. Sidney M. Milkis and Jerome M. Mileur, 1–39. Amherst: University of Massachusetts Press, 1999.

———. "Franklin D. Roosevelt, the Economic Constitutional Order, and the New Politics of Presidential Leadership." In *The New Deal and the Triumph of Liberalism*, ed. Sidney M. Milkis and Jerome M. Mileur, 31–72. Amherst: University of Massachusetts Press, 2002.

Milkis, Sidney M., and Michael Nelson. *The American Presidency: Origins and Development, 1776–2002*. 4th ed. Washington, DC: Congressional Quarterly Press, 2003.

Miller, Eugene F. "Democratic Statecraft and Technological Advance: Abraham Lincoln's Reflections on 'Discoveries and Inventions.'" *Review of Politics* 63, no. 3 (Summer 2001): 485–515.

Morrisey, Will. "Theodore Roosevelt on Self-Government and the Administrative State." In *The Progressive Revolution in Politics and Political Science*, ed. John Marini and Ken Masugi, 35–71. Lanham, MD: Rowman and Littlefield, 2005.

Mowry, George E. *Theodore Roosevelt and the Progressive Movement.* Madison: University of Wisconsin Press, 1946.

Moynihan, Daniel Patrick. *The Negro Family: The Case for National Action.* Washington, DC: Office of Policy Planning and Research. U.S. Department of Labor, 1965.

Murley, John A. "On the 'Calhounism' of Willmoore Kendall." In *Willmoore Kendall: Maverick of American Conservatives*, ed. John A. Murley and John E. Alvis, 99–139. Lanham, MD: Lexington Books, 2002.

"A News Report of Four Campaign Speeches in Monmouth County, New Jersey." *Newark Evening News*, October 12, 1911.

Nichols, David K. *The Myth of the Modern Presidency.* University Park: Pennsylvania State University Press, 1994.

Nichols, James H., Jr. "Pragmatism and the U.S. Constitution." In *Confronting the Constitution: The Challenge to Locke, Montesquieu, Jefferson, and the Federalists from Utilitarianism, Historicism, Marxism, Freudianism, Pragmatism, Existentialism . . .* , ed. Allan Bloom and Steven J. Kautz, 369–88. Washington, DC: American Enterprise Institute Press, 1990.

Noble, David. "Herbert Croly and American Progressive Thought." *Western Political Quarterly* 7 (December 1954): 537–53.

———. *The Paradox of Progressive Thought.* Minneapolis: University of Minnesota Press, 1958.

Noonan, Peggy. "Conceit of Government: Why Are Our Politicians So Full of Themselves?" *Wall Street Journal*, June 29, 2005.

Oates, Stephen B. "Abraham Lincoln: Republican in the White House." In *Abraham Lincoln and the American Political Tradition*, ed. John L. Thomas, 98–110. Amherst: University of Massachusetts Press, 1986.

Obama, Barack. "What I See in Lincoln's Eyes." *Time*, June 26, 2005, at http://timeinc8-sd11.websys.aol.com/time/magazine/article/0,9171,1077287,00.html (accessed September 21, 2010).

———. *The Audacity of Hope: Thoughts on Reclaiming the American Dream.* New York: Three Rivers Press, 2006.

———. "Announcement for President." Speech at Springfield, Illinois, February 10, 2007, at http://www.nytimes.com/2007/02/10/us/politics/11obama-text.htm (accessed September 21, 2010).

———. "To Form a More Perfect Union." Speech at Philadelphia, Pennsylvania, March 18, 2008, at http://www.nytimes.com/2008/03/18/us/politics/18text-obama.html (accessed September 21, 2010).

———. "Victory Speech." Speech at Grant Park, Chicago, Illinois, November 4, 2008, at http://www.nytimes.com/2008/11/04/us/politics/04text-obama.html (accessed September 21, 2010).

———. "What the People Need Done." Remarks at the 102nd Abraham Lincoln Association Annual Banquet, Springfield, Illinois, February 12, 2009, at http://www.whitehouse.gov/the_press_office/Remarks-of-President-Barack-Obama-What-the-People-Need-Done-Abraham-Lincoln-Bicentennial-Springfield-Illinois (accessed April 20, 2009).

"Offers Recall Amendment; Senator Bristow also Proposes to Embody the Initiative in Constitution." *New York Times,* December 5, 1912.

Olsen, Otto H. "Abraham Lincoln as Revolutionary." *Civil War History* 25, no. 3 (September 1978): 213–24.

Owens, Mackubin Thomas, Jr. "Alexander Hamilton on Natural Rights and Prudence." *Interpretation* 14 (1986): 331–51.

Parenti, Michael. "The Constitution as an Elitist Document." In *How Democratic Is the Constitution?* ed. Robert A. Goldwin and William A. Schambra, 39–58. Washington, DC: American Enterprise Institute Press, 1980.

Parrington, Vernon L. *Main Currents in American Thought: An Interpretation of American Literature from the Beginnings to 1920.* 2 vols. New York: Harcourt Brace, 1927.

Pestritto, Ronald J. "Why Progressivism Is Not, and Never Was, a Source of Conservative Values." Claremont Institute, August 2005, at http://www.claremont.org/publications/pubid.439/ pub_detail.asp (accessed September 21, 2010).

———. *Woodrow Wilson and the Roots of Modern Liberalism.* Lanham, MD: Rowman and Littlefield, 2005.

Peterson, Merrill D. *Lincoln in American Memory.* New York: Oxford University Press, 1994.

Ragsdale, Lyn. *Presidential Politics.* Boston: Houghton Mifflin, 1993.

Rainwater, Lee, and William L. Yancey. *The Moynihan Report and the Politics of Controversy.* Cambridge, MA: MIT Press, 1967.

Rietveld, Ronald D. "Franklin D. Roosevelt's Abraham Lincoln." In *Franklin D. Roosevelt and Abraham Lincoln: Competing Perspectives on Two Great Presidencies,* ed. William D. Pederson and Frank J. Williams, 10–60. Armonk, NY: M. E. Sharpe, 2003.

Roosevelt, Franklin D. *Complete Presidential Conferences of Franklin D. Roosevelt.* Edited by Jonathan Daniels. 25 vols. New York: DaCapo Press, 1972.

———. *The Public Papers and Addresses of Franklin D. Roosevelt.* Edited by Samuel I. Rosenman. 13 vols. New York: Random House, 1938–1950.

———. "The Forgotten Man Speech." Radio address, Albany, New York, April 7, 1932. In *Public Papers,* 1:624–27.

———. "A Concert of Action Based on Fair and Just Concert of Interests." Address at Jefferson Day Dinner, Saint Paul, Minnesota, April 18, 1932. In *Public Papers,* 1:627–39.

———. "'I Pledge You—I Pledge Myself to a New Deal for the American People': The Governor Accepts the Nomination for the Presidency." Chicago, Illinois, July 2, 1932. In *Public Papers,* 1:647–59.

———. "New Conditions Impose New Requirements upon Government and Those Who Conduct Government." Campaign address on progressive government at the Commonwealth Club, San Francisco, California, September 23, 1932. In *Public Papers,* 1:742–56.

———. "We Are Through with 'Delay'; We Are Through with 'Despair'; We Are Ready and Waiting for Better Things." Campaign address on a program for unemployment and long-range planning, Boston, Massachusetts, October 31, 1932. In *Public Papers*, 1:842–56.

———. "We Are Moving toward a Greater Freedom, to Greater Security for the Average Man." Second Fireside Chat of 1934, September 30, 1934. In *Public Papers*, 3:413–22.

———. "'A Tribute to Abraham Lincoln,' to Be Read on His Birthday." Letter to the Lincoln Association of Cleveland, Ohio, January 25, 1936. In *Public Papers*, 5:68.

———. "We Are Fighting to Save a Great and Precious Form of Government for Ourselves and the World." Acceptance of the renomination for the presidency, Philadelphia, Pennsylvania, June 27, 1936. In *Public Papers*, 5:230–36.

———. "In 1776 the Fight Was for Democracy in Taxation. In 1936 That Is Still the Fight." Campaign address at Worcester, Massachusetts, October 21, 1936. In *Public Papers*, 5:522–29.

———. "Campaign Address at Wilmington, Delaware on 'Liberty.'" October 29, 1936. In *Public Papers*, 5:557–58.

———. "Introduction." In *Public Papers*, 7:xxii–xxxiii.

———. "We in Turn Are Striving to Uphold the Integrity of the Moral of Our Democracy." Address at the Jackson Day Dinner. Washington, DC, January 8, 1938. In *Public Papers*, 7:37–45.

———. "Avoiding War, We Seek Our Ends through the Peaceful Processes of Popular Government under the Constitution." Address at the dedication of the memorial on the Gettysburg battlefield, Gettysburg, Pennsylvania, July 3, 1938. In *Public Papers*, 7:419–21.

———. "The Democratic Party Will . . . Continue to Receive the Support of the Majority of Americans Just So Long as It Remains a Liberal Party." Address at Denton, Maryland, September 5, 1938, in *Public Papers*, 7:512–20.

———. "On Jackson Day Every True Follower of Jackson Asks that the Democratic Party Continue to Make Democracy Work." Address at Jackson Day Dinner, January 7, 1939. In *Public Papers*, 8:60–68.

———. "The Future Lies with Those Political Leaders Who Realize That the Great Public Is Interested More in Government than in Politics." Address at Jackson Day Dinner, January 8, 1940. In *Public Papers*, 9:25–35.

———. "'Unless There Is Security at Home, There Cannot Be Lasting Peace in the World.' Message to the Congress on the State of the Union," January 11, 1944. In *Public Papers*, 13:32–44.

———. "We Are Not Going to Turn the Clock Back." Campaign address at Soldiers' Field, Chicago, Illinois, October 28, 1944. In *Public Papers*, 13:369–78.

Roosevelt, Theodore. *The Works of Theodore Roosevelt*. Edited by Hermann Hagedorn. National Edition. 20 vols. New York: Charles Scribner's Sons, 1926.

———. "The New Nationalism." Speech at Osawatomie, Kansas, August 31, 1910. In *Works*, 17:5–22.

———. "A Charter of Democracy." Address before the Ohio State Constitutional Convention at Columbus, Ohio, February 21, 1912. In *Works*, 17:119–48.

———. "The Right of the People to Rule." Address at Carnegie Hall, New York City, March 20, 1912. In *Works*, 151–71.

———. "The Recall of Judicial Decisions." Address at Philadelphia, Pennsylvania, April 10, 1912. In *Works*, 17:190–203.

———. "A Confession of Faith." Address before the National Progressive Party Convention, Chicago, Illinois, August 6, 1912. In *Works*, 17:254–99.

———. "The Future of the Progressive Party." Speech at Chicago, Illinois, December 10, 1912. In *Works*, 17:349–57.

———. *An Autobiography*. New York: Macmillan, 1913. Reprinted as *Works*, vol. 20.

———. "The Heirs of Abraham Lincoln." Speech at the Lincoln Day Banquet, New York City, February 12, 1913. In *Works*, 17:359–78.

———. "Progressive Democracy." A review of Herbert Croly's *Progressive Democracy* and Walter Lippmann's *Drift and Mastery*, November 18, 1914. In *Works*, 12:232–39.

———. "Washington and Lincoln: The Great Examples." In *Works*, 19:48–61.

Rossiter, Clinton. *The American Presidency*. Revised edition. 1956. New York: Harcourt, Brace, and World, 1960.

Rucker, Philip. "A Familiar Precedent for a President-elect," *Washington Post*, November 19, 2008.

Ruiz, George W. "The Ideological Convergence of Theodore Roosevelt and Woodrow Wilson." *Presidential Studies Quarterly* 1 (Winter 1989): 159–77.

Rustin, Bayard. "From Protest to Politics: The Future of the Civil Rights Movement." *Commentary* 39 (February 1965): 25–31.

Sandburg, Carl. "Abraham Lincoln, 1809–1865." In *There Were Giants in the Land: Twenty-eight Historic Americans as Seen by Twenty-eight Contemporary Americans*, ed. Henry J. Morgenthau, Jr., et al., 226–42. New York: Farrar and Rinehart, 1942.

Schlesinger, Arthur M., Jr. *The Age of Roosevelt: The Coming of the New Deal*. Boston: Houghton Mifflin, 1958.

———. *The Age of Roosevelt: The Politics of Upheaval*. Boston: Houghton Mifflin, 1958.

———. *The Imperial Presidency*. Boston: Houghton Mifflin, 1973.

Schneider, Thomas E. *Lincoln's Defense of Politics*. Columbia: University of Missouri Press, 2006.

Schwartz, Barry. *Abraham Lincoln and the Forge of National Memory*. Chicago: University of Chicago Press, 2000.

———. *Abraham Lincoln in the Post-Heroic Era: History and Memory in Late Twentieth-Century America*. Chicago: University of Chicago Press, 2008.

Siemers, David J. "Principled Pragmatism: Abraham Lincoln's Method of Political Analysis." *Presidential Studies Quarterly* 34, no. 4 (December 2004): 804–27.

Skowronek, Stephen. *The Politics that Presidents Make: Leadership from John Adams to Bill Clinton*. Cambridge, MA: Belknap Press, 1997.

Smith, J. Allen. *The Spirit of American Government*. 1919. Reprint, Cambridge, MA: Harvard University Press, 1965.

Sowell, Thomas. *A Conflict of Visions*. New York: Basic Books, 2002.

Stephens, Alexander. "Cornerstone Speech," Savannah, Georgia, March 21, 1861, at http://www.historicaldocuments.com/ CornerstoneSpeech.htm (accessed May 4, 2007).

Stewart, Judd. "Abraham Lincoln on Present-Day Problems and Abraham Lincoln as Represented by Theodore Roosevelt." Letter to the Members of the Ohio State Constitutional Convention, Columbus, Ohio. February 1912. Illinois State Historical Society.

Stourzh, Gerald. *Alexander Hamilton and the Idea of Republican Government*. Stanford, CA: Stanford University Press, 1970.

Strauss, Leo. *Natural Right and History.* Chicago: University of Chicago Press, 1953.
Sunstein, Cass R. *The Second Bill of Rights: FDR's Unfinished Revolution and Why We Need It More Than Ever.* New York: Basic Books, 2004.
Tarcov, Nathan. "A 'Non-Lockean' Locke and the Character of Liberalism." In *Liberalism Reconsidered*, ed. Douglas MacLean and Claudia Mills, 130–40. Totowa, NJ: Rowman and Allanheld, 1983.
Thomas, Evan, and Richard Wolffe. "Obama's Lincoln." *Newsweek*, November 24, 2008.
Thurow, Glen E. "Voice of the People: Speechmaking and the Modern Presidency." An address delivered at Wake Forest University, October 1, 1979.
Tocqueville, Alexis de. *Democracy in America.* Edited by J. P. Mayer, translated by George Lawrence. New York: HarperCollins, 1988.
Tulis, Jeffrey K. "The Decay of Presidential Rhetoric." In *Rhetoric and American Statesmanship*, ed. Glen E. Thurow and Jeffrey D. Wallin, 99–110. Durham, NC: Carolina Academic Press, 1980.
———. *The Rhetorical Presidency.* Princeton, NJ: Princeton University Press, 1987.
———. "The Two Constitutional Presidencies." In *The Presidency and the Political System*, ed. Michael Nelson, 91–123. 4th ed. Washington, DC: Congressional Quarterly Press, 1995.
"An Untrammeled Judiciary." *New York Times*, August 16, 1911.
Weisberger, Bernard A. "The Great Arrogance of the Present Is to Forget the Intelligence of the Past." *American Heritage* (September/October 1990): 97–102.
West, Thomas G. "Misunderstanding the American Founding." In *Interpreting Tocqueville's Democracy in America*, ed. Ken Masugi, 155–77. Savage, MD: Rowman and Littlefield, 1991.
Williams, T. Harry. "Abraham Lincoln: Principle and Pragmatism in Politics." *Mississippi Historical Review* 40 (June 1953): 89–106.
———. "Abraham Lincoln: Pragmatic Democrat." In *The Enduring Lincoln*, ed. Norman A. Graebner, 23–46. Urbana: University of Illinois Press, 1959.
Wills, Garry. *Nixon Agonistes: The Crisis of the Self-Made Man.* Boston: Houghton Mifflin, 1970.
———. *Inventing America: Jefferson's Declaration of Independence.* New York: Doubleday, 1978.
———. *Lincoln at Gettysburg: The Words That Remade America.* New York: Simon and Schuster, 1992.
Wilson, Woodrow. *The Papers of Woodrow Wilson.* Edited by Arthur S. Link. 69 vols. Princeton, NJ: Princeton University Press, 1966–1993.
———. "Cabinet Government in the United States." *International Review* 7 (August 1879): 146–63.
———. *Congressional Government: A Study in American Politics.* 1884. Reprint, New York: Meridian Books, 1956.
———. "The Study of Administration," November 1, 1886. In *Papers*, 5:357–80.
———. "Leaders of Men," June 17, 1890. In *Papers*, 6:644–71.
———. *Division and Reunion, 1829–1909.* 1893. Reprint, New York: Longmans, Green, 1916.
———. "A Calendar of Great Americans," February 1894. In *Papers*, 8:368–81.
———. "Leaderless Government," September 1897. In *Papers*, 10:288–305.

———. *The State: Elements of Historical and Practical Politics.* 1898. Reprint, Boston: D. C. Heath, 1918.

———. *Constitutional Government in the United States.* 1908. Reprint, New York: Columbia University Press, 1961.

———. "'Abraham Lincoln: A Man of the People.' An Address in Chicago on Lincoln's Birthday," February 12, 1909. In *Papers*, 19:33–46.

———. "A Campaign Address in Asbury Park, New Jersey," October 15, 1910. In *Papers*, 1:328–34.

———. "An Address to the Los Angeles Jefferson Club," May 12, 1911. In *Papers*, 23:32–40.

———. "An Address in Chicago to Democrats on Lincoln's Birthday," February 12, 1912. In *Papers*, 24:151–62.

———. "Address in the Williams Grove Auditorium, Williams Grove, Pennsylvania," August 29, 1912. In *Crossroads*, 52–61.

———. "Human Rights." Address delivered at the Parade Grounds, Minneapolis, Minnesota, September 18, 1912. In *Crossroads*, 185–95.

———. "Lessons from Lincoln." Address delivered at the Coliseum, State Fair Grounds, Springfield, Illinois, October 9, 1912. In *Crossroads*, 394–98.

———. "Remarks in Springfield, Illinois, on the Main Issue of the Campaign," October 9, 1912. In *Papers*, 25:390–92.

———. "Government for the Average Man." Delivered at Clarksburg, West Virginia, October 18, 1912. In *Crossroads*, 445–52.

———. "An Inaugural Address," March 4, 1913. In *Papers*, 27:148–52.

———. *The New Freedom: A Call for the Emancipation of the Generous Energies of a People.* 1913. Reprint, Englewood Cliffs, NJ: Prentice-Hall, 1961.

———. *A Crossroads of Freedom: The 1912 Campaign Speeches of Woodrow Wilson.* Edited by John Wells Davidson. New Haven, CT: Yale University Press, 1956.

Wolfe, Christopher. "Woodrow Wilson: Interpreting the Constitution." *Review of Politics* 41, no. 1 (January 1979): 121–42.

Yarbrough, Jean M. "Theodore Roosevelt and the Stewardship of the American Presidency." In *History of American Political Thought*, ed. Bryan-Paul Frost and Jeffrey Sikkenga, 536–48. Lanham, MD: Lexington Books, 2003.

Zarefsky, David. "Lyndon Johnson Redefines 'Equal Opportunity': The Beginnings of Affirmative Action." *Central States Speech Journal* 31, no. 2 (Summer 1980): 85–94.

———. "Presidential Rhetoric and the Power of Definition." *Presidential Studies Quarterly* 34, no. 3 (September 2004): 607–19.

Zentner, Scott J. "Liberalism and Executive Power: Woodrow Wilson and the American Founders." *Polity* 26, no. 4 (Summer 1994): 579–99.

———. "President and Party in the Thought of Woodrow Wilson." *Presidential Studies Quarterly* 26, no. 3 (Summer 1996): 666–77.

Zuckert, Catherine, and Michael Zuckert. *The Truth about Leo Strauss: Political Philosophy and American Democracy.* Chicago: University of Chicago Press, 2006.

Index

"Abraham Lincoln: A Man of the People" speech (Wilson), 75–77, 84
Abraham Lincoln and the Second American Revolution (McPherson), 11
affirmative action, 148, 151
American Youth Congress, 106
Audacity of Hope: Thoughts on Reclaiming the American Dream, The (Obama), 158–59, 163–64, 166–67, 169, 172
Autobiography (Roosevelt), 33

Basic Symbols of the American Political Tradition, The (Kendall and Carey), 14, 15, 17
Beer, Samuel, 150
Belz, Herman, 21, 88
Bennett, Lerone, 147
Berle, Adolf, 107, 120–22, 129
Boritt, Gabor S., 44–45
Bowers, Claude, 100
Bradford, M. E., 14
Bristow, Joseph, 54
Brokaw, Tom, 170
Brown, John, 161–62
Brown v. Board of Education of Topeka (1954), 149
Bull Moose Progressive Party, 6, 33
Burke, Edmund, 77
Burns, Ken, 11, 98–99

"Calendar of Great Americans, A" (Wilson), 76
Calhoun, John C., 81, 107
capital, 36, 41–46, 68
Carey, George W., 14, 15–17, 23, 31, 88, 92, 95, 129

Ceaser, James, 20, 79, 88
Charter of Democracy address (Roosevelt), 37, 49
Chicago Tribune, centennial editorial, February, 1909, 35
Churchill, Winston, 149
Civil Rights Act of 1964, The, 138–41, 143, 149, 151, 176
civil rights movement, the, 134, 139
Clay, Henry, 25
Clinton, Hillary, 156
"Commonwealth Club" address (Franklin Roosevelt), 113, 120, 122–24, 126–128
Conkling, James C., 143
Constitution, U.S., 40, 54, 56, 66–68, 86–87, 89–91, 108, 112, 143, 151; Article II of, 28, 90, 163
Constitutional Government in the United States (Wilson), 86
Croly, Herbert, 6, 56, 58–63, 71, 91, 106–107, 112–113, 116, 121, 156, 177
Cuomo, Mario, 99

Darwin, Charles, 67, 76
Darwinian principles, 67–68
de Alvarez, Leo Paul S., 17
Declaration of Independence, 3, 6, 21, 31, 39, 62, 69–71, 74–75, 77–80, 109–10, 115–116, 118–20, 123, 125, 130, 147, 158–59, 163–64, 167, 177; as founding document, 13, 14, 15, 17, 31; meaning of equality in, 16, 18, 20, 30, 96, 98, 112, 138, 146
Democracy in America (Tocqueville), 30, 139
Democratic Party, 36, 73, 83, 93, 100, 137, 157

Dewey, John, 103, 107–112, 122–24, 169
Dietze, Gottfried, 88
DiLorenzo, Thomas, 12–13
Division and Reunion, 1829–1909 (Wilson), 80
Donald, David, 3, 100, 174
Douglass, Frederick, 161
Douglas, Stephen, 20, 21, 26, 40, 54, 62–63, 78, 83, 107, 162
Dred Scott v. Sandford (1857), 16, 18, 37, 54–58, 78, 80, 162

Ebony magazine, 147
Eden, Robert, 108–111, 115, 120–23
egalitarianism, modern, compared to Lincoln's understanding of equality, 4–5, 9–31 *passim*, 99, 151–53, 175, 177–78
Ellis, Richard J., 93–95
Emancipation Proclamation (Lincoln), 29, 134, 137, 139, 141
entitlements, 127, 131, 145, 169–71
equality: Bradford on, 14; Johnson on, 141–53, 171; Kendall on, 15, Lincoln on, 4, 9–31 *passim*, 47, 70, 74, 107, 107, 178–79; Obama on, 154, 166–71, 173; progressives on, 97, 98, 131, 133, 175; Wilson on, 74, 95–96
equality of opportunity, 21–23, 35, 41–42, 46–49, 96, 99, 110–112, 117, 119, 126, 129, 136, 138, 148, 150–51, 154, 168, 170
equal protection law, 11

faction, 62, 65, 68–69, 87, 130, 176
Federalist, 51, 67, 69; no. 10, 22
Fields, Barbara, 11, 98
Fifteenth Amendment, 10, 143
Fitzhugh, George, 43, 45
Fletcher, George P., 10, 12
Fornieri, Joseph, 13, 22, 26, 28, 29
Founders, the, 49, 59, 62–68, 74, 79, 84, 102, 109, 121, 130, 132, 155, 160, 163, 166, 173; on the Constitution, 9–11, 12, 13; on equality, 19, 20, 38, 78, 80, 134, 151; on property, 22, 46, 127; on the presidency, 87, 92; on slavery, 26–27, 83, 162–63
Fourteenth Amendment, 10, 12
Fragments on Government (Lincoln), 45, 103, 131, 166–67, 169

Garrison, William Lloyd, 161–62
Gaughan, Anthony, 71
Gettysburg Address (Lincoln), 4, 11, 12, 15, 18, 31, 35, 73, 75, 104, 135–37, 155, 172
Goodwin, Doris Kearns, 156
Great Depression, 99, 100, 115
"Great Society" (Johnson), 134, 136, 144–45, 147, 150–53, 176

Hamilton, Alexander, 62
Hammond, James, 43
Hay, John, 33
Hayward, Steve, 11, 15, 98
Hegel, G. W. F., 6, 64, 68, 80
"Heirs of Abraham Lincoln, The" speech (Roosevelt), 35, 37, 41, 42, 48, 49, 50, 53–55, 58
historicism, 62, 68–69, 71, 91, 120, 123, 178–79
Hofstadter, Richard, 24, 147
Holzer, Harold, 99
Hoover, Herbert, 4, 100, 105
human brotherhood, as an end of American democracy, 58–61
human nature, 20, 23–24, 96, 109, 153; Lincoln on, 60–61, 63, 130, 140–41, 175, 178–79; Wilson on, 68–69, 122–23
human rights, 31, 36, 41, 46, 77–78, 131, 136, 143

Individualism Old and New (Dewey), 109
initiative, 48–51
Inventing America: Jefferson's Declaration of Independence (Wills), 13

Jackson, Andrew, 34, 93, 99, 103–5
Jacksonian era, 30, 80, 93, 94
Jaffa, Harry V., 19, 22, 23, 132

Jefferson, Thomas, 62, 70, 93, 99, 103, 121–22
Johnson, Lyndon, 7–8, 134–153, 177; on equality, 144–53, 171, 176; on justice, 140–41; on suffrage, 142–44; the "Great Society," 144–45, 176

Kansas-Nebraska Act (1854), 20, 36, 40, 60, 79
Kendall, Willmoore, 14–15, 22, 88, 92, 95, 129
Kesler, Charles, 115, 120, 123, 163, 169–70
King, Jr., Martin Luther, 134, 142, 172
Kirk, Stephen, 93–95
Kleinerman, Benjamin, 90
Krannawitter, Thomas, 32, 166–67

labor, 21–22, 36, 41–47, 68, 81, 101–2, 119, 125, 138, 152, 166, 170
"Laws of Nature" 20, 38, 74, 115, 129, 132, 164
leadership, 59, 66, 73, 77, 84–85, 106–107, 111, 119, 155, 176
"Lectures on Discoveries and Inventions" (Lincoln) 81
Lerner, Max, 105
"Lessons from Lincoln" speech (Wilson), 73–74
liberalism, 24, 107–11
liberals, 9, 10, 15, 29, 88, 92, 99, 100, 103–5, 110, 122, 158, 169, 171, 178
liberty, 22, 101–2, 125–26, 161, 167
Lincoln: draft laws, 25; equality, 3–5, 9–31 *passim*, 47, 48, 71–72, 74, 80, 96, 97–98, 107, 127, 129–30, 135–39, 145, 150, 153, 165, 170–71, 175–78; free labor, 4, 43–45, 81, 138, 152, 166; human nature, 60–61, 63, 130, 140–41; liberty, 125–126, 129; mob rule, 30; the presidency, 84–96; natural rights, 38–39, 77, 81, 96, 130, 153, 165, 171; progress, 79–84; prudence, 25–29; purposes of government, 113, 118, 132; recall of judicial decisions, 51–58; recall of public servants, 50–51; rights of freed slaves, 29; slavery, 26–29, 52–53, 60, 70, 94–95; statesmanship, 25–26, 58, 77, 111, 129; technological innovation, 81–83, 138, 166, 171; "Young America" 82–83
—Lincoln's speeches: address at sanitary fair, Baltimore (April 1864), 101, 125; at Chicago (1858), 57; at Cincinnati (1859); on colonization to a deputation of Negroes (1862), 45; to Congress in special session (July 4, 1861), 23, 88; to Congress, annual message (December 1861), 43, 50, 51; on the *Dred Scott* decision (June 26, 1857), 16, 78; First Inaugural (1861), 50, 54, 57, 158; at Hartford, Connecticut (March 5, 1860), 21; at New Haven, Connecticut (March 6, 1860), 21, 43; to New York Workingmen's Democratic Association (March 21, 1864), 22; at Peoria (October 16, 1854), 29, 60, 79; "Response to Serenade" (November 10, 1864), 61; Second Inaugural (1865), 172; Speech at Cooper Institute, 83; at Springfield (July 20, 1858) 21; State of the Union Address (December 6, 1864), 94
Lincoln (Sandburg), 106
Lincoln and the Economics of the American Dream (Boritt), 44
Lincoln at Gettysburg: The Words that Remade America (Wills), 12
Lincoln-Douglas debates of 1858, 21, 25, 54–55, 63, 76–78, 162
Lincoln Reconsidered (Donald), 3
Lind, Michael, 100
Locke, John, 19, 21, 22, 89, 109, 121–22, 126
"Lyceum Address" (Lincoln), 30, 90, 122

Machiavelli, Niccolo, 122
Madison, James, 22, 51
Manifest Destiny, 83
Marshall, John, 53
McCain, John, 169
McPherson, James, 11, 12, 21

Meyer, Frank, 13–14
Milkis, Sidney, 108, 120, 127–28
Miller, Eugene, 81
Montesquieu, 67
Moynihan, Daniel Patrick, 148–51
"mud-sill theory" (Hammond), 43
Murley, John, 17, 31–32

Nation, The, 35
National Bank Bill, 34
natural equality, 18–20, 22, 26, 30, 80
natural rights, 6, 21, 29, 32, 38, 62, 64, 69–71, 74–75, 81, 96, 97, 99, 107, 109–10, 115, 118, 120, 125, 129, 132–33, 141, 153, 164–66, 171, 173, 175, 177–79
"negative liberty," 21
New Deal, 3, 5, 7–8, 96, 99, 100, 102–109, 112–14, 117, 119, 120–29, 131, 134, 137, 166, 169, 174–75
"New Freedom" (Wilson), 64, 72, 73, 75, 114–15, 123
"New Nationalism" (Roosevelt), 41, 46, 64
New Republic, 58, 105, 109
Newton, Isaac, 67
Nicholson, Meredith, 114–15
Nixon, Richard M., 151

Obama, Barack, 3, 8, 154–73; on "absolute truth," 160–61; on the Founders, 158–60, 162–63; on Lincoln, 154–57, 161–62, 166–68; on the purposes of government, 166–68; on "values," 157–60
On the Origin of Species (Darwin), 76
"Opinion on the Draft" (Lincoln), 25
original intent conservatives, 12
Our Secret Constitution: How Abraham Lincoln Redefined American Democracy (Fletcher), 10

Pestritto, Ronald, 62, 71, 77, 80, 85
Peterson, Merrill D., 71
Plato, 82
plebiscitary presidency, 7, 15, 88–95, 98, 122–23, 176

"positive liberty," 21, 22
practical equality of opportunity. *See* "equality of opportunity"
pragmatism, 26, 31, 107–113, 120–23, 127–31, 166–67
Preliminary Emancipation Proclamation (Lincoln), 28
prerogative, 34, 89, 121–22
presidential mandate, 87–88, 92–95, 98, 122, 138, 139
private property, origin of, 21, 22
Progressive Democracy (Croly), 56
Progressive Party, 36–38, 41–43, 51, 64
progressives, 5–9, 15–17, 29, 31–32, 33, 36–47, 54, 61, 65, 68, 78, 84, 90–103, 108–9, 112–16, 120, 122, 127, 136, 140, 146–47, 156, 169–73, 175–78
progressivism, 6, 15, 17, 24, 31–32, 52, 64–65, 71, 76, 78, 81, 95, 97, 103, 121, 178
Promise of American Life, The (Croly), 58, 59
prudence, 5, 25–26, 164–65, 169
public opinion, 29, 86–92
Public Papers and Addresses (Roosevelt, Franklin), 103

"race of life," 13, 16, 23, 36, 41, 43, 65, 72, 137, 150–53, 168, 170–71
recall of judicial decisions, 51–58
"Recall of Judicial Decisions, The" speech (Roosevelt), 53, 54
recall of public servants, 48–51
Reconstruction, 94
Reconstruction Amendments, 3, 10, 11, 56, 135, 143, 160
redistribution of wealth, 47
referendum, 48–51
"Report on the Negro Family" (Moynihan), 149–50
Republican Party, 4, 33, 36, 39, 40, 72, 100, 155, 157
Republicans, 35, 36, 72, 73, 94, 105
Rietveld, Ronald, 102, 106
Roosevelt, Franklin, 4, 6–7, 14, 15, 88, 97–133, 147, 166–67, 169–71, 176; and

economic rights, 124–31, 145, 167, 169, 170; on individual freedom, 126; on liberty, 126, 167; on the purposes of government, 113–24, 126–28, 138, 152, 169
Roosevelt, Theodore, 4, 15, 64, 71, 88, 99, 102, 103, 106, 113, 117, 121, 136, 178; and the Constitution, 33–34; and executive power, 34, 89; and Lincoln, 33–63 *passim,* 84, 91; and natural rights, 38–39, 113; speech to the Ohio Constitutional Convention (1912), 55

Sandburg, Carl, 106
Schlesinger, Jr., Arthur, 108
Schwartz, Barry, 35, 71
"Second Bill of Rights"(Roosevelt), 124–31
Second Treatise of Civil Government (Locke), 19, 89
separation of powers, 4, 13, 40, 62, 65–66, 97–98, 107, 109, 111, 130, 178–79
Sherman Antitrust Act, 53
slavery, 19–20, 21, 81, 83, 94, 160. See *also* Lincoln on slavery
"standard maxim" of equality, 18, 22, 24–25, 28, 29, 31, 78, 129, 137, 140, 152, 171, 173, 177
Stephens, Alexander, 81
"stewardship theory" of executive power, 34
suffrage, 29, 50, 135, 141–44
Sunstein, Cass, 128
Supreme Court, 11, 13, 15, 53–55, 57

Taft, William Howard, 4
Taney, Roger B., 18, 26, 55, 57, 78, 80, 83, 107, 162

Taylor, Zachary, 93
Team of Rivals: The Political Genius of Abraham Lincoln (Goodwin), 156
Thirteenth Amendment, 10
Tocqueville, Alexis de, 30, 47
tyranny, majority, 13, 47–48, 56, 62–63, 102

United States Constitution. See Constitution
United States v. E. C. Knight Co. (1895), 53

"values," 12, 117, 157–60, 164–65, 167
Voting Rights Act of 1965, The, 141–44, 149, 176

war on poverty, 137–38, 143
Washington and Lincoln: The Great Examples (Roosevelt), 42, 44
welfare state, 13–14, 16, 21
Whigs, 36, 39, 45, 67–68, 87, 93–94
Wills, Garry, 12–14
Wilson, Woodrow, 4, 6–7, 15, 64–96 *passim,* 99, 102, 103, 106–8, 112, 114–15, 121, 124, 148, 163–64, 171, 176–77; presidential leadership, 84–92, 167; purpose of government, 72, 117–18, 123, 130, 169
World War II, 99
Wright, Jeremiah, 162

Yarbrough, Jean M., 46

Zarefsky, David, 151